BRUCE SPRINGSTEEN
ON TOUR
1968–2005

The early 1970s

BRUCE SPRINGSTEEN
ON TOUR
1968–2005

DAVE MARSH

BLOOMSBURY

For Joan Dancy, an inspiration, and for Terry Magovern,
who never fell behind

Contents

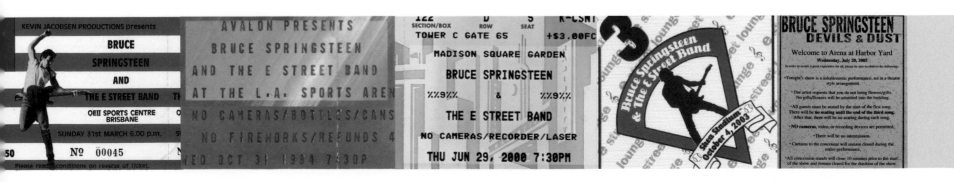

Acknowledgments

I T'S CUSTOMARY TO THANK the subject last, if at all, but that won't work here. Bruce Springsteen maintains the highest standard of personal and professional behavior of anyone I know. It's an inspiration to me and to thousands of others.

The people who work with Bruce live up to that measure, too. That includes the various band members over the years and the road crews who support them with amazing daily diligence. Thank you one and all for the assistance and many kindnesses.

Rock and roll can be portrayed as an awful and irresponsible business, but that is not the case with the people who have worked longest and most closely with Bruce. Jon Landau remains not only my friend but also a paragon of artistic enthusiasm who has been an encyclopedia and a university for me.

I make an attempt in this book at doing some justice or at least giving some credit to George Travis and what he's achieved backstage over the past three decades. It would require a book of its own to do the job right. He's both a puzzle and a beacon. He works harder than just about anybody I've ever met, he's honest in a singular way that involves never answering a question directly, and I've never seen him let anyone down. He lives the craziest schedule imaginable and still created one of the finest families I know. (Some major credit here to Lenore Travis.)

Frank Barsalona and Barry Bell have been my mentors over many years of trying to grasp the concert business. The errors here are mine alone, but many of the best ideas about how the rock world works are theirs.

THE INFORMATION EXPLOSION accompanying the advent of the Internet has created a situation exactly the opposite of the one that existed when I wrote *Born to Run*. Then, teasing out any kind of information about events you didn't see was extraordinarily difficult. Now, we have many Web sites. For me, the foundation is Brucebase, at http://www.brucebase.org.uk—a complete list of virtually every show Bruce has played, as well as some he hasn't, by way of dispelling rumor, with song lists, and detailed transcriptions of many of his stage raps. It's an astonishing resource and reflects the commitment Bruce inspires.

Holly Cara Price researched Bruce's early career for me. She was virtually the only person I would have trusted to do this, and I'm lucky she was free for the task. Holly also contributed the timeline, so I could dwell on other things. Thanks, Holly.

My Bruce Springsteen family extends off the largest page we could create. I need to mention an online discussion group to which I belong, the Stratlist, which includes a hard core of Bruce fans who also share an avid interest in music, politics, food, and unmentionables. We also have the Holler If Ya Hear Me blog at www.hollerif.blogspot.com. Lou Cohan, Lauren Onkey, Matt Orel, and Chris Papaleonardos shared an expertise in some areas of Bruce's live work that outstrips mine, and they were incredibly generous with their time and their recorded archives. But everyone on that list shares ideas freely and with great vigor, and my thinking here often boils down my interpretation of very long dialogues with each person there.

Daniel Wolff, Danny Alexander, Craig Werner, Lauren Onkey, and Susan Martinez, all Stratlist members, and Mary Erpenbach read all or part of the manuscript and provided insight and encouragement. Lew Rosenbaum, Strat's most literary member, did the best set of transcriptions I've ever received, from the Sirius Radio interviews I did with Bruce, Jon, and Steven Van Zandt in 2005.

Other Bruce fans who helped out include Stephanie Casella, Karen Chapman (an amazing mix CD, *Bruce on War*), Barbara Hall, and Chris Phillips, whose editorship of the fanzine *Backstreets* has turned it into another fount of good information and sharp thinking about Springsteen and related matters.

I TELL MORE STORIES here about my personal Springsteen experiences than I have in any of the other books, because finally, if this book was going to work at all, it had to be from the voice of a fan. Also because the work was done by people who are important parts of my extended family.

Sandy Choron has guided my career for more than twenty-five years, with unflagging devotion, conviction, and care. She has never let me fall behind, and believe me, there have been some close calls. Her continual patience, above all, shows what a remarkable human being she is.

One reason this book was fun was the presence of Harry Choron, whose ideas always stimulate me (probably more than I let on to him) and who matches his wife's conviction and devotion. This book is beautiful above all else, and its beauty comes from them, much more than me.

Daniel Wolff's generosity, wisdom, intelligence, insight into writing, and musical judgment affect all my writing and have for years. Our long discussions about what Bruce's work means, how it fits into a broader political vision, and where it may help us go are at the core of this book. In particular, a long drive we took from my house in Connecticut to Williamstown, Massachusetts, in October 2005 generated some of the best stuff here. Daniel's *Asbury Park, 4th of July: A History of the Promised Land* affected everything I wrote about Bruce in New Jersey and a fair amount of what I said about his involvement in various political issues.

A second book that shaped my political vision of Bruce Springsteen was Craig Werner's *A Change Is Gonna Come: Music, Race, and the Soul of America,* to my mind the most indispensable single volume about contemporary American popular music. My conversations with Craig were as fundamental to the writing as those with Daniel.

Partly because of Craig and Daniel's shared interest, I have come to see much of what Bruce sings and says through the lens of James Baldwin, not a friend, but nevertheless a moral, literary, and political beacon. For me, the measure of Bruce Springsteen's music is that he could merit the use of the quotation from Baldwin's "Sonny's Blues," which is, for me, the quintessential story of our sonic culture.

In the end, books like this happen because there are still some publishers out there who champion the causes of writers and who are prepared to go to bat for books that matter. Karen Rinaldi and her team at Bloomsbury, Lindsay Sagnette and Penny Edwards in particular, renew our faith in the process, and I join others who worked on this book in expressing heartfelt thanks.

BARBARA CARR PLAYS a minor role in this story—in part because she doesn't much like seeing her name in print—and the most major role in my life. One of her many gifts to me is the constant reminder that there is more to life than work. You'd think a rock and roll guy would get that straight off but I don't. In a true sense, I have a life because Barbara loves me enough to make sure I have one. I love her back—it ain't much, but it's what I've got to offer.

Sasha Carr, our daughter, and her late sister, Kristen, are the ones who have done the most to teach me the meaning of living that life. I am ever grateful to have been such a well-loved father and husband.

Additional Acknowledgments

THE EDITORS WISH TO THANK the following for their invaluable assistance in assembling the artwork included here: Kirsty Arkell; Robert Bader; Kenny Barr; Bob Benjamin; Paolo Calvi; Charlie Cross; René van Diemen; Danny Federici; Joe Grushecky; Patti Hallead; Marc Zakarin, Debra Zakarin, and Larry Marion of ItsOnlyRocknRoll.com; Judi Johnson; Paul Kaytes; John Leach; Greg Linn; Lauren Onkey; Matthew Orel; Chris Phillips; Carrie Potter and Dan Eitner; Retna; John Sasso; Billy Smith; Don Stine; George Travis; Salvatore Trepat; Cathy Vocke; David Wade; and Michael Waldman. A special thanks to Drew Laura, a true rock and roll hero.

BRUCE SPRINGSTEEN ON TOUR 1968–2005

Don't that man look pretty . . . at the Bottom Line, New York City, August 1975.
From left: Clarence Clemons, Bruce Springsteen, Garry Tallent.

Leaving for the Land of Hope and Dreams

"It ain't no sin to be glad you're alive."

BRUCE SPRINGSTEEN ISN'T a noun. It's a verb.

But then, so is music.

In English, *music* is a noun, a thing, even though it is intangible and extremely diffi-cult to define as an object. The problem's in the language. Music is not something that just lies there—the guitar or the compact disc is not music. Music is an action. An action is a verb.

Seen this way, all the activity around the music is part of it, too: dancing, listening, working, playing, kissing, contemplation. There is no "background music." Music is sound that captures present space and time, helps organize it or drive it or make sense of it. If it doesn't do that, it's not music, it's life's daily racket.

Bruce Springsteen currently exists as a middle-aged father of three living in central New Jersey, who spends most of his days quietly. This Bruce Springsteen is the anti–Ozzy Osbourne, but well short of sainthood. The man Bruce Springsteen is a noun. You could touch him.

The Bruce Springsteen that interests people is a verb—the activity labeled Bruce Springsteen (to be found in a comprehensive thesaurus as a specific type of the verb music). Bruce Springsteen may be at times the most active verb in the English language, although there is a secondary func-tion of the term, which slows the pace long enough for survival. When engaged in the activity known as *Bruce Springsteen*, grown men and women have been known to roll up their eyes and emit a mighty roar, thus: *"BROOOOOCE!"* repeated so often that it could be taken for the lowing of cows overdue for milking. This is a part of the musical activity. Dancing is too, sort of, though

3

most of the really strenuous dancing takes place on the stage, not in the aisles.

People—myself prominent among them—have spent a great deal of time trying to fix this Bruce Springsteen phenomenon in some form in which it can be held down on a page or within a CD, DVD, or some other storage medium, up to and including the Dual Disc. All such recordings of Springsteen the verb, whether aural or visual, recorded in print or electronic form, fail. At best, they catch the shadow of the verb Springsteen. That's not surprising, since it applies to all verbs in this class, such as James Brown, Robin Williams, and Muhammad Ali. But if we are going to explore Springsteen the verb, we need to hold fast to the idea that to discuss and observe rolling one's tongue is a lot different from sliding both sides up and over toward the middle. For instance, some can't. Although it is widely believed that only pot-bellied middle-aged men in white T-shirts and jeans and a few similarly attired romantic females can Bruce Springsteen, close observation in Barcelona, Milan, and Stockholm demonstrates otherwise.

ALL THAT'S TRUE. Our task is basic: to slow down the Springsteen phenomenon for a little while and see if catching it at a new angle will help find a way to hold on to a bigger piece of all that activity. If we can do that, or at least come close, maybe we can figure out what it all means anew. If your conviction is that pop stars and rock music exist only to be experienced, not thought about, have a great time looking at the pictures and the rest of us will catch up to you at the show. But if you believe, as I do, that one reason we return to the song is because it shows us new sides of itself and its maker and ourselves, too, then maybe we can have a little fun on the journey.

You can have it both ways. You can think and dance (though doing so at the same time requires a lot of skill and even more practice). The question is what to think about. You can't think about the dancing or you'll fall over your own feet. But you might think about what it is that makes you dance and what makes this dance different than all the others. Or some of the others. Or none of the others.

Springsteen's concerts exhibit a kind of life different from that in his songs, taken by themselves, and even more different from his records of those songs. What happens if we do our best to push his writing and recording aside and concentrate on what he does onstage? What do we learn about the music, the concerts, the past thirty or forty years of popular music, the noun version of Bruce and, not least, the people who love him and what he does? (Since his involvement in the 2004 election, maybe that should be love him and/or what he does.)

Talking about Springsteen this way refocuses the story—it doesn't change what happened, what's still happening, but it gives some of it different meanings. Which is the main reason I decided to tackle writing a third book after two biographies (*Born to Run*, from 1979, and *Glory Days*, its 1987 sequel, which are updated through 2003 in a volume called *Two Hearts*). I wrote the first book because I thought that he was the paradigmatic case of how an honorable man might become a rock star and, more particularly, how a

man without credentials, working in a form without respectability, becomes an artist. I wrote the second because I wanted to see what happened when that star tested his artistry on the broadest imaginable canvas. (This became known in certain quarters as me "inventing the myth of Bruce Springsteen." Hey, if you think I'm that good, thanks. And by the way, you're welcome to come over to the house and listen to one of the twenty-four million copies of *Born in the U.S.A.* that I bought and hoarded as part of the scheme.) Well, I do have to admit that it seemed to me that if you do what I do for a living, one of the coolest jobs you could have is watching a bunch of Bruce shows and listening to his records incessantly and talking to him and the people around him about it once in a while. I was pretty much right, too.

After that job was done, though, I kept watching, and what I've seen has not so much changed my mind as my focus. As he has more than once so generously done, Bruce accommodated this project by creating what may be his most interesting show of all, certainly his most curious, and one of his deepest. The *Devils & Dust* tour of 2005 left town as a quick venture designed to promote his wordiest and musically driest album. The *Devils & Dust* tour that is coming to its conclusion as I write involved an exploration and reinterpretation that rummaged through his entire song catalog, a set of musical and emotional high-wire acts that placed him in new territory. Was it a success? As he finished the last version I saw of the concluding number, a version of the no-wave punk band Suicide's "Dream Baby Dream," I thought I had never seen an artist or an audience so free, so charged, so ready for what's next.

That is how he has always defined success.

In my opinion, this had very little to do with the specific songs on *Devils & Dust* and a very great deal to do with why Bruce Springsteen is the greatest rock and roll stage performer since James Brown. It's one thing to try on a lot of new faces and discard them, whether they work or not: As Neil Young regularly proves, not just Bob Dylan can do that. Bruce Springsteen does something else. He wears the same face and keeps changing what's inside it, keeps excavating new possibilities from that single persona, and then, and this is the part I can never quite believe until I'm standing there, heart pumping, seeing it—he does the one thing you'd never think a Big Official Rock Star would do: *He shares this power.* He invites you to be a verb, too. He insists that you are one, if you'd only act the part. And he does his best to show you how, and to show you why it's okay if once in a while you fall on your face.

To start with, it's your face. Which he convinces you is so by wearing his own. If you think that's not a scary wire to walk, ask Bob Dylan or Neil Young. Or get yourself to the next Bruce Springsteen show.

ROCK AND ROLL *IS* ART. At its best, it is the art of planned spontaneity. Bruce Springsteen onstage epitomizes this.

Palace Amusements, Asbury Park, 1992

Anyone who's seen a Bruce show (just one single show; you don't have to go to dozens, though plenty of those tramps like us will drop everything else in their lives as soon as a tour is announced) can tell that some parts are carefully rehearsed, planned well in advance of the moment, and some are products of his total immersion in the moment: this moment, right *now!* But anyone who's seen a single rehearsal (or just a bunch of shows on the same tour) knows that the obvious first guess about which are the planned parts and what just happened to fall into place tonight isn't that simple. For one thing, sometimes something will happen in the moment, and he'll find a way to keep it, expand upon it. It could even become a central element of what Bruce does next.

About a month into the *Ghost of Tom Joad* solo tour in 1995, Bruce began playing an acoustic version of "The Promised Land," a song he'd done at virtually every perform-ance since he debuted it on May 25, 1978, the first show of the *Darkness on the Edge of Town* tour. He toyed with "The Promised Land" a little, slowing it dramatically, or, rather, slowing it to pull out the inherent drama, to change its flavor: The rock version wrung the bitterness out of the situation that produced it; the acoustic version fingered the wounds from which that bitterness oozed.

It wasn't just the instrumentation that dictated the way he sang the song. The acoustic version also had to do with being middle-aged and with being famous, with understanding that it was, in many ways, these agonies of alienation that had helped make him famous or, for that matter, make it to middle age. It was even more alienated, but it also accepted the fact of alienation.

On January 11, 1996, after another month of shows, Springsteen played the Fox Theater in Detroit. The night was charged by the presence of striking Detroit newspaper workers, whose side Bruce took with a brief comment and a dedication to the strikers that managed to honorably avoid trashing the scab jour-nalists. Then he played "The Promised Land."

By now, the acoustic "The Promised Land" had what one would assume was going to be its perma-nent solo arrangement. But that night, the song seemed to grab Bruce in a new way at the end, and he issued a high-pitched wail, a banshee sound, as lonesome as the lyrics, and equal in its desperation to any-thing he conveyed in words in those songs from the *Joad* album—in that moment, "The Promised Land" became of a piece with the new songs he was doing.

More important in the long run, it also broke new ground vocally.

As far as I can tell, Bruce himself didn't quite know where he'd pulled that voice from—I mentioned it to him after the show, and he seemed as fascinated as I was that it had popped up. That doesn't mean he didn't know it was in him. He knew he had a "head voice" (falsetto), he knew he could sing wordlessly. He just didn't know that it would emerge from this context quite so powerfully or have the effect it did. He hadn't planned it.

The *River* tour, 1981

From the early 1980s

Over the next decade, that falsetto voice became a regular part of his performances, not only (or always) of "The Promised Land" but also as a new touch to other songs, old and new. 2005's *Devils & Dust* featured "All I'm Thinkin' About," in which he sang the complete song in his head voice, though without the spooky quality.

Springsteen is notoriously and correctly regarded as a great songwriter, especially as a great lyricist, and he deserves to be. But for him, the song remains a pliable device—there might be a dozen different preliminary versions of the song that we now know as "Thunder Road," and the residue turned up in three or four other songs. *Tracks*, his 1999 box set of leftovers, amply displays the results of such tinkering, and not only with "Thunder Road."

In a sense, the recordings of the songs—or at least of the most important songs—serve as sketches, diagrams that can be referred to for comparison. I think he uses the relatively flat surfaces of the recorded music the way an architect uses a drawing—to build something three-dimensional. From "Rosalita" to "Mary's Place," to hear the record is not necessarily the best way to know the song.

Early on, Bruce treated the stage as a rehearsal hall. Songs appeared and then disappeared into the maw of his studio perfectionism, so that something like "Frankie," now just a stray cut on *Tracks* that he occasionally hauls out in the middle of a set, acquired legendary status among his fans.

Even now, he rewrites when it suits his purpose—a beautiful new verse he added to "Blood Brothers" for the final appearance of his 1999 E Street Band reunion tour, for example. He still tinkers with arrangements frequently, though it's rare to have a song transformed as radically as "Born in the U.S.A.," which he shifted from the hard-rocking, defiance-in-defeat stance of the electric version to the pared, knife-edge acoustic one, with its acknowledgment of loss and the

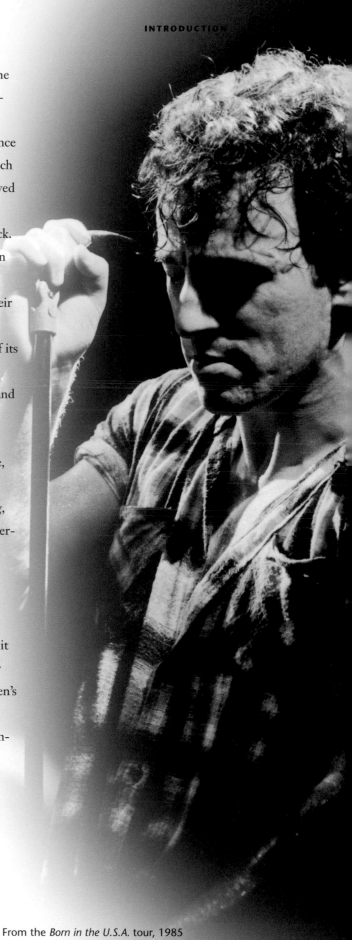

defiance apparent only in the fact that such a battered character could still will himself to sing at all. (The resemblance to what he did with "The Promised Land" is unmistakable. It's part of how he has comfortably grown old—well, older—as a great performer in a young man's game.)

The most important thing about the songs for the live show is that they exist as potential performance pieces. One of Springsteen's great records, *Tunnel of Love*, for instance, stymied him onstage because much of its best material isn't really suitable to be played live by a rock band. Most of the material was conceived of solo: In a reversal of his usual procedure, he grafted the band parts after recording his own voice and guitar tracks. Those grafts blossomed, particularly Nils Lofgren's brilliant guitar playing on the title track. But onstage, there was something about the material that never quite fit. Very little of it would remain in his set after the *Tunnel of Love* tour. Surprisingly, he played literally every song from that album on the *Devils & Dust* tour, though. It was a solo tour, so perhaps he saw the chance to take the tunes back to their origins. Perhaps in the edgy questions he asked about romance on *Tunnel*, Bruce saw a link to the edgy questions he asked about life on *Devils*. Or maybe, he felt musical links—*Devils & Dust* also had much of its music added late in the production process.

But whatever the reasons, those songs got mixed into the setlists gradually, as Bruce tried first one and then another of them on for fit during the tour. This is the opposite process from what happened with "The Promised Land": Its foundation is plan.

People who think that music ought to be all spontaneity, and they are as numerous as they are naïve, have trouble with such calculations, with the way in which Springsteen's plan for a show can be seen. Its overarching themes and rhythms are meant to be understood; the show is meant to add up to something, and that something is not just a feeling or a spirit but a set of ideas that propel what he does as a stage performer beyond the realm of mere excitement into something much more nourishing.

YOU CAN OVEREMPHASIZE PLAN, too, which is why people who write about music are so fixated on Springsteen as songwriter, by which they seem always to mean lyricist. In the early twenty-first century, it has become fashionable to regard him as a writer of poetry. Which is not entirely nonsense, since poetry started out, in the Homeric period, as a species of song. But way too much current analysis of Springsteen's work relies on looking at pages, rather than listening to sounds. It begins to seem as if his proper antecedents are Philip Roth and Raymond Carver (interestingly, almost all of the comparisons are to non-poets) rather than Chuck Berry, John Lennon, and Bob Dylan. At least, I don't remember any essays on why his most influential structural contribution to American songwriting may be his use of multiple bridges (middle 8s to the Anglophonic).

Springsteen's songwriting in midcareer (which I presume is about where he is temporally if not

From the *Born in the U.S.A.* tour, 1985

From the *Born in the U.S.A.* tour, 1985
From left: Clarence Clemons, Max Weinberg,
Bruce Springsteen, Nils Lofgren, Garry Tallent,
Roy Bittan, Patti Scialfa, Danny Federici

commercially) does owe an increasing debt to literary sources. In part, that's because the increasingly streamlined structure of his songs—and their increasing use of truncated melodic phrases—calls more attention to the words. In part, that's because he's become more respectable as the generation influenced by his work reaches a greater position of influence. In part, it's because he's unafraid of tackling big, important subjects that are ordinarily not discussed in songs and, when they are, are usually reduced to agitprop, caricature, or incoherence. The clarity and psychological insight of his lyrics are beautiful, startling, and for many, profoundly moving, because they bespeak the human heart as keenly as an earlier generation of music writers believed that only educated musicians could.

But that doesn't mean Springsteen as a writer can be best or fully understood on the page. For one thing, he doesn't write exactly what he sings, or more to the point, sing exactly what he writes. At its most complex, the process works something like this: Springsteen plays a new song live, with one set of words;

he alters them—sometimes a lot, sometimes hardly at all—during further performances; he records a near-final set of words; he looks over the differences and comes up with the version that gets printed on the album, in the sheet music, and on his Web site.

Beyond that, though, what's on the page is flatter than it is in performance. Sometimes, it hardly seems to bear weight at all: "Cadillac Ranch" is one of the smartest songs ever written about the inevitability of death, but you can't find that in the lyric sheet; you need to experience the exuberance of the music, too.

Take the finest song on his *Lucky Town* album, "If I Should Fall Behind." The couplet that opens the third verse is: "Now everyone dreams of a love lasting and true / But you and I know what this world can do."

On the page, this is a little awkward—there are twelve syllables in the first line, ten in the second. But when they are sung, they're beautiful, with Springsteen quickening the cadence a little bit—but not rushing it—as he goes through the near-cliché of the first line and then relaxing the tension as he spills out the insight of the second. When Dion demonstrated that the song was even better sung as doo-wop, with emphasis on open-mouthed vowels and an extremely legato cadence, Springsteen took the song apart and put it back together again on the '99 reunion tour, parceling out the lines to the singing E Streeters—Clarence Clemons, Steven Van Zandt, Nils Lofgren, Patti Scialfa—as they took the center stage mic one by one until Bruce joined in for the last three lines of this verse and the others, the group forming a shimmering chord on the last words, "Wait for you."

Not a bit of that can be read in those twenty-three words and their spacing on the page. Even this explanation of what they did fails to convey how they did it. If there's language for that, I don't have it.

Well, actually, I do: "Listen to this!"

But even just listening doesn't give you the full song. Jonathan Demme directed a live video of "If I Should Fall Behind." The stage is black, except for a single spotlight, which falls on the center microphone. Clarence Clemons, dressed all in white, approaches the mic, which is set too low. He leans very far forward and intones the first words of each verse. He steps aside, and Steven Van Zandt, his opposite in clothes and size, cranes his neck into the mic, as if it's set too high. He sings the next line and steps aside. Nils Lofgren has to stand on tiptoes to reach the mic, and he sings half of the third line before Patti Scialfa steps in to complete it. Then Bruce leans across so that his head is in the midst of the rest of them (his body is held back, strumming the guitar), and they sing that chord.

IT'S A HELL OF a video.

But it's not the same thing as seeing the song performed live, at all. There, it emerges from a pattern. It typically appeared during the encores, which means both the band and the audience has undergone

more than two hours of strenuous activity, proving that *Bruce Springsteen* is a verb. The two songs that precede "If I Should Fall Behind" are screaming signature songs that embody all of Bruce's rock and soul hijinks as well as setting a driving pace: "Born to Run" and "Thunder Road." The lights have been full up in the arena for fifteen or twenty minutes now.

And then the darkness falls and the white spot hits the mic at center stage while the band members lurk in the shadows, and Clarence steps to the mic and the pageant begins.

And when it ends, the band slams into the final song of the night, the gospel-based "Land of Hope and Dreams." And the true power of it is the clash between the ideas in that final quartet of songs—between the guileless convictions of youth and the wary lessons of maturity, and the hopes and the dreams that carry us through nevertheless.

There isn't any easily available video that shows this sequence, but even if there were, you wouldn't be surrounded in your house by fifteen thousand other people, each of them lost in their heads and fully awake in the moment, screaming and concentrating at the same time.

And if that isn't a very good description of why the stuff doesn't work on paper . . . QED.

ONE REASON THAT SPRINGSTEEN gets celebrated in literary terms is that it's a lot simpler for a writer to describe him that way, and another is that literature remains in our official culture the highest caste of all art forms. Besides, as I found out when writing those other books, those songs often do make sense when put down on paper. (Don't try it with "Sherry Darling" though.) I don't think that the Bruce-is-literature types know that, since it happens onstage, not on record, and the monologues and semitheatrical set pieces aren't in the songbooks.

Springsteen is the greatest rock and roll storyteller and not only in songs. The legends he spun in the seventies and eighties concerts riveted his audience for five or ten minutes at a time, while he told what amounted to barroom boasts and shaggy-dog stories of crappy cars, broke-down radios, gypsy women, and a gigantic saxophone player blown into his life by a howling wind. The stories sometimes weren't much; the props and costumes that occasionally accompanied them never broached the bounds of the junior high theatrical.

It didn't matter. Springsteen told his tales without any need for pencil or paper, and if you chained his hands and refused to let him strum his guitar or gesture to the Mighty Max to accent the next phrase, that wouldn't have made much difference, either. He just knew how to spin a yarn, turn a late-night encounter between three guys at a closed gas station into an epic that somehow illumined a corner of the world—his world, yours too—that you'd always suspected had unexplored kinks of *some* kind.

Asbury Park, 1999, the reunion tour

Asbury Park, 1999

Mic stand calisthenics on the *Rising* tour, 2002

Springsteen absorbed the hangdog everyman postures of Art Carney in *The Honeymooners* the way the young Bob Dylan absorbed the shambling gait of Charlie Chaplin's Little Tramp. He soaked up the elaborate double-take of Jack Benny, the psychotic stare of DeNiro in *Taxi Driver*, the pelvic havoc of Elvis, and the gesticulations of every TV preacher from Reverend Ike to Jack Van Impe. Rolled into a quasi-comedic, melodramatic ball, it came out as an unforgettable extension of his stage persona—all without plucking a string or singing a note.

He might introduce a song with a story or stop a song midway through (or very near the end) to go into what fans call stage raps but which are really serio-comic rock and roll–drenched answers to the fables of Uncle Remus.

All that adds to his unique ability to give his concerts dramatic structure without imposing a quasi-operatic overlay requiring what amounts to program numbers to advance the plot. There is no overt plot—the fables are discursions, not the way of driving home the main point. Like a lot of his social commentary, the overarching narrative of Springsteen's shows is almost gnomic—you have to pay attention, think back, make connections across the span of the evening or sometimes his career.

An easy example is Springsteen sometimes singing "Lost in the Flood" just before "Born in the U.S.A."—two songs inspired by the war in Vietnam, written ten years apart. An easier one yet more descriptive of his typical art is the Atlantic City show that began with "Atlantic City" and ended with "Roll of the Dice," with stops along the way for "Jersey Girl" and "My City of Ruins." But to really understand that set you'd have to hear the differing stresses in songs like "Out in the Street," "Dancing in the Dark," and "Saint in the City," sung amidst the urban-development scam that Atlantic City has become.

It's all there, and on a lucky night for you, or a very good one for Bruce and the boys in the band, you'll catch all of it as it flies by. More likely, in the car on the way home, someone will fill in the gaps for you as you do for them. I don't believe there is another artist who consistently assembles shows in this way. It simply requires two things most performers don't have: an instinctual gift and a body of work sufficiently adaptable to these occasions.

It's EASY TO UNDERESTIMATE Bruce Springsteen's musical equipment—I don't mean his guitar or his teleprompter, I mean his voice, his skills as a band leader, and his guitar playing.

It's even easier to undervalue Springsteen's attributes in this area if all you've got to go by are his records, where his performances are stiffer, less free than in his shows and where the band has fewer

opportunities to show its agility at responding both on cue and in the spirit of a moment.

Springsteen's musical virtues aren't derived from technical prowess. His triumphs come from mastery of the vernacular aspects of music, which people who compare rock singers to Elizabethans and short-story writers don't always know exist, let alone appreciate. (If you doubt me, you can always dive into Christopher Ricks's book about Bob Dylan—see if you can figure out from that whether Bob ever picked up a guitar.)

Virtuosity, as producer Chuck Plotkin once remarked about some other musicians than Bruce and the E Street Band, is a cheap commodity in the music industry, simply because there is so much of it. In popular music, the issue isn't how many notes you can hit but how expressively you can hit them (or come close to them). There are hallowed singing voices from Ray Price and Jackie Wilson to Mitch Ryder and Whitney Houston, but range itself isn't why those singers are memorable. A sense of drama and timing, the ability to use dynamics and timbre, the gift of a singular personality, more than range, are the things that make Johnny Cash, Marvin Gaye, Donna Summer, Madonna, Prince, Willie Nelson, Eddie Vedder, and Tupac Shakur memorable and compelling vocalists.

Springsteen's vocal personality is as distinct as any of these, and he has shown increasing command of his voice over the span of his career. He loves Pentecostal preaching at least as much as gospel vocalizing, but as far as one can hear, his propensity to shout and holler like Richard and Ryder and his antihero Jimmy Swaggart has taken surprisingly little toll on his larynx. It's been a while since he recorded a rock vocal as overpowering as "Badlands," but onstage, he hasn't toned it down at all and still manages to evoke the necessary emotional subtleties in more somber songs like "You're Missing"; and he can still reach the notes required to sing early '80s songs derived from girl groups and frat-rock bands: "Sherry Darling," "Hungry Heart," "Janey Don't You Lose Heart," and the like.

His guitar playing is summed up by one of his most famous lyrics: "I got this guitar and I learned how to make it talk." Like Louis Armstrong, B. B. King, and Jack Teagarden, he uses his instrument to converse with his singing voice, to support it, to ad lib from and comment on the bedrock of the vocals. This doesn't make him a lesser guitarist—I have never discussed his playing with an electric guitar virtuoso who isn't impressed by his use of rock and roll ready-mades to create both a stylistic signature and a wide variety of effects. But as he himself says, he's not the best guitarist in the E Street Band anymore—that'd be Nils Lofgren. It doesn't matter. When he rips into the solo from "Prove It All Night" or the guitar break in "Thunder Road," no one can doubt that the defining sound of the E Street Band is his voice and his guitar. It does talk.

NOTHING I'VE TOLD YOU amounts to something that anybody who's seen a couple dozen Springsteen shows doesn't already know. Sort of. But most people who love Bruce Springsteen are never going to see him, especially since a lot of them live in places like Greece or Israel or Hong Kong where he may play once in his lifetime (he's never played any of those). The function of the photographs and artifacts here is to get us close and to jog our memories, to offer a tangible expression of what those who have seen the show up close and personal—which can mean at the back end of a soccer stadium—experienced (I sat at the rear of the stadium on purpose once, in Barcelona; well, for a while). They are here so that when people tell us we're nuts, we can at least turn to them and convince ourselves that it really did feel like your best birthday ever, Easter morning, Christmas Eve, and all eight days of Hanukkah wrapped up into one celebration.

It's a feast for the eyes as well as the ears, this Springsteen show. And Springsteen works very hard to make it a mental banquet, too. He does so too earnestly for those who believe that the essence of the game is hedonism and decadence (not that there isn't any hedonism; decadence, it depends on how you define it).

When you get this far into what Bruce Springsteen has accomplished, it's hard to believe that he, like any prime mover, hasn't always been there. But another reason I wanted to tell this story is that not only Springsteen, but also the rock concert is far from eternal.

When Springsteen joined his first band, the rock concert as we think of it now had yet to be invented. The venues were completely different, smaller and grubbier, harder to locate or even to find out about. The sound and lighting equipment didn't exist. A rock band's performances were brief, counted in the number of minutes—not hours—it took to play a handful of songs. What bands could do or even what they imagined doing was conceptually very narrow.

The audiences were different, too. To begin with, everybody was young, which is not true at many different kinds of rock shows today, not just Bruce Springsteen's. More to the point, everything was amateurish, simply because there was no professionalism, or as Bruce's longtime agent, Frank Barsalona, the man who began the professionalization process, said after the dust had begun to settle, "Back then, rock really was the asshole of show business, lower than the rodeo."

Over the course of Bruce Springsteen's career, you can see all that changing, and in fact, given his resistance to some of the changes, such as larger venues and ticket prices deliberately designed to force the nonrich out of their seats, there's hardly a better lens anywhere with which to see them. The stands he has taken on principle are nearly as legendary as the shows themselves.

SHOW'S ABOUT TO START. Let's get in there.

Chapter One

Where the Bands Were

"Well my feet they finally took root in the earth but I got me a nice little place in the stars."

B RUCE SPRINGSTEEN DID NOT, as is commonly supposed, spring from the head of the muse. He worked a long time in the New Jersey clubs and bars, formed many alliances, skipped a lot of meals, and slept on a lot of couches before he became the verb we know today. In songs like "Rosalita," "Where the Bands Are," and "Mary's Place," he tells a lot less than all his story. While everything he says about the music, its effect on him and his comrades, and the exhilaration of playing it is absolutely true, it's still less than half the story. Work was involved and so was—no surprise—growing up.

Let's just say that in terms of the hours it takes to learn to be good at it, rock and roll is 10 percent excitement, 90 percent drudgery. Which makes it about 10 percent better than lives without rock and roll or some similar sound but about 90 percent shy of the myth.

One reason I keep returning to the story of Bruce Springsteen's version of the sixties and early seventies is that his 90 percent is, for a certain time, archetypal. The battles he fought, with himself and the world, the choices he made, represent the battles and choices of a whole generation of musicians—and to some extent, their audiences, too. His singular intensity, his ability to never lose focus on the most important things about the music, his urge to keep growing, and his willingness to change are the reasons this story has additional chapters.

Because this is a thrice-told tale, you may know much of what's in this chapter. For me, it always feels new in some ways, maybe because I wasn't there and have to imagine what it was

Bruce in a Castiles publicity shot, June 1965

like to be a teenager in a park in Long Branch and hear amazing music where I'd come expecting only a rehash. In some ways, this version is new, since so much information has been unearthed since the last time I went through it. It is anything but a digression.

Anyway, considered in terms of the story of Bruce live—well, at the time this part of the story takes place, live was the only Bruce there was.

It begins in the usual fashion. . . .

ON A DARK AND STORMY night in the spring of 1965, Tex Vinyard answered a knock on the door of his two-family house in Freehold, New Jersey. Tex, a blustering, slope-shouldered man, opened the door to a deluge—"It was raining like a cow pissing on a flat rock," he liked to say. Standing there he found a soggy, scrawny, pimply fifteen year old holding a guitar. He let the kid in.

They'd met the night before. The kid wanted to become the guitar player in the Castiles, a teenage band Tex managed. Vinyard had told the kid to come back when he knew at least five current rock hits.

Overnight, the kid had learned how to make that guitar talk. "This damn kid sat down and knocked out five songs that would blow your *ears*," Tex said. "He

said, 'Oh by the way, I learned a couple more . . . I learned on the radio.'" Bruce Springsteen had passed his first audition.

The Castiles, like most high school bands, began as a bunch of kids with hopes but no plans and few skills. Bart Haynes, the drummer, who lived in the other half of Tex's house, could play some. Vinny Roslin, the bassist, could play very well. The others were less talented, less committed, and their incessant starting and stopping of songs without ever reaching the end drove Tex a little nuts.

Tex Vinyard didn't know anything about managing. Although he and his wife Marion were childless, what they knew was that the hopes and dreams of the kids who formed bands deserved respect. He laid down the basic law: You showed up for rehearsal on time, you paid attention and learned as much as you could, and if you started a Goddamn song, you didn't stop til you'd finished it. Several of the band members didn't survive this tutelage.

The Castiles were a garage band. The term is generic. It doesn't mean they rehearsed in a garage, since a basement, an attic, or a spare bedroom often served the same purpose. The Castiles used the Vinyard dining room.

Garage bands played a specific kind of music—basic

Aug. 1965 – Woodhaven Swim Club, Freehold, NJ
Bruce's first paid public gig with the Castiles. The band's fee for the night is thirty-five dollars. The show's setlist is not known, but the final song is a rock and roll rendition of "In the Mood."

Rock'n Roll - Rhythm'n Blues

"The Castiles"

Management:
Gordon Vinyard

After 5 P.M.
(201) 462-5107

Oct. 8, 1965 – N.J.I.B. Club, Howell, NJ
The Castiles open for New York band the Florescents. Believed to be their first publicly advertised nightclub appearance, it is organized by area promoter Norman Seldin, who in 1972 would have his own band, Norman Seldin and the Joyful Noyze, featuring Clarence Clemons.

three-chord rock. In 1965, that meant British Invasion hits by the Beatles, the Rolling Stones, the Who, the Kinks, the Yardbirds, and so on, plus "Louie Louie" and its cosmically crude ilk. In fits of ambition, garage bands often tried some Motown and other R&B, too. In the spring of 1965, Bruce might have learned the Animals' "Bring It On Home to Me," the Yardbirds' "For Your Love," the Beatles' "Ticket to Ride," the Rolling Stones' "The Last Time," maybe even Bob Dylan's "Subterranean Homesick Blues."

Garage bands didn't stick to the basics out of commitment to pure simplicity or simple purity, but because the basics were their limit. It's also true, though, that the basics, done right, always, in every era, offer kicks and thrills.

The garage-band world sparked by the British Invasion didn't stay that innocent, that free of harassment, or that insulated for long. But it was glory while it lasted, pumping out your own group's interpretation of the riffs from the big hits, trying out your Mick Jagger wiggles, learning to sing harmony at the mic without bashing heads, checking out the chicks who were checking you out, finding out how much camaraderie could be created by sharing the shape of a fourth chord or a hint about how to phrase a tricky vocal line.

Being in a band meant being in the world, and for a lot of outsiders, that was more than enough.

BRUCE SPRINGSTEEN GOT his first guitar at nine, but his hands were too small to play it. He resumed playing in earnest as soon as he heard the Beatles, but until the Castiles, he'd never been in a band, although he might have jammed with a couple.

With Bruce added, the Castiles got a lot better right away, even after Vinny Roslin left to join the area's most popular band, the Motifs. Tex added Frank Marziotti, a twenty-five-year-old country-western guitarist whom Tex persuaded to play bass. Bruce was a natural. "Every time I showed him something, he'd come back the next day and show me how he did it," Marziotti says in the documentary *Becoming the Boss.* (Tex also recruited a second vocalist, Paul Popkin, to carry some straight pop material. Bruce sang one song, the Who's "My Generation.")

By July, Tex declared the band ready to play its first gig. He took them to a local music store and helped them buy their first serious equipment: a Danelectro 310 amp with full reverb, a couple of voice microphones, and a 50-watt Bogen amp for the PA system.

They played that first show in August at West Haven Swim Club. By the time the band played its final number, Glenn Miller's "In the Mood," a Tex favorite rearranged by Bruce for rock quartet, they knew they were good enough to do more. Between then and the summer of '68, the Castiles played teen clubs, wedding

Aug. 14, 1966 – Surf 'n' See Club, Sea Bright, NJ

This is the final show of a three-day Surfer's Holiday concert series. The Castiles share the bill along with Steven Van Zandt's band, the Shadows, opening for headliners Little Anthony and the Imperials.

Dec. 1, 1967 – Cafe Wha, New York, NY

The Castiles begin a two-month club residency at the Cafe Wha, performing Friday, Saturday, and Sunday afternoons from 1:00 to 6:00 P.M., during which time the club is an alcohol-free, teens-only discotheque.

Aug. 10, 1968 – Le Teendezvous, Shrewsbury, NJ

The final public performance of the Castiles

"This damn kid sat down and knocked out five songs that would blow your *ears*."
—Tex Vinyard

receptions, at least one supermarket opening, the Matawan-Keyport Roller Drome, Loew's Drive-in in Hazlet (opening for *The Russians Are Coming, The Russians Are Coming*), high school dances, an elementary school, and a series of gigs at the Surf 'n' See Club in Sea Bright. Sometimes they played at shows put on by Gary Stevens, one of WMCA's "Good Guys," the most popular radio deejays around. Frank Marziotti left after a night at the all-teenage Le Teendezvous club, where a girl asked him, "Are you Bruce's daddy?" The new bassist, Chris Fluhr, became the Castiles' surfer-blonde heartthrob. Sometime in 1966, Bart Haynes quit, replaced by Vinny "Skibotts" Manniello, the first of many Springsteen collaborators with colorful nicknames. The Castiles developed a following and even played one original song, "Sidewalk," which Springsteen had a hand in writing.

Few name bands played in the area, and both New York and Philadelphia were too far away for the teenage audience. Bands like the Castiles slaked the local thirst for beat music, and the best of those bands grew followings and, maybe more important, forged bonds among themselves that encouraged innovation.

It was a scene still amateurish enough to produce a periodic battle of the bands, pitting as many as twenty-five bands against one another in a single evening, with cash prizes for the top three groups. At the one in April 1966 at the Roller Drome, the Castiles came in third, after the Rogues and the Starliters, pocketing twenty-five dollars. As late as the summer of 1967, the Surf 'n' See Club advertised "Soul Music and Go Go Cages" along with appearances by groups including the Castiles. The names of the other bands suggest that the local rock culture incorporated greaser, fratboy, surfer, Anglophile, protobiker, and protopsychedelic subcultures: the Shadows, the Dekes, the Beau Mondes, the Henchmen, the Blue Denims, the Prisums, the Ascots, the Pubs, the Gremlins, and the Brew-Masters.

The teen clubs came out of attempts to capture and control pop-culture energy, a noble but doomed effort on the part of that minority of American adults who could stand what adolescents were creating for themselves.

That it didn't work can be seen in the repertoire of the Castiles. No recordings exist of the band onstage in '65 or '66, but setlists do, and in addition to rock songs ("For Your Love," "I Got You, Babe," "What'd I Say," "Wipe Out," and such Stones standards as "Play With Fire," "The Last Time," and "Satisfaction"), a lot of straight pop shows up: "Stranger on the Shore," "Moon River," "Summertime," even "Sentimental Journey."

But by mid-September 1967, a month after Bruce saw his first show by a major British Invasion act, the Who, the Castiles were playing a set suffused in psychedelic guitar rock. We know what the

The Castiles outside the Cafe Wha in Greenwich Village, New York, 1967. *From left:* Vinnie Maniello, George Theiss, Curt Fluhr, Bruce, Paul Popkin.

band sounded like then because of a gig at a club called the Left Foot, which was run by the Freehold Episcopal Church. Father Fred Coleman liked the Castiles enough to record two of their sets. They included Eric Burdon's "San Franciscan Nights," Jimi Hendrix's "Fire," the Beatles' "With a Little Help from My Friends" and "Eleanor Rigby," the psyche-punk classic "Hey Joe," Jeff Beck's "Jeff's Boogie," Moby Grape's "Omaha," as well as such folk-rock as "Catch the Wind," by Donovan, and Leonard Cohen's "Suzanne." They also did hard rock like Bo Diddley's "You Can't Judge a Book by Its Cover," soul like Sam and Dave's "Hold on I'm Comin'," and even a couple of unremarkable originals. Bruce sang almost all the songs, and his guitar was the group's other dominant voice. If that music is innocent teenage stuff, it's innocent in a very different way than "Wipe Out" or even "Satisfaction."

You could see where the Castiles would be popular —their version of rock's cutting edge expertly mimicked the originals. You could see why it was a dead end— nothing the band performed did more than gloss over someone else's original ideas. They had a hot guitarist and a cute bassist but not a sound to call their own. In an effort to keep things going, if not growing, they found a Greenwich Village booking at a little club called Cafe Wha.

The Castiles played at Cafe Wha on weekend after-

noons from 1:00 to 6:00 P.M. as part of a teens-only (no alcohol) discotheque. They played every week from the beginning of December 1967 through January 1968. It was a step up, they handled it well, but nothing really came of it.

THE JERSEY SCENE CHANGED in mid-February 1968 with the addition of a new club in Asbury Park, the Upstage. Run by an eccentric bohemian couple, Tom and Margaret Potter, the Upstage took over the second floor of the Green Mermaid teahouse, a folk club opened the previous spring. Upstairs, Margaret fronted the house band, Margaret and the Distractions. The sound was a roar because the entire back wall was speakers: "Maybe a hundred fifteen-inch speakers, thirty twelves, ten eights, and little Bassman heads in front of it. You plugged into those amplifiers with the speakers behind you," Danny Federici remembered. It was, for that day, an ungodly amount of decibels. Also on the stage were a little Farfisa electric keyboard and a drum kit.

Musicians loved the Upstage for the jam sessions that took place after all the local bands' gigs were done for the night. The Potters kept the club open until 5:00 A.M. on weekends. It was a chance to stretch musically, far beyond the jukebox-like efforts the teen clubs demanded. It was also a place to meet other local musicians and whatever

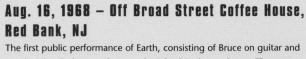

Aug. 16, 1968 – Off Broad Street Coffee House, Red Bank, NJ

The first public performance of Earth, consisting of Bruce on guitar and vocals, John Graham on bass, and Michael Burke on drums. They were possibly also joined by Castiles organist Bob Alfano. Graham, Burke, and Springsteen are believed to have met in May of this year at this Red Bank venue and had been jamming for a few months prior to this gig. All three were to enter Ocean County College that fall.

Nov. 1968 – Manhattan Diplomat Hotel Ballroom, New York, NY

Earth plays a 1,800-capacity venue in New York City. The show is a near sellout and this is the largest audience Bruce Springsteen has played to at this point in his performing career.

minor stars might be working in the area, to learn some licks, make friends, scout new collaborators. Over the following four years, the Upstage served as headquarters for the musicians who became the E Street Band. No one's ever described it better than Bruce, in the liner notes to the first Southside Johnny and the Asbury Jukes album, *I Don't Want to Go Home*:

"Everybody went there 'cause it was open later than the regular clubs and because between one and five in the morning, you could play pretty much whatever you wanted, and if you were good enough, you could choose the guys you wanted to play with.

"Tom Potter . . . plastered the walls with black light and pinups and showed fifties smokers to the kids in between the bands. . . . It was a great place. He'd slip you five or ten bucks to sit in, and you could work it so you'd never have to go home, 'cause by the time you got out of there it was dawn, and you could just flop on the beach all day, or you could run home before it got too light, nail the blankets over the windows of your room and just sleep straight through till the night.

"There were these guys . . . Mad Dog Lopez, Big Danny, Fast Eddie Larachi, his brother Little John, Margaret and the Distractions . . . Black Tiny, White Tiny, Miami Steve and assorted E Streeters, plus the heaviest drummer of them all, in terms of both poundage and sheer sonic impact, Biiiig Baaaaad Bobby

Williams, badass king of hearts, so tough he'd go the limit for you every time, all night . . . they're names that deserve to be spoken in reverence at least once, not 'cause they were great musicians (truth is, some of them couldn't play nothin' at all) but because they were each in their own way a living spirit of what, to me, rock and roll is all about. It was music as survival and they lived it down in their souls, night after night. These guys were their own heroes and they never forgot."

Most young musicians were in bands as a schoolboy lark. As they ceased to be schoolboys, the lark ended and those who remained had to get serious about what they were doing. Freehold and the other little towns in central New Jersey were the kind of places that turned out cannon fodder. Bart Haynes had enlisted in the Marines in September 1966, was sent to Vietnam, and a year later, in November, news came that he had died there. The Motifs' lead singer, Walter Cichon, had been drafted, and he, too, died in combat.

You couldn't really make a living being in a garage rock group. Admission to the teen clubs was stuck at a dollar or two; there was no bar to generate additional cash. The bars at the beach wanted Top 40 hits, none of this "underground rock" experimentation. The work was seasonal, too: A huge influx of tourists hits the Jersey Shore every year from Memorial Day to Labor Day, but from September to May, there's hardly anyone around.

Feb. 14, 1969 – Italian American Men's Association Clubhouse, Long Branch, NJ
The last Earth show is advertised as the St. Valentine's Day Massacre. Originally planned for the Paddock Lounge, the location was changed to the larger IAMA due to ticket demand.

Mar. 28, 1969 – West End Park, Long Branch, NJ
Child's debut performance, an outdoor show

June 1969 – Student Prince, Asbury Park, NJ
The first documented Springsteen performance at the newly opened club.

NOW APPEAR
ay - Saturday -
AT THE
udent Pr
Kingsley St., Asbu
Tel. 776-9837

The Castiles in New York City, 1967

So everybody had day jobs, or lived at home with their folks while they finished school, or both. Only Bruce stuck to music alone, and that kept him the poorest as well as the best, crashing where he could and eating sporadically. He kept on the lookout for something, and if the price included a little starvation, he'd pay it.

Yet the Castiles persisted a few more months. After Cafe Wha, they played most at the Hullabaloo clubs in Asbury, Freehold, and Middletown, and at Le Teendezvous, in New Shrewsbury. In June of '67, promoter-bandleader Norman Seldin staged another battle of the bands, this time at the Long Branch YMCA, and the Castiles served as guest judges. (They also closed the show by playing one number.)

Bruce began playing occasionally as a solo act at a club in Red Bank, the Off Broad Street Coffeehouse. (The whole band played Off Broad Street in July, backing local singer Jeannie Clark.) In August, with college looming for some and marriage for others, the Castiles disintegrated. Everybody except Fluhr and Popkin remained a musician; only one made any kind of career in music.

An ad for the August 10 show at Le Teendez-

Sept. 20, 1969 – Free University, Richmond, VA
Final show in which the band is billed as Child. Bruce changes the name to Steel Mill after hearing that another band named Child already has an album out on Roulette Records.

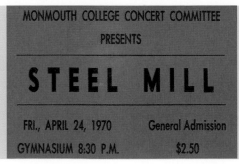

MONMOUTH COLLEGE CONCERT COMMITTEE
PRESENTS

STEEL MILL

FRI., APRIL 24, 1970   General Admission
GYMNASIUM 8:30 P.M. $2.50

Feb. 28, 1970 – Free University, Richmond, VA
Steel Mill drives nonstop from California to Richmond to make it to this show on time, with Vini Lopez and Tinker West doing most of the driving. This is Vinnie Roslin's final show as bass player for the band; he is soon replaced by Steven Van Zandt.

vous announced: "'The Castiles' will now perform as 'The Earth Band.'"

BY 1968, IT WAS obvious that in the nooks and crannies of hit songs lurked not just sex but rebellion, and even darker things. For the boldest, most talented, most antisocial, and, yes, loneliest kids in garage bands, rock and roll—now just "rock"—appeared as more than a pastime. It offered a life.

Springsteen formed Earth, the first band that he created for himself, for his own ideas, for his own songs, to get closer to the core. Initially, he worked with John Graham on bass and Michael Burke on drums—the trio format suggests a group inspired by the Jimi Hendrix Experience and Eric Clapton's Cream. In 1968, such power trios abounded. A list of Earth's material from the period includes Hendrix's "Foxy Lady," "Purple Haze," and "Fire," the Yardbirds' proto–jam band "Shapes of Things" and "Jeff's Boogie," Traffic's "Dear Mr. Fantasy," Ten Years After's "Help Me," and a pack of Cream numbers, including their blues tropes, "Spoonful" and Robert Johnson's almighty "Crossroads."

Bruce met Graham and Burke at Off Broad Street, and they jammed there through the summer. All three were scheduled to enter college that fall. In September, they did a show at Ocean County College, where Bruce had enrolled, the first of several gigs they played at OCC that winter. Other than that, Earth mostly played the same old circuit: Le Teendezvous, the Red Bank Coffeehouse (where Bruce still occasionally did acoustic shows), the Freehold Hullabaloo.

It was garage rock with a joint between its lips. Even Earth's November gig at the Diplomat Hotel in New York, later one of the redoubts of the New York Dolls, came together out of Jersey naïveté. Two OCC students had booked the 1,800-seat venue. Since it was about five years too early for anyone outside of central Jersey to know Bruce Springsteen, fewer than a hundred tickets had been sold the week before the show. Somehow, the promoters convinced the school administration to hire busses as part of the ticket price and the gig became an OCC field trip to Times Square. The show almost sold out. It was by far the largest crowd Bruce had ever had, and the peak of the power trio's career. By Valentine's Day 1969, Earth was through.

THERE'S NO RECORDING of Earth, but images do exist from the period that extends from the late Castiles through Bruce's third band, Child. They don't show the canny, quirky, mobile frontman who became famous.

STEEL MILL
FORMERLY CHILD of NT

Aug. 14, 1970 – Seventh and Marshall Street Parking Deck, Richmond, VA
Triple bill headlined by Steel Mill, with Mercy Flight as one of the opening bands. This outdoor show was probably modeled on the Beatles' rooftop concert in *Let It Be,* which was then showing in theaters. Shortly after this show, Bruce invites Mercy Flight lead singer Robbin Thompson to join the band.

Sept. 11, 1970 – Clearwater Swim Club, Atlantic Highlands, NJ
The infamous Clearwater Swim Club show. An outdoor show, five hours long, including four bands headlined by Steel Mill. It is the debut performance by new vocalist Robbin Thompson. Mercy Flight drummer Dave "Hazy Davy" Hazlett fills in because Vini Lopez is absent. Local police order the band's power to be shut off and arrest several audience members for using drugs. Keyboardist Danny Federici gets his nickname, "The Phantom," when he "disappears" for a few days after being pursued by police for some actual and some alleged damage to the venue.

"Everybody went there (the Upstage Club) 'cause it was open later than the regular clubs and because between one and five in the morning, you could play pretty much whatever you wanted, and if you were good enough, you could choose the guys you wanted to play with."

—BS

They show a scrawny teenager with long, kinky hair flowing past his shoulders, often with his head down as if he were playing straight into his guitar pickups. In offstage photos from the period, Springsteen also seems aloof or, more accurately, insular.

Bruce's charisma was already in play, though. His two classmates booked the Hotel Diplomat because they knew they'd found a rock star. At the Upstage jam sessions, Bruce remembered Garry Tallent pulling a chair out into the middle of the room, so he could stare at Springsteen more closely, and Garry wasn't the only one staring.

A week after Earth's final show, a quartet came together in the middle of the night at the Upstage: Bruce Springsteen on guitar, Vini "Mad Dog" Lopez from Sonny and the Starliters on drums, Danny Federici, a freelancer from Flemington, on organ, and Bruce's old chum from the Castiles, Vinny Roslin, on bass. After a couple of weeks of what amounted to rehearsals with an audience, this band named itself Child and played an afternoon gig at a park in Long Branch. Vini Lopez remembers a big crowd and that Child, though not the closing act, "caused a scene." After that, they tried to play on the steps of Monmouth College. "There were a lot of people, three, four hundred people at the bottom of the stairs, and when we started putting up our equipment, they all came toward us," Lopez said. "They wanted to get right around where we were. And we got scared. We all ran inside Monmouth College, saying 'What the hell's going on here?' We thought they were gonna attack us, like we saw in them Beatles movies. We really thought that. Then we came out and set up and played."

Such local stardom didn't translate when it came time to look for a job, though. Child took a gig at the Pandemonium Club for several weeks and began working the grueling marathon of adult clubs: five sets, a total stage time of two and a half hours.

Then it was back to the circuit: Le Teendezvous, the Asbury Hullabaloo (soon to become the Sunshine In), a few more nights at Pandemonium, including one opening for bluesman James Cotton, one gig at OCC, another at Monmouth College, lots of shows in area parks.

A new mentor turned up: Carl "Tinker" West, a California émigré who ran the Challenger East surfboard factory in Wanamassa, New Jersey. West came from the fringes of the early West Coast hippie scene and he recognized Child as something special. "Something was going on and it felt right," he said in *Becoming the Boss*. "I thought it was great basic rock and roll. Not a lot of fancy effects, not a lot of BS. It was rock and roll, and that's what worked."

Of course, it was not the rock and roll of Elvis or the Beatles. It was the underground rock of Cream, Hendrix, and Traffic, a thicker soup of sound, more given to extended soloing than concise three-minute hit tunes. But this was Bruce's band now. "Bruce would write these songs on a daily basis," said West. "When he finally got [the song] where he thought it would work, he'd get [the group] all together in a pile and they'd play with it 'til they got [an arrangement]."

West had ideas about lights, sound equipment, and promotion. Mainly, he believed that groups should play all original music. West also thought that the band needed to play more college dates and that it should travel outside Jersey to find them. He also got them work as the opening act when such stars as Ike and Tina Turner, Grand Funk Railroad, Jethro Tull, and Black Sabbath played the Shore. The group already had been playing shows at area parks.

On June 1, 1969, Child traveled to Richmond, Virginia, for a free concert in Monroe Park. The set included Jimi's "Voodoo Chile" and a Springsteen original, "Jennifer." Although Child went straight back to the Jersey circuit, West's plan established a Virginia beachhead.

In mid-September, Child went back to Richmond, playing at the Free University's student center, later known as the String Factory. A rough recording of one of those shows features a batch of original songs: "Sister Theresa," "Garden State Parkway Blues," "Resurrection," and the instrumental "KT-88." Springsteen's lyrics showcased his renegade Catholicism, but mainly, Child's material served to set up elaborate, improvised instrumental virtuosity. The songs used basic blues structures heavily influenced by, among others, the Allman Brothers and the post-*Tommy* Who—the bluesier end of jam band music.

There were two routes for a band now. One was playing clubs, sticking to cover versions, sneaking in an original or two, basically becoming a background for drunks and dancers and a lot more of the former than the latter. Five sets a night, night after night, 'til you were old and gray and began to long for a wedding gig.

The other option was the new rock scene, easy enough if your base was a city like New York or London or even Detroit, where there were psychedelic ballrooms and hip clubs that encouraged playing original music. Tinker West figured out that this hard-rock universe could be accessed by emphasizing colleges. On October 15, Child played at Monmouth College's Vietnam Moratorium program, and by November 1, they were back in Richmond, playing at Virginia Commonwealth University.

They came home to find that another band—another Jersey band—called Child had released an album. They decided to become Steel Mill for reasons nobody recalls. The sound and the personnel remained Allmanized blues.

A local Richmond band, Mercy Flight, became Steel Mill's sidekicks; the two bands played many

Bruce at the Upstage, ca. 1969

A snapshot taken at the Upstage in 1971 after Steel Mill's final show. *From left:* Bruce, unidentified fan, Vini Lopez, Robbin Thompson, Steven Van Zandt, Danny Federici.

gigs with one another. Bruce became particularly close to its leader, Robbin Thompson, a guitarist and singer. Drummer Dave Hazlett, later immortalized as Hazy Davy in "Spirit in the Night," also spent a lot of time with Steel Mill.

Tinker West decided Steel Mill's next move would be revisiting his old California haunts. In December, they played a fundraiser for the trip at the Wanamassa surfboard factory, their rehearsal hall (and Bruce's frequent crash pad), and headed west the next day. They traveled in a van overcrowded with people and equipment. It frequently broke down, so they traveled slowly.

Just before New Year's, they arrived at the Esalen Institute in Big Sur, California. Esalen, a temple of group therapy and alternative lifestyles, represented the kind of place that suburban New Jersey kids thought existed only in their finest hallucinations. "I'd never been out of Jersey in my life," said Bruce. "Suddenly, I get to Esalen and there's all these people walking around in sheets." Steel Mill played as an added attraction at Esalen's New Year's Eve party, then hung out, cribbing in a log cabin, doing another show on January 2. At their next stop, in Oakland, Steven Van Zandt says they slept in a garage. They were too broke to be sure of having enough money for the tolls to San Francisco.

A January 8 audition at the Avalon Ballroom flopped. Steel Mill then played the College of Marin before going to work at the Matrix, one of the birthplaces of acid rock, opening for Boz Scaggs one night and Elvin Bishop another.

Phil Elwood of the *San Francisco Examiner* caught them at the Matrix, playing to about fifty customers. In his review, Elwood called it "one of the most memorable evenings of rock in a long time," adding, "I have never been so overwhelmed by an unknown band." He especially liked the songwriting and "a fascinating juxtaposition of stop-time solos, interesting lyrics, and a heavy, heavy ending" in "Lady Walking Down by the River."

The review—or Bill Graham attending the Esalen party—got them two nights at Fillmore West, a week apart, and a recording session for Graham's Fillmore label. Graham offered Steel Mill a thousand-dollar advance on a long-term record deal. Tinker West convinced the band to turn it down.

After a final gig at the College of Marin on February 23, they made a pell-mell, multibreakdown drive to Virginia, where they had String Factory gigs, then went home.

The shows at the String Factory were the first in which Springsteen debuted two of the most important Steel Mill songs, "Goin' Back to Georgia," which has an Allmans-like grandeur, and "Send

That Boy to Jail," with its Lynyrd Skynyrd–like narrative and guitar chops (albeit nobody north of Georgia heard of Lynyrd Skynyrd until 1974).

You went to see Steel Mill, like other such bands, mainly to hear the music, not to dance or to drink. This wasn't music best suited to clubs anymore. Groups like Steel Mill played concerts.

Listening, not dancing or screaming, as the main audience activity, broke sharply with previous rock and roll. So the shows could be—not that they always were—presented as primarily musical events: concerts. This meant, in turn, that the shows became longer, sometimes much longer (twenty-minute sets gave way to two-hour performances). These shows were meant to do some of the same things that classical music and jazz did, in terms of challenging perceptions, digging deep into the talents and psyches of the players and singers, and asking something similar of the audience. As all concert events do, they also provided the audience and the performers with an identity.

Newfangled as it seemed, the music played at these rock concerts was based in anachronism: The blues—not just the country blues of Son House and Robert Johnson but the city blues of Muddy Waters and Howlin' Wolf, too—had mutated years before into the more profusely syncopated R&B of James Brown or merged with gospel to become the soul music of Stax and Motown. Heavy underground rock represented both the persistence of the blues and its deteriora-

Bruce, ca. 1969

tion, since perhaps one in a hundred rock musicians (Johnny Winter, say) could play it with something like the old fervor and nuance. By 1969, blues-rock musicians like Eric Clapton had already begun to move on. But in Asbury Park, isolated as it was, the form held sway much longer. The musicians in such spots made their own rules, though, and Asbury's musicians remained open to rock and roll from the fifties and the British Invasion.

After the Beatles did the last of the great screamer tours in 1966, "psychedelic ballrooms" arose: Fillmore West and Fillmore East set a pattern for the Boston Tea Party, Detroit's Grande Ballroom, and Philadelphia's Electric Factory. Their underground-rock concept traveled rapidly, abetted by recordings like *Super Session*, by Al Kooper, Michael Bloomfield, and Stephen Stills, and *The Who Live at Leeds*. The influence of both can readily be heard in Steel Mill.

In March, Steven Van Zandt, from Middletown, an Upstage regular who'd been in several bands, became Steel Mill's new bass player. Steven wasn't a bassist but Bruce wanted to play with him, and turning a guitarist into a bassist is practically rock tradition (ask Ronnie Wood). From what can be heard on the many tapes of Steel Mill, an indication of the band's popularity, adding Van Zandt didn't make much change in the music.

Steel Mill brought Mercy Flight to a Jersey college date in May. Steel Mill headlined a Memorial Day battle of the bands at the Virginia State Fairgrounds. For the rest of the summer, the two bands played back and forth from Richmond to Asbury Park. On August 14, they played a still-discussed concert on the seventh-floor roof of a Richmond parking lot. "It was after that concert that Bruce said, 'I'm thinking about another singer in the band. Why don't you come up and try out for it?'" Thompson said in *Becoming the Boss*. "It very much took me aback. I couldn't figure out why he needed anybody else." But Thompson went to New Jersey and rehearsed with Steel Mill for the better part of a week. "Then they all went into a room and left me outside and came out and said, 'Okay, we think this'll work.' So I quit school and moved to New Jersey."

Thompson feels Springsteen wanted the freedom to play more lead guitar and that he needed help with the background singing. "I wasn't the lead singer frontman. A lot of times I just played tambourine," Thompson recalled. "They also thought they could teach me to play bass for a few songs." But Robbin didn't necessarily come to New Jersey for that. Thompson recognized that Steel Mill, or at least Springsteen, had a future. "He had a way about him onstage. You knew something was gonna happen with the band or at least with him. . . . You noticed right off that it's a natural thing for him to be doing what he's doing."

Oct. 10, 1970 – Centennial Park, Nashville, TN
All-day show starting in the afternoon with Steel Mill, among other bands, supporting headliner Roy Orbison. Bruce referenced this show in his speech inducting Roy Orbison into the Rock and Roll Hall of Fame in 1987. "In 1970 I rode for fifteen hours in the back of a U-Haul truck to open for Roy Orbison at the Nashville Music Festival. It was a summer night and I was twenty years old, and he came out in dark glasses, a dark suit, and he played some dark music. . . ."

Steel Mill Churns Out
A Roomful of Good Music

Nov. 27, 1970 – Sunshine In, Asbury Park, NJ (two shows)
Steel Mill opens for Cactus and headliner Black Sabbath.

Thompson's first show with the band came at the Clearwater Swim Club in Middletown, Van Zandt's hometown. For that show, Mercy Flight drummer Dave Hazlett filled in for Vini Lopez, still dealing with a bust for hassling authorities at a Virginia Commonwealth concert.

Middletown cops were always unfriendly to hippie kids. At an earlier Clearwater show, which drew four thousand, a dozen cop cars lined the road outside the club, ticketing illegally parked cars. These police were specially trained in "riot control," which seems to have taught them how to create a riot.

At the September show, shielded and armored police surrounded the venue from a hilltop perch. As Steel Mill began playing, the police moved in to search for drugs. The cops also ordered the power shut off. Danny Federici blew his top and pitched his speakers down off the stage, right onto a passing policeman. Amidst the chaos, Federici escaped. He was immediately and forever after dubbed the Phantom.

A Child publicity photo. *From left:* Bruce, Danny Federici, Vini Lopez, Vinnie Roslin

WHY THE HELL DID the Middletown police force have riot gear?

In the wake of the rebellions in Newark, Watts, and Detroit, paranoia rampaged through segregated

Jan. 8, 1971 – Upstage Club, Asbury Park, NJ

Bruce joins Steven Van Zandt & Friends during the first of two shows. The other musicians besides Bruce and Steven are Garry Tallent, Danny Federici, Southside Johnny, Joe Hagstrom, and Bobby Williams. Steven puts the show together to help Bruce come up with new ideas for his next band.

ROCK ALL NITE
UPSTAGE CLUB
702 COOKMAN AVE.
ASBURY PARK, N. J.
FRI. & SAT.   PRESENTS   FRI. & SAT.
MAY 21 & 22   MAY 21 & 2
BRUCE SPRINGSTEEN

Jan. 23, 1971 – Upstage Club, Asbury Park, NJ

Advertised as Steel Mill's last show.

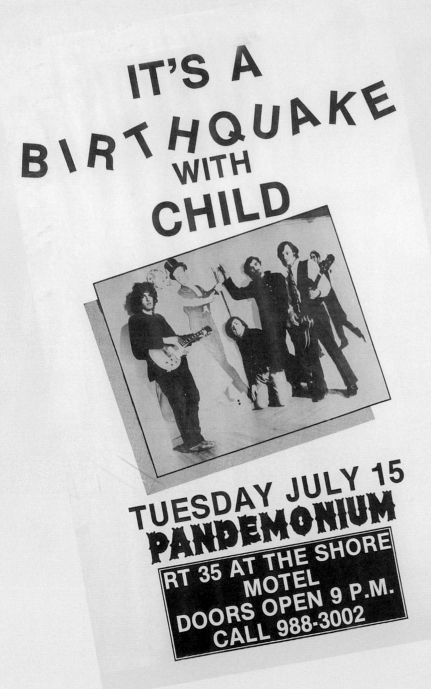

suburbs. In Monmouth County, there was even a known flashpoint: Asbury Park, where racial and class segregation were so extreme that they became the subject of a book, Daniel Wolff's fine *4th of July, Asbury Park: A History of the Promised Land.* The city had endured a minor eruption in July 1967, a rebellion associated with the much larger one in Newark.

In 1970, 30 percent of Asbury Park's year-round population was on welfare. The amusement park strip up at the beach, the cruising circuit on Kingsley and Cookman avenues thrived. The West Side ghetto all but starved.

On the Fourth, a Saturday, Ten Years After played Convention Hall, drawing over a thousand almost exclusively white teenagers, and a teen dance was held on the West Side. A melee began later that night in the heart of the ghetto, Springwood Avenue. It ended soon enough, but the next night, a series of police skirmishes with crowds of up to two hundred kids led to looting, and before the sun came up, eight buildings were destroyed. This time it didn't end and it didn't stay isolated to the West Side. On Tuesday, the plate glass windows of the Thom McAn shoe store below the Upstage shattered as the rebellion moved to the white East Side and the cops started shooting. On Friday, the riot was finally "contained." By then the West Side was, as Wolff wrote, "torched, gutted, and left for dead." The city refused to negotiate over any of the demands of the impoverished black community.

Wolff writes that when Bruce heard about the riots, he climbed a water tower and watched the city burn. Some of his musician friends paid virtually no attention; the Upstage remained intact, and it was still safe territory,

Child poses on Tinker West's truck,1969. *From left:* Vini Lopez, Vinnie Roslin, Bruce, Danny Federici.

even for a black player like David Sancious. Others, Steven Van Zandt told Wolff, only cared about "some kind of sacred, mystical shaman thing." Wolff calls this attitude "the heart of rock and roll," but rock and roll has several hearts, and one of them was in big trouble.

The police assault on the Clearwater show dispelled the notion of the music as a safe space. The burning of Asbury Park dispelled the notion of the boardwalk city as sanctuary. Steel Mill traveled as far as Nashville and up to Newark, a rare foray into north Jersey. There was now an Asbury club called the Sunshine In, where they could play some original music, so the pretense may have been that nothing had changed or even that things were getting better. Consciously or not, Springsteen knew from what he'd seen from the water tower that this could not be true.

He decided to join his family in California for Christmas. He told the band that Steel Mill was over.

SOMETIME THAT WINTER, Bruce saw a Van Morrison show. After that, he drowned himself in *His Band and the Street Choir*, the album Morrison released in January 1971.

Springsteen knew Morrison's early albums with the British Invasion group, Them, the most cosmic of all British R&B groups. The music Bruce set out to make in early 1971 wasn't that guitar-led blues rock, though. It had more to do with *Street Choir*'s "Call Me Up in Dreamland," "Domino" (a tribute to early R&B titan Fats Domino), "Blue Monday," and "If Ever I Needed Someone." The arrangements feature a horn band with slinky grooves. It's an album filled with sunshine right down to its gloom, an effortless synthesis of Celtic melancholy and African American R&B ecstasy. Morrison sought a way out of pretension through pastoralism, but he retained a rock and roll edge. The best comparison remains the solo albums made by Curtis Mayfield after he left the Impressions, which helped define black rock.

When he got back from California in January 1970, Springsteen played with Van Zandt and others under various noms de guerre: Steve Van Zandt and Friends, Steve Van Zandt and the Big Bad Bobby Williams Band. He even did a couple of gigs with Steel Mill—a small notice in the *Asbury Park Press* declared the January 23 show at the Upstage their last. Bruce also played solo at the Green Mermaid. He sat in every night that the Upstage was open.

The Bruce Springsteen Band (Bruce didn't like the name; everyone else did) played its first gig at a dance in Deal. The group included Van Zandt, Lopez, David Sancious—the black pianist from Belmar—and on bass, Upstage regular Garry W. Tallent, a young, white vet-

Mar. 27, 1971 – Sunshine In, Asbury Park, NJ (two shows)

Allman Brothers headline, three bands total, opening set by Bruce Springsteen and the Friendly Enemies (Steven Van Zandt on guitar, Garry Tallent on bass, David Sancious on keyboards, Vini Lopez on drums and vocals, Southside Johnny on harmonica and vocals, Al Tellone on sax and vocals, John "Hotkeys" Waasdorp on electric piano, Bobby Feigenbaum on tenor sax, Bobby Williams on drums and vocals, and Tinker West on congas). During the two shows played on this date, four Asbury denizens (Kevin Connair, Bruce Greenwood, Danny Gallagher, and Big Tiny, the bouncer at the Upstage) sit on stage and play Monopoly. There is a point in the set where Bruce joins them at the Monopoly table and sings. Backstage, Duane Allman (who dies later this year) shows Steven some slide guitar licks.

eran of a bunch of West Side soul gigs.

Springsteen wanted a bigger group, keeping the rock and roll rhythm section but featuring horns and backup singers. Why? Tinker West thinks he was bored, and heavily affected by the rise not only of Morrison but of the big band Leon Russell built around Joe Cocker for the Mad Dogs and Englishmen tour. Maybe. Maybe Bruce just saw more possibilities with this music—you can play heavy guitar solos in a horn band. You can't conjure horns in a three-piece jam band.

At the end of March, the Allman Brothers were coming to the Sunshine In (the renamed Hullabaloo Club), and Bruce wanted desperately to be the opening act. He just didn't have a band. So he put together Bruce Springsteen and the Friendly Enemies, which quickly acquired the snappier name Dr. Zoom and the Sonic Boom.

It was as much a troupe as a rock band. The musicians included Bruce, Van Zandt, Lopez, Sancious, Tallent, Southside Johnny Lyon on harp and vocal, an electric keyboardist, two saxophones, Big Bad Bobby Williams as a second drummer, and Tinker West on congas. Dr. Zoom also included the Sonic People, a chorus who also did skits; a baton twirler; and Big Tiny, the Upstage bouncer; and a couple other guys playing Monopoly. Bruce actually sat at the Monopoly table and sang during one song. "It was basically taking the feel of the Upstage club and bringing it out into a concert setting, on a large scale," said sax player Albee Tellone in *Becoming the Boss*.

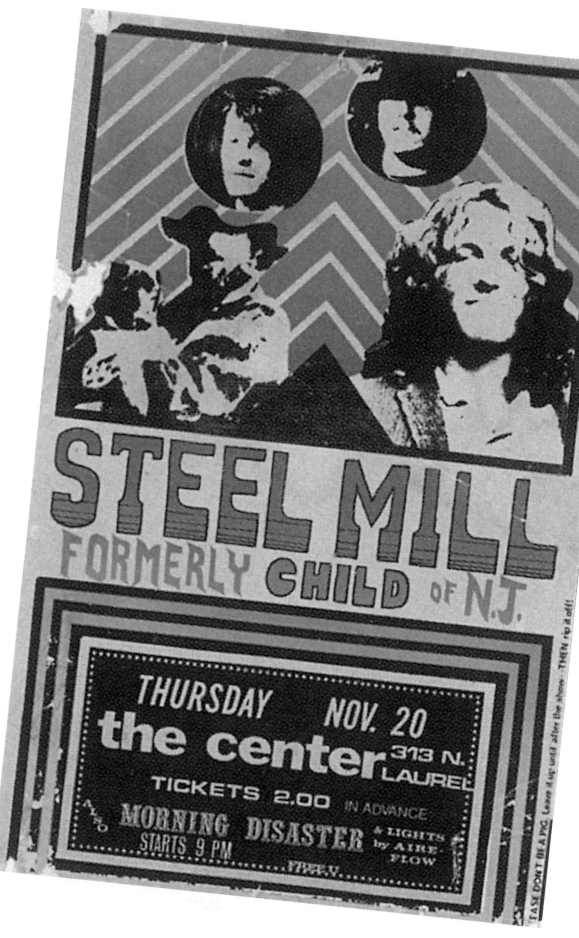

Dr. Zoom and the Sonic Boom, 1971

Bruce in Steel Mill, 1970

To judge from the bootleg *The Bruce Springsteen Story Vol. 5*, Dr. Zoom was the first band to sound something like the Springsteen we know. The expansively tender version of the Shirelles' "Will You Still Love Me Tomorrow" highlights Bruce's girl-group influence. (He could be described in this mode as the male Ronnie Spector.) "Jambalaya" has no relation to the Hank Williams song; the guitar riff is closer to the Move's glam-rock "Do Ya," though most of the song bows in the direction of *Street Choir*. But in the "Jambalaya" approach to a rock and soul synthesis and the song's eight-and-a-half-minute length are familiar to concert-goers who know "Rosalita" and "Mary's Place." The lyric's fusion of legend and lunacy—"She's built like Marilyn Monroe but she walks like Smokey Stover"—comes straight out of *Greetings From Asbury Park, N. J.*

In May, the same club hosted Dr. Zoom and the Sonic Boom without the Monopoly players and a few of the other nonmusical elements, and with more female backup singers. Their setlist was about half old rock and R&B hits (Dylan's "It Takes a Lot to Laugh, It Takes a Train to Cry," "Cry to Me" from Solomon Burke, a Chuck Berry medley to close) and half leftover Steel Mill originals. Dr. Zoom also did a show at Newark State College at the first annual Ernie the Chicken Festival. Then it was back to grinding out five sets a night as the Sundance Blues Band.

Finally, on July 10, the full-scale Bruce Springsteen Band debuted at Brookdale Community College in Lincroft, New Jersey. Here were all the musical pieces from Dr. Zoom, plus a third horn (Harvey Cherlin's trumpet) and a pair of first-rate female gospel-soul singers, Delores Holmes and Barbara Dinkins. Plus a ten-piece band featuring a setlist with a whole lot of classic R&B, "Goin' Back to Georgia" and one of the first Springsteen songs that lasted long enough to get professionally recorded, "You Mean So Much to Me," a feature for Holmes (and later a single for Ronnie Spector of the Ronettes).

At their second gig, the BSB opened for Humble Pie, whose coleader Peter Frampton reportedly offered Springsteen the opening slot on the rest of the tour and an A&M Records audition. West turned him down on the spot, without rebellion from Bruce. The BSB also played at Lincoln Center's Damrosch Park—part of a culture series held daily that summer—and on the Jersey circuit.

"Everybody talks about the Asbury sound," said Vini Lopez. "Well, there's the beginning of it. The change from Steel Mill to that band, with the horns. Nobody did that before—maybe a sax player, but not a horn section."

You don't just throw a ten-piece band onstage. Its elaborate arrangements require extensive rehearsals. It's not ten times harder than playing solo—but it's a hundred times harder than running a jam.

You also don't just put a ten-piece-band on the road. "All that went through my mind was, if you

"Everybody talks about the Asbury sound. Well, there's the beginning of it. The change from Steel Mill to that band, with the horns. Nobody did that before—maybe a sax player, but not a horn section."

—Vini Lopez

have ten people, how're we gonna book this, on the level we're on," said Tinker West. "Because if we get two thousand dollars a night, that's two hundred dollars gross per individual. . . . How you gonna put them up in a hotel room? With a four-piece band, I could find people who would put us up. We had no overhead. . . . The things we did with no money—sure it was hard. *But we didn't have any debts.* But when the ten-piece came in, I didn't resign. I just looked at the economics of the whole thing and said, 'Forget it.'" Tinker wasn't out of the picture; he still played congas sometimes and he ran the soundboard. But he wasn't going to be responsible.

From what can be discerned from the few BSB relics, Springsteen didn't have an original synthesis. He had a fine core band, and Delores Holmes was a marvelous singer. But he hadn't written his breakthrough material. Anyway, the economic issues really were insurmountable. By late August, when the Bruce Springsteen Band began a forty-date residency at Asbury's Student Prince, the group was down to Bruce, Sancious, Van Zandt, Tallent, and Lopez.

Sometime in early September, on another dark and stormy night, part of the solution wandered into the Student Prince. Norman Seldin and the Joyful Noyze had a gig at the nearby Wonder Bar, and on that evening, their tenor sax player, Clarence "Big Man" Clemons, decided to go take a look at Springsteen. Those who were there say it was so wet and windy that the door really did almost come off its hinges when Clarence entered that night. Nothing came of the encounter, but Bruce and Clarence kept in touch.

On October 29, Springsteen led a jam session from 2:00 to 5:00 A.M. at the Upstage. The next night, the club closed forever. Bruce was already in Richmond (with a band featuring Delores Holmes), opening for Cactus at Virginia Commonwealth. But most of the work he found was back home in Asbury, where he remained a local hero. A Student Prince place mat featured an "unravel the Springsteen titles" game.

After the Student Prince gig on December 19, Bruce left for Christmas in California with his folks. He said he might not come back at all. Finding no one he could connect with enough to form a new band, he came home before the end of January. The BSB reunited for one show at the Captain's Garter.

That show typifies the problem with the Jersey music scene. The Bruce Springsteen Band in full array, with Sancious and Tallent in the mix, packed the house, closed the show without having top billing. (No one ever wanted to follow Bruce onstage.) The music, Springsteen felt, was about the best he'd ever made. He and Steven eagerly approached club manager Terry Magovern. "We'll get a regular gig out of this," they reassured one another.

Instead, they ran straight into bar-band reality. "I can never hire you again," said Magovern.

"What do you mean?"

"I can never hire you again," he repeated.

"But the joint was packed. Everybody'll come back, too."

"Yeah, but nobody drank."

Van Zandt claims they didn't even get paid. (Terry Magovern is now the most indispensable member of Springsteen's crew, on and off the road.)

They finagled a February residency at the Back Door, in Richmond. Bruce's songs now dominated the setlist. One of them, "When You Dance," was later rewritten for Southside Johnny and the Asbury Jukes, and "Cowboys of the Sea" and "Down to Mexico" had the wordplay and loose but tight arrangement style characteristic of pre–*Born to Run* Bruce albums.

Back in Jersey, it was high schools and bars. But West had bumped into a couple of writers from Wes Farrell's Brill Building song shop, Mike Appel and Jim Cretecos. On Valentine's Day, Springsteen went into Manhattan and auditioned. Appel, who did the talking, suggested he come back when he had more and better songs. A month or two later, Springsteen did. This time Appel got excited.

The songs Bruce played Appel, or more particularly, the way he played them, fit in as a careening version of the then fashionable singer-songwriter style. Appel saw Bruce as a new Dylan. In any event, they worked out a deal—Appel gained control of management, publishing, and recording. Bruce suggested calling John Hammond, the talent scout who had discovered Dylan. So Appel called him.

At the May 2 audition, Hammond heard enough to arrange for Springsteen to do a live showcase at the Gaslight Au-Go-Go in Greenwich Village. Bruce played four or five songs, among them "Growin' Up" and "It's Hard to Be a Saint in the City." He went on before the billed attractions, blues harpist Charlie Musselwhite, and a New York City singer-songwriter with much in common with Springsteen, Garland Jeffreys. Sure that he had not only a writer but a performer on his hands, Hammond offered a recording deal. This one, Springsteen accepted.

Bruce in the Bruce Springsteen Band, 1971

The mid-seventies

Chapter Two

No Time to Get Cute

"If it don't work out, I ain't lame, I can walk."

TO GET INTO MAX'S KANSAS CITY, you walked up a long, steep, very narrow staircase. On his way up those stairs to see Bruce Springsteen in February 1973, John Hammond had a heart attack. They took him down to the restaurant part of Max's, and an ambulance came. He lived another fifteen years.

I went up those stairs on July 18, 1973, healthy and eager. I was twenty-three years old and had lived in New York City for two weeks. My first weekend, I saw Tito Puente, Aretha Franklin, and Ray Charles on one bill. Music that amazed me, changed my way of looking at the world, seemed to lay in wait everywhere.

I'd mainly come to see the Wailers: Bob Marley, Peter Tosh, and Bunny Wailer. Already the legends of reggae, they'd never been to the States before, and as a trio, they never came again. Reggae still meant nothing in the United States, so they were playing this club that couldn't have held more than 150 people.

The Wailers had plenty of record company money behind them. Nevertheless, to my surprise, the Wailers were the opening act. Bruce Springsteen would close the show.

To me, Springsteen was the extra added attraction. The Wailers were proven—their *Catch a Fire*, with "Concrete Jungle," "Stop the Train," and "Stir It Up," was smart, intense, original. In Jamaica and England, they had made hits for years, legendary music like "Trenchtown Rock." Springsteen, whose first album I'd loved because of the ways it defied "new-Dylan" hype and whose second did its best to conjure an American voice to equal Van Morrison's, remained a bundle of possibilities.

The Wailers met all my expectations with a fine show.

Springsteen lit magic and danced while it burned. After the first show, I ran home—about a mile—and wrote my five hundred–word review for the next day's *Newsday* as quick as I could type. I didn't really get him right, but I got him some: "[His music has] only the visionary ramblings of Dylan and maybe Van Morrison as its precedent. I'm not quite sure whether what I saw is believable, but if it is, Bruce Springsteen is one of the most healthful signs of post-sixties rock, a polysyllabic punk who walks it like he talks it."

I rushed because I wanted—needed—to get back to Max's for his second set. His charisma grabbed me that tightly.

I sat through that second show on the edge of my chair and this time, preoccupied by only the songs and the singer, I believed it. There was a ton of music up there on that stage. Vini Lopez's runs across his drum kit, the ragged but right harmonies, the touches of tuba and flute and accordion that Springsteen used like a poor boy's orchestra, the ringing guitar, the insistent sax, the roisterous organ, and most of all, the soul-man intensity he brought to the singing of those madman lyrics.

This crazy charisma pulled me back that night. But it didn't make me into one of his crazy fans. For the next

eight months, I played the record once in a while and occasionally looked forward to seeing him again.

IN JANUARY 1974, I moved to Boston to work for the *Real Paper*, one of the city's alternative weeklies. One of the things I did there was edit a column written by Jon Landau, the record reviews editor of *Rolling Stone*, who I'd known since he'd produced the MC5's second album, *Back in the U.S.A.*

I went up there in February, and I was back working for *Newsday* by about Labor Day. In between, I saw Bruce Springsteen again, and this time, my life changed.

In April, Springsteen scheduled a three-night stand at a bar in Massachusetts called Joe's Place in Cambridge's unfashionable Inman Square. Bruce had played the joint in January and bonded with owner Joe Spadafora. When the Inman Square place burned down a week before the April dates, Bruce agreed to move the shows to Charlie's Bar, in more upscale Harvard Square. He and opening act Mighty Joe Young, a young blues singer, agreed to play the dates as a benefit for Spadafora.

Strong buzz preceded these shows, at least in the Boston music scene. Landau's column that week raved about *The Wild, the Innocent, and the E Street Shuffle*, then six months old, as if it were a brand-new record, which it might as well have been for all the attention it got after the

Apr. 16, 1971 – Upstage Club, Asbury Park, NJ

Billed as the Bruce Springsteen Jam Concert, they are actually Bruce's chance to audition potential members for his next band. These shows will ultimately result in the formation of the Bruce Springsteen Band and the Sundance Blues Band (Southside Johnny, Garry Tallent, Bruce, Steven, and Vini).

May 14, 1971 – Sunshine In, Asbury Park, NJ, and May 15, 1971 – Newark State College, Union, NJ

The only two shows played by the Dr. Zoom and the Sonic Boom configuration. The band is anchored by Bruce, Steven, David Sancious, Garry Tallent, Vini Lopez, and Southside Johnny. They are joined by a female vocal troupe of six (the Zoomettes) led by folksinger Jeannie Clark. Vaudeville skits and cameos during the sets feature Shore legends Danny Gallagher, Al Tellone, Kevin Kavanaugh, and others.

first week or two. The album couldn't have sold fifteen thousand copies. Still, Charlie's was smaller than Max's—a capacity of maybe seventy-five or one hundred. (Joe's Place wasn't much bigger.) I made a reservation for Friday night and counted myself lucky to be there.

On Wednesday night, I was rustling up dinner, getting ready to watch *Kojak*, the hit of the season, when Landau called me. "I want to go see this Bruce Springsteen," he said. "And I know you've met him."

"I only just said hello to him. I'm going Friday night. And tonight's *Kojak*."

"C'mon, I'll buy you dinner." Jon was a friend I wanted to know better. The music would be good. I said sure.

We walked up to the bar on narrow Bow Street, and in front of it stood a guy wearing as yet unfashionable torn jeans and a black leather jacket, bouncing up and down in the cold. He was reading Landau's column, which somebody had posted in the window. "Guess they *aren't* sold out," I thought.

"That's him," said Landau, while we were still out of earshot. "Introduce me."

I walked up, reintroduced myself, and explained who Jon was, without mentioning the column.

Landau gestured to the review in the window. "Pretty good, huh?" he said jocularly.

Bruce waited a beat. "I've read better," he said. Then he let loose his now-familiar hoarse chuckle.

About then, a guy who looked like a pugnacious Paul McCartney came out of the bar and told Bruce that it was just about showtime. Bruce introduced us to his manager and producer, Mike Appel.

Appel's reputation as a fanatic had become part of the buzz around Bruce. He'd dared the Super Bowl to make Bruce its half-time attraction, playing the unrecorded song "Balboa the Beast-Slayer." Mike alienated CBS Records with continual demands that Bruce be given more support and attention. He assaulted radio stations that wouldn't play Bruce's records and continuously cajoled those few that did.

Bruce held a scalpel in hands that belonged to an inexperienced but talented surgeon. Appel wielded a hammer like a journeyman carpenter with a bad temper.

The four of us sat at a table near the door. Appel pulled up the chair across from Landau; Bruce sat on the same side as Mike, across from me. I don't think Bruce and I exchanged ten sentences in the next twenty minutes. We just watched Appel and Landau spar. Jon had been explicitly critical of the record production. Appel defended himself with subdued belligerence. It didn't look like a fight but it looked like no fun. I thought, "Well, maybe I'll see this show Friday night after all."

But when it came time for Bruce to go on, courtesy resumed. The crew placed two chairs—ordinary barroom chairs with vinyl backs and seats—right up next to the

In the Bruce Springsteen Band, 1971

band. I was maybe two feet from David Sancious's left elbow. When Sancious started to play, I shifted back in my chair in case he needed room.

Sancious played a prelude from Mozart, I think, that developed into one of the epics from *The Wild, the Innocent, and the E Street Shuffle*, "New York City Serenade." Just the two of them played while the rest of the band sat poised for action and took none. The song settled Springsteen's command of the room. His charisma burned now as his voice conjured the story and his interplay with Sancious drove home the blooming emotion within it. When he finished the coda—the junkman "singing . . . *siiiinging . . . siiinging*"—he owned that crowd, little as it was. He'd have owned Fenway Park.

Before we could think about recovering, Bruce turned to the band and the group exploded— "Spirit in the Night," maybe, or maybe it was "Let the Four Winds Blow," although that's more likely what they ended with. It was like the show all happened in one moment—the great shows always do. Rather than sitting on the edge of my seat, I felt pressed back as if the night literally accelerated. I took no notes and I'm not sure my hands would have cooperated if I'd tried.

We walked out of there in a daze. It must have been three o'clock in the morning—the bar closed at two, then we talked with the band awhile. The next morning, Jon and I were on the phone again. I said my thighs were sore, from pounding them all night. Jon said his were, too. I asked him if that had really happened. He assured me it really had.

Now I was a convert. Hell, now I was ready for an audition as a disciple.

David Sancious at the Main Point, early 1970s

THERE WAS A HUGE difference between Springsteen's music at Max's and his music at Charlie's Bar. It started with a fistfight between road manager Steve Appel—Mike's brother—and Vini Lopez. Neither of the Appels was a band favorite. At first, Mike Appel didn't even want Bruce to have a band, and John Hammond felt even more strongly against it. When Bruce insisted on his Asbury Park band playing on his first album, *Greetings From Asbury Park, N. J.*, Appel told them they had to work for free. (They didn't.) Mike saw Bruce as the only one who mattered.

July 10, 1971 – Brookdale Community College, Lincroft, NJ
The first show played by the Bruce Springsteen Band (Bruce, Steven, David, Garry, Vini), in which they headline an outdoor concert called the Second Annual Nothing's Festival. Delores Holmes and Barbara Dinkins are the backing singers; Bobby Feigenbaum on sax and Harvey Cherlin on trumpet join in on some songs.

July 11, 1971 – Sunshine In, Asbury Park, NJ
The new Bruce Springsteen Band opens for then-popular Humble Pie.

CONCERT HALL PRESENTS

Steve Appel was his brother's surrogate and not especially good at being a road manager. Bands take things out on their road managers, and up to a point, they get away with it.

Before a gig at the University of Kentucky on February 12, 1974, Vini Lopez, who Bruce called Mad Dog, punched out Steve Appel. After the show, Bruce and Mike Appel spent the rest of the night on the phone. Sometime before dawn, Springsteen called Vini to his room and fired him.

The band was frantic for a new drummer—two dates in Ohio had to be cancelled, and in those days, not playing meant not eating. David Sancious immediately proposed Ernest "Boom" Carter. Carter had played with both Sancious and Garry Tallent in a group in Richmond after Bruce split up the band to go to California. He was now in Atlanta but immediately flew to New Jersey.

Rehearsals couldn't go quickly because not only did Carter need to learn the material but Carter's playing meant a new style for the group. Boom had more drive and more finesse than Lopez (as he amply demonstrated when they recorded "Born to Run"). The rest of the band tightened up around him. Songs that had scampered and romped—"Kitty's Back," "Spirit in the Night"—now charged and exploded.

After a week, they still weren't ready, but Bruce had a booking that couldn't be cancelled. He told the story a couple of weeks later in Houston.

"This is a pretty nice place. . . . It's funny because we just came from playing this place in Jersey, near Fort Dix, this place called the Satellite Lounge. Really. And it was run by this guy named Carlo Rossi. And we just got a new drummer, he'd only been with us about four days and we were gonna cancel out the gig because we weren't ready, and Carlo calls up my manager and says, 'Tell 'em to get down here,' and he said he was gonna kill me if I didn't come *[laughter]*. So we called up these cats we know—Tyrone and Rocky *[laughter]*—and these cats run another place, they run this joint called the Erlton Lounge, which is like another little chapter, you know, about twenty-five, thirty miles up. We said, 'Tyrone, man, this cat Carlo, he's gonna kill Bruce unless we . . . you know.' And Tyrone says, 'Be there. Go' *[chuckles]*. And it's funny because a week before . . . this band Foghat played there and [Rossi] came out and he told them to turn down, and they didn't listen to him. He came up again and told 'em to turn down, and they didn't listen to him. So the third time he comes up, he says, 'I told you guys to turn down,' pulls out a gun, and shoots the amps *[laughter]*. That's a true story . . . pulls out a gun, blows the amps away, right *[chuckles]*. So I was there on Saturday night. But yeah—Satellite Lounge, don't ever go there."

Carter's presence galvanized the music. The E Street Band of August 1973 played Van Morrison style arrangements well. The E Street Band of April 1974 blazed its own path—it became a unique rock band, and it helped push Springsteen into a different realization of his vision.

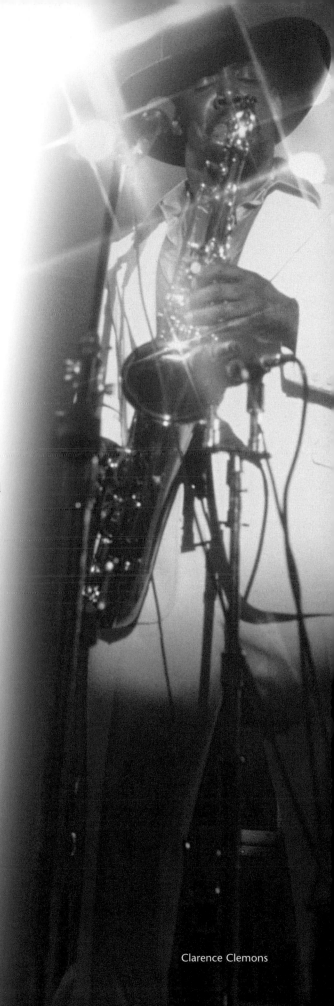

Clarence Clemons

"When his two-hour set ended I could only think, 'Can anyone really be this good; can anyone say this much to me, can rock 'n' roll still speak with this kind of power and glory?' And then I felt the sores on my thighs where I had been pounding my hands in time for the entire concert and knew that the answer was yes."
—Jon Landau

BRUCE GOT HIS RECORD contract by stripping away to the basics: one man, his guitar, his songs, his voice.

For the first few months after signing his Columbia Records contract, Bruce sat in with various bands to make his rent. But Appel and Hammond both heard him as a solo act; they wanted to showcase his lyrics. Bruce was writing prolifically—or he was exposing more of the songs he wrote, maybe because they were better songs. In a scene dominated by soft rock, playing solo made sense.

Bruce was good at it. When he played Max's Kansas City at a special late-afternoon show over Labor Day weekend, 1972, David Blue, an important singer-songwriter of Bob Dylan's period, heard him and brought him to his own gig at the Bitter End in Greenwich Village.

Jackson Browne was the headliner. "David Blue walks in before the show with this guy in tow," Browne, who had just released his own first album, remembered years later. "'Jackson, this is Bruce, and . . . Jackson, you *gotta* hear him. Can he do a guest set tonight?' So I said, 'Sure.' He went out there for about an hour and proceeded to do the greatest songs I've ever heard, with just his guitar and [my] piano. When he got offstage, I said, 'Man, where the hell have *you* been hiding?'"

Nevertheless, Bruce showed up for his recording session with a concise version of the Bruce Springsteen Band: Vini Lopez, Danny Federici, Garry Tallent, David Sancious, and newcomer Clarence Clemons. For the recording, the producers brought in two New York jazz pros—Richard Davis, who played bass on one track, and Harold Wheeler, who contributed piano on two. The sessions finished quickly—when you don't have much money, you can't use much studio time. In late October, Bruce rehearsed his road group—the Asbury guys from the sessions, minus Sancious. They played Bruce's first date at West Chester College in Pennsylvania on October 28, 1972, came back home to play a Halloween party at the Long Branch Armory, then hit the road in earnest, playing colleges and clubs, opening for everybody from Sha Na Na and David Bromberg to the Paul Winter Consort and the Persuasions, and in the few places where they could sell tickets, with some even less-known act opening for them. They played a lot of colleges—between 1972 and 1975, sixty-five dates at fifty-five different schools. They played California, Texas, and Arizona.

Dozens of bands paid those dues. From the mid-sixties to the mid-eighties, when the record company idiots decided to divert their tour-support dollars to music-video budgets, playing such live dates was how the music industry made stars. But nobody pays off on potential.

Mar. 17, 1972 – Richmond Arena, Richmond, VA
The Bruce Springsteen Band opens for Mitch Ryder and the Detroit Wheels (four bands total on the bill). About 1,000 people attend in a venue that holds 4,500. Ryder's "Detroit Medley" would become a Springsteen concert staple many years in the future.

May 2, 1972 – Gaslight Au-Go-Go, New York, NY
This show was hastily booked following Bruce's audition with John Hammond the same day. Bruce's four- or five-song set takes place hours before the regular show, Garland Jeffreys and Charlie Musselwhite, is to start. John Hammond attends the show and asks Bruce to come in the following day to record audition demos.

Opening acts didn't make much more than bar bands in New Jersey, and living on the road is expensive. Sets could be brutally short, soundchecks hard to come by. They worked out from their base in New Jersey: Bruce played better than half of his shows in the Northeast (of those college dates, about a third were in Pennsylvania alone). He played the Philadelphia singer-songwriter haven, the Main Point, eight times between January 1973 and February 1975 (when he played a benefit because the club had gone broke). The band traveled by station wagon or van, the equipment following in a rented truck. They stayed in dumps or drove 'til dawn to get home, even though they had to do the same thing the next night.

Sometimes people paid attention: During his first run of Boston shows, disc jockey Maxanne Sartori did a long live interview with Bruce. "An engrossing opening act," read Lynn Van Matre's entire comment in the *Chicago Tribune.* Mostly, Bruce and the band moved on not knowing whether they'd expanded their audience or not. But promoters wanted them back.

Fellow artists provided another gauge. Spurred by Jackson Browne's raves, Don Henley of the Eagles, who'd already made some hits, made sure to see Springsteen when both bands played the Ohio Music Festival in April 1973. "He was just a warm-up act at this show. After watching him, I remember thinking to myself that this was a guy that wasn't gonna be warming up the crowd for us—

or for anybody—for very long," Henley said.

Others put it a different way: David Bromberg opened for Springsteen in January 1973. That November, he found out he'd be taking the stage after Bruce at a New Jersey date and elected to cancel.

Greetings and then *The Wild, the Innocent, and the E Street Shuffle* provided most of Bruce's material but not all of it. There are a dozen or more "lost" songs from this period, some of which eventually showed up on his *Tracks* collection, although just as many didn't. Bruce also rummaged through older rock and roll for material—"Let the Four Winds Blow" was one example out of a dozen.

The reason, Garry Tallent thinks, was purely practical. "You're out on the road, and you've only got one or two albums' worth of songs—maybe two. So naturally, you start going through older songs you could do."

The original songs kept getting better. "Rosalita" entered the setlist in January 1973, almost a year before its release on *The Wild, the Innocent.* It was a kind of omnibus song—at first he did it as a medley with the Beach Boys' "Fun, Fun, Fun" or Junior Walker's "Shotgun." Then it began to stand on its own but with an extended middle section in which, among other things, he introduced the band. For the next ten years or more, he used it like that, the last song of his show. Well, the last song before the encores.

Not only did Bruce play more and more different

July 5, 1972 – Red Bank Cinema III, Red Bank, NJ
A box office poster verifies that Bruce did a solo benefit concert for presidential candidate George McGovern prior to the regularly scheduled movie that night. The suggested donation was three dollars.

Aug. 9, 1972 – Max's Kansas City, New York, NY [two shows]

Bruce is the first of two solo opening acts for headliner Dave Van Ronk, who was encouraged to add him to the bill through friend John Hammond. These shows were likely Bruce's first New York appearances after being signed by Columbia Records.

Oct. 28, 1972 – West Chester College, West Chester, PA

The first known public appearance of the E Street Band. Cheech and Chong are the headliners, with Bruce and the ESB opening the show for the Persuasions.

Jan. 5, 1973

Columbia Records releases *Greetings From Asbury Park, N.J.*

Apr. 24, 1973 – Main Point, Bryn Mawr, PA
Broadcast locally on WMMR, this is Bruce's first live radio concert.

Apr. 28, 1973 – University of Maryland, College Park, MD
Springsteen and band open this sold-out show, Jerry Lee Lewis follows them, and Chuck Berry headlines. Bruce and the E Streeters, including Southside Johnny, back Berry. They perform without even a sound check, as this is not included in Berry's contract.

October 26, 1973, Hobart and William Smith College, Geneva, New York

A HISTORY MAKING PHOTO!
AT MAIN POINT VISITING DAVID SANSCIOUS' "TONE"

THIS IS THE NO BULLSHIT LAST FUCKING PHOTO OF BRUCE WITH A BEARD!!! THE NEXT DAY HE SHAVED AND THAT WAS IT!!

The photographer, the late Phil Ceccola, tells his own tale about this "history-making" shot, taken at the Main Point in Bryn Mawr, Pennsylvania, the night before Bruce shaved off his trademark beard. *From left:* David Sancious, Ernest "Boom" Carter, Bruce.

songs, his shows got longer and longer. As he developed a few places where he could play as the sole act or as a headliner, he'd cram all the music he used to do in four or five sets on the Jersey circuit into one marathon, often clocking in at close to two hours, sometimes longer.

That reemphasized the original material issue. In four sets, you can play "Kitty's Back" four times. In one long set, if you want to do all your own tunes and don't have many good ones, you want a way to stretch some of them. For an earlier generation of musicians, it worked the other way around. They trimmed their lengthy live arrangements to three minutes or less to fit on 78 RPM records.

Bruce had never been known for talking a lot on stage before 1974, but now he became a yarn spinner. He'd drop these stories into songs, changing the details to fit the occasion, or move them from one song to another. The ones supposedly about what the songs said often just rambled. "Gonna do a song now about a bishop, his wife, and a violin player in West Virginia," he said, introducing a song called "Bishop Danced." "How they lost their daughter to mathematics while on a business trip in Detroit . . . 'bout James Garner, during his well-known, very popular stint as TV's, uh, very own Maverick . . . 'bout a little boy, says the Indians are still in the woods, only nobody sees 'em . . . 'bout the sexual pathos of elderly choirboys in Puke, Montana . . ." he said, and then played "Wild Billy's Circus Story."

June 6, 1973 – Spectrum, Philadelphia, PA
Bruce and the band open for Chicago. Possibly the only time ever that Bruce is booed in the city of Philadelphia.

June 15, 1973 – Madison Square Garden, New York, NY
The final show on the Chicago tour. Bruce tells manager Mike Appel that he never wants to play big venues again.

JUNE 14 & 15
8PM
Chicago
With Special Guest
Bruce Springsteen

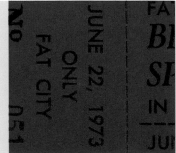

NO
051
FAT CITY
ONLY
JUNE 22, 1973

FA
BI
SI
IN
JU

Some of the stories drew on his real life, blown up to comic proportions, like the classic about Ducky Slattery, the guys Ducky hung out with at a gas station in Freehold, and how Bruce got out of Vietnam. Or the one about the trip that he and his father had taken to Mexico, both funny and frank about his writing process: "This is a newer song," he said one night at the Main Point. "I was in California last winter, and I went down to Mexico. That's a funny place, Mexico, 'cause, uh . . . you drive across the border . . . all these bumps in the road, *grrrr, grrrr,* you're driving down the street, and the Mexicans are smart, they—like I said, I was telling these people last night—they got all these old cars and they drive like maniacs, they just drive all over the place. And the big thing, the big rage right now is they have auto body shops. I mean more auto body shops than you've ever seen in your life and the whole thing is metal flake upholstery, you know—do some of the best work you've ever seen. The funniest thing about it is, soon as you drive across the border, there's cats waving you into these places, these auto body shops. We're driving a brand-new car—my father bought a new car—I was driving. I was going down to Mexico with my father—and you drive across the border and all these cats are waving us into these auto body shops, I think they hire cats to smash into you in Tijuana—really I think they do. . . . I don't know. Anyway, I was able to shake off the reality of the situation—as usual—and I romanticized myself into writing a tune down there . . . this is, uh . . . I think this is it . . ." The band played "Santa Ana," which Bruce played only occasionally at the time and not again until 2005.

Sometimes the stories coalesced into something bigger—transitions into other songs, or allusions to other songs, or invocations of the power and glory of rock and roll. Sometimes they became an occasion for skits of sorts—Bruce could and did fascinate an audience by using his ski cap as a prop. The shows, whose original set piece was Bruce playing two songs solo before bringing the boys on, became more and more theatrical.

He built a following that was loyal enough to trek considerable distances to see the shows, and fanatic once it got there. His reputation as a great live act grew, even if record sales and airplay didn't. Bruce opened for Dr. John in July 1974. By October, Dr. John opened for him. The same thing happened with Richie Havens and the Persuasions. The fervor of his performances simply made it impossible to take the stage once he'd finished—he was what groups on the gospel circuit used to call a housewrecker.

Vini Lopez in Steel Mill, Free University, Richmond, Virginia, February 27, 1970

At the Main Point in Bryn Mawr, Pennsylvania

What you have, in effect, is a best-of-all-worlds synthesis of rhythm and blues, jazz roots and straight soul in the musical end and Dylan's surreal knack for lyrics, adulterated with a young-punk outlook, in the words.

But don't let this highflown language fool you: Bruce Springsteen and his band produce what is, to my mind, the best rock and roll available today. Period.

Springsteen draws the

Oct. 13, 1973 — Eisenhower Theater / Kennedy Center, Washington, DC

Start of the *Wild and Innocent* tour. The album has not yet been released. All seven songs on the album are played at this show.

Nov. 6–10, 1973 — Max's Kansas City, New York, NY

Roy Bittan, who is playing keyboards in Niki Aukema's band, meets Bruce for the first time at these gigs.

Dec. 17, 1973 — Student Prince, Asbury Park, NJ

The first of a three-night stand and the only E Street Band shows ever to be held at this venue. Bruce had not played there since 1971.

Dec. 23, 1973 — Rova Farms Function Center, Cassville, NJ

Admission to the congregation center for the local Russian Orthodox Church is five dollars and includes all the beer you can drink. A huge audience fight erupts during the song "Santa Claus Is Coming to Town," and the police almost stop the show. The promoter convinces them to let it proceed.

Feb. 12, 1974 — University of Kentucky, Lexington, KY

Vini Lopez's final show as drummer for the E Street Band.

Feb. 23, 1974 — Satellite Lounge, Cookstown, NJ

First show with new drummer Ernest "Boom" Carter, who supposedly has not yet been able to learn any of Bruce's songs. The appearance is almost cancelled for this reason but goes on because of threats by the club owner. The set consists entirely of cover songs.

In August 1974 at the Schaffer Music Festival in Central Park, Springsteen was booked to open for Anne Murray. Murray was in the midst of a ten year string of hit singles, a smooth and accomplished if not dynamic performer. When promoter Ron Delsener booked Springsteen to close the show, her managers sneered. When booking agent Barry Bell told them that whoever got top billing, Murray did not want to follow Bruce, especially not in front of what amounted to a hometown crowd, they dismissed him as an arrogant raver. Bruce was, however, granted a headliner-length, eighty-minute show. Before Bruce had been onstage an hour, Murray's managers tried to bully Mike Appel into cutting his show short. Now it was Appel's turn to sneer. Of the five thousand people crammed into Wollman Ice Rink that night, somewhere around four thousand came to see Bruce. Murray was left not only in the position of trying to follow a housewrecker but without much of a house left—when Bruce was done, maybe a thousand people stuck around.

It wasn't just Murray. Bonnie Raitt had to fight to be heard after Bruce finished his set opening for her in Harvard Square that spring. And Harvard Square was Bonnie's home turf.

Bruce felt bad about it. And word got around. For the rest of his career, Springsteen never opened for another artist. Within a few months, he wouldn't have an opening act himself. He did one big show, usually with an inter-mission, with a total stage time of more than two hours, the same as in the Jersey clubs.

Songs had started to emerge in a flood, and one reason he attracted such a passionate fan following was the way he varied not just the songs he played, but the way he played and sang them. He must have come up with a dozen different arrangements and lyrics for what became "Thunder Road." "Jungleland" came in various versions, too, and "She's the One" could sometimes contain the whole history of rock and roll. Of the new material he showcased in 1974, the only song he didn't tinker with much was "Born to Run." That one didn't need tinkering.

The music felt more honed now, the jam-band elements losing ground to rock songs with tighter, though often still elaborate, structures and much more rhythmic propulsion.

The stories got edited, burnished, more rehearsed without sacrificing their absurdist rock and roll air. Here's a monologue from the midst of "Rosalita" that Bruce delivered on February 11, 1973, at Virginia Commonwealth:

"There I was, I was eight years old in Alabama. I'd been hitchhiking around the country for five years . . . I was something else . . . and just by coincidence, I got arrested for loitering, and they put me in the same cell, by sheer coincidence, as was James Brown. It was amazing, here I was, eight years old, with James Brown sitting next to me and he looked me in the face and he said, 'Ungh, aah

Feb. 25, 1974 – Main Point, Bryn Mawr, PA
The final night of a two-night stand. Bruce has the flu and so performs the entire show sitting on a chair. He stands for "Rosalita."

Mar. 16, 1974 – Armadillo World Headquarters, Austin, TX
Bruce and band's first ever Austin show. The openers (Alvin Crow and the Pleasant Valley Boys) are a Western swing band and there is concern that the two styles won't mesh well. The show is reviewed by *Rolling Stone* magazine.

. . . ain't it funky now?' And the next time he opened his mouth to say something, it was the funniest thing. Out came [some James Brown–style music]. Then he walked away. Just by sheer coincidence, in that very next cell, sitting there with his surfboard was Dennis Wilson of the Beach Boys. I said, 'Dennis, what are you doing in that cell with a surfboard?' Said he was looking for the perfect wave. All right, he came up to me, looked me in the face and said [the band does "Fun, Fun, Fun"]. Then he split. By sheer coincidence, with a cop, with a policeman on both sides, they brought in Wilson Pickett—for being, uh, too funky or something, I forget. I forget the exact charge but he came up to me, he said, 'Son.' 'Mr. Pickett.' He said, 'If you're ever in trouble, all you got to do is'—and then he showed me this. . . ."

And then he sang Pickett's hit "634-5789" before swinging back into "Rosalita."

As you know if you saw him over the next decade, when he still closed the show with "Rosie," every version after this one merely varied the theme.

It was this sense of continual growth within the known that drew in Springsteen's particular fan base—or to be blunt, cult. You knew what you were going to get, but you had no idea in what style.

The growth continued even after a major shakeup in the band, when David Sancious left (because he'd been signed to Epic Records to make a jazz album) and took

Boom Carter with him. Auditions for a new drummer and bassist yielded Max Weinberg, whose approach was rock and roll theatrics, which blended perfectly with what had been evolving, and Roy Bittan, who was, like Sancious, a virtuoso talent but approached being in a band from a pop rather than a jazz and classical viewpoint.

Bruce often sat at the piano by himself at the start of the show and sang "New York City Serenade" or "Thunder Road," but once the band was onstage, his presentation grew more and more physical—he crawled out into the audience, and when they played on a stage that gave him room, he leaped off the piano, bounded over to Clarence, and cavorted like a kid turned loose at the carnival. At Lincoln Center in October 1974, fans mobbed him, and the stage collapsed. The show ended in exultant chaos.

BRUCE'S SHOWS MIGHT HAVE been going over, but his first two records didn't sell, John Hammond's influence was practically nil because corporate policy would force him to retire in 1975 at age sixty-five, and in early 1973, CBS Records chairman Clive Davis, the most important Springsteen supporter, was fired in an expense-account scandal.

The label's new regime perceived Springsteen as a Hammond folly who'd probably never have a hit, and in a post-Davis regime, being one of Clive's darlings became a

Apr. 10, 1974 – Charlie's Bar, Cambridge, MA
Music critic Jon Landau attends this show (second of a four-night stand) and meets Bruce outside as he is reading Landau's review of *The Wild, the Innocent* album posted on the club's door.

Apr. 27, 1974 – University of Connecticut, Storrs, CT
The afternoon show (a free event) takes place outdoors in the Ice Hockey Arena parking lot. Three bands open the show—Fatback, Fairport Convention, and Aerosmith. This is the only time Aerosmith will ever share a bill with Bruce. Each band plays full sets. After the show, Springsteen, band, and crew hit the road to drive to Hartford for another show that evening at the University of Hartford.

May 9, 1974 — Harvard Square Theater, Cambridge, MA [two shows]

Bruce Springsteen and the E Street Band opens for Bonnie Raitt. The set opens with a long story introduction to "The E Street Shuffle." A new song, "Born to Run," is performed.

July 12, 13, 14, 1974 — Bottom Line, New York, NY

Bruce's first appearances at this venue, which has recently opened. "Jungleland" is performed for the first time during these shows.

July 27, 1974 — Celebrity Theater, Phoenix, Arizona

Due to strong ticket demand, a second show is added and both sell out. Biggest fee ($11,500 plus a percentage of the gate) paid to date for a concert by Bruce and band. This is almost triple their best payday up to this point.

At the University of Connecticut, April 27, 1974

Aug. 3, 1974 – Schaffer Music Festival / Wollman Ice Rink, Central Park, New York, NY

The lineup is Brewer and Shipley, Bruce, and Anne Murray headlining. Originally Bruce is scheduled to headline, but Murray's managers protest due to her commercial success at the time, and the schedule is shifted the week before the show. Most of the audience leaves after Bruce's set concludes. This is the last time that Bruce opens for another artist.

Springsteen
and The "E" Street Band

Aug. 14, 1974 – Carlton Theater, Red Bank, NJ

Final shows with David Sancious on keyboards and Ernest "Boom" Carter on drums.

Sept. 8, 1974 – Stone Pony, Asbury Park, NJ

Bruce's first known appearance at the legendary club, which has opened recently. The Blackberry Booze Band (later to become Southside Johnny and the Asbury Jukes) are joined onstage by Bruce for a lengthy jam. Garry Tallent and Vini Lopez also join in the jam.

Hobart and William Smith College, Geneva, New York, December 7, 1974

Garry Tallent, 1974

liability. Some people even thought that the record company would drop Springsteen from its artist roster before he made a third album.

Record company execs didn't look forward to confrontations with Mike Appel, for one thing. Mike correctly understood that Bruce's commercial potential couldn't be measured by listening to his records. He even got it right that sticking to the standard record-business way of doing business wouldn't work with Springsteen. But if you're working outside the boundaries, you need diplomatic skills and you need allies on the inside.

In January 1974, Appel learned that a CBS Records sales convention would be held in Nashville. All the local and regional sales personnel would be in town. So Mike arranged a Nashville Springsteen gig, opening for bluesman Freddie King, at Muther's Music Emporium. Then he printed up a handbill and delivered the leaflet to every room in the hotel where the sales reps were staying. He apparently didn't know that the reps weren't free at such conventions, even at night. Almost no one at all turned up at the shows, but the leaflets, taken back to the company's Black Rock headquarters, would make Appel seem, once again, a profitless renegade.

Columbia executives denied that Bruce was in trouble, when reporters asked, but one promotion man went around the country telling the few stations that played *The Wild, the Innocent, and the E Street Shuffle* to take it off the air and add Billy Joel's new album instead. There were also Columbia Records staffers who championed Springsteen; one wrote a ten-page, single-spaced, in-house memo touting his merits.

Standard "artist development" in the record business argued for the third album as the commercial breaking point for new artists. The first two releases might not sell well, but they served to establish an identity and to acquaint the performer with the methods of record making, pretty much the obverse of the spontaneous, direct, ever-changing ways in which live music is made. (And they'd sell plenty if the third one took off.) By that time, the system encouraged the artist to have done a great deal of live work, for little or no money, in an attempt to build a following. The unwritten theory was, by the third time around the circuit, the artist either had a base live or on radio, or probably never would.

Although Bruce had developed a strong live base, it was strictly regional—the Northeast and Atlantic coast, from Maine to Ohio to Virginia, with a couple of pockets outside it, in Houston, Austin, and

Sept. 19, 1974 — Main Point, Bryn Mawr, PA
First public performances with new band members Roy Bittan and Max Weinberg

Oct. 4, 1974 — Avery Fisher Hall, Lincoln Center, New York, NY
First appearance by Suki Lahav, the wife of 914 Sound Studios engineering manager Louis Lahav, on violin. First known performance of "She's the One." The stage collapses at the end of the show.

Phoenix. His shows were small; his one attempt at working as an opening act, on a three-week tour with the horn band Chicago in early 1973, failed so miserably that Bruce said "never again"—not to working with more popular bands but to playing cavernous sports arenas. In the early 1970s, sports arenas were new and somewhat controversial venues for rock shows. To some, it looked like nothing more than a bigger place to throw the party (and rake in the proceeds); to others, it seemed like the destruction of all that the "underground" strove to build. Early results were mixed: The Stones never sounded better or more present. Dylan was a distant, muttering speck.

Springsteen, at twenty-four, kept his own counsel on many matters, but when he got his back up, he displayed an impressive stubbornness. Arena rock was a place where he took a semipublic stand. Clubs and theaters—and the occasional college gymnasium or outdoor facility—were big enough for him. Playing arenas was anathema. Playing a stadium . . . well, that was so far off the map, it's doubtful anyone even fantasized about it.

BRUCE HAD A BUNCH of stuff going for him. In less than two years on the road, he had already become a legendary live performer, as formidable to other performers on the national circuit as he had been to other guitar slingers in New Jersey. Much of the press adored him. His fans were fanatic. His stand against ever again playing arenas, the exhausting length of his concerts, his continual innovations in arranging his songs, his explorations of several sets of lyrics for the same tune, his tale-telling, his stagecraft all began to build a reputation.

He'd made one of the most enduring rock and roll records of all time, too, but only a handful of people knew it. "Born to Run" made its live debut at a show at the Harvard Square Theater. Landau heard it and "Jungleland" and wrote a raving column about the show, emphasizing Springsteen's new material.

Bruce had worked for over a year writing the song, and he would work for months recording it. When they had what sounded to Mike Appel like a finished version, he sent tapes to a select group of disc jockeys, all of whom aired it. In Cleveland, Kid Leo adopted it as the last song he played each week, kicking off the weekend with those four minutes of rumble.

Columbia Records needed an album, not a single, but Bruce couldn't satisfy himself with the track, adding new elements, remixing it, and tinkering for months. The other songs had to get in line behind it. Eventually he brought in Landau as a coproducer, but it took until late summer 1975 to finish the album.

Appel's strategy of selectively releasing "Born to Run" paid off. It was among several factors that not

At the University of Connecticut, Storrs, Connecticut, April 27, 1974

only made Columbia keep Springsteen on its roster but made *Born to Run* one of the most anticipated albums in years.

The live show was the most important. Then "Born to Run" itself. Virtually no one who heard it and loved rock and roll could resist its power, its innocence, its sheer determination, its articulation of a dream. And "Born to Run" had already achieved the grail of record promotion—airplay on influential radio stations, even if only a handful.

Then there was Landau, not as a producer but as a writer. A second *Real Paper* column in May included three sentences that changed Bruce's history and his own; they might be the most famous sentences ever written by a rock critic:

"Last Thursday, at the Harvard Square Theater, I saw my rock and roll past flash before my eyes. And I saw something else: I saw rock and roll future and its name is Bruce Springsteen. And on a night when I needed to feel young, he made me feel like I was hearing music for the very first time."

Springsteen as rock and roll future—almost always misquoted as "the future of rock and roll," losing the thread of the Dickensian case made by Landau's essay—made a great advertising hook, and Columbia Records didn't waste time exploiting it. It coalesced the buzz around Bruce, even if it also alienated those with differing opinions. From that moment, Springsteen became a controversial figure, and the ability to excite that controversy confirmed his significance.

SOMEONE ELSE SAW a Bruce show and played a role, too. Irwin Segelstein, the caretaker chief of CBS's record division, was a television executive who knew little about music. But he had a college-age son who went to a Bruce show at his school in Pennsylvania. Or maybe he saw him on Halloween night at the Main Point, when Bruce introduced "4th of July, Asbury Park (Sandy)" with this:

"Like I went into Columbia. You go in the elevator, right, and they take you up. You see the clouds passing you by, you walk out, and there's all these cats in white robes—no, no, I'm not jiving you now. They're all up there, all the presidents, they're all up there in those long white robes. And the contract with the little gold letters, and they say, 'Sign here, son' [*chuckles*]. And first thing they did, they'd say, 'Hit 'em in their hearts. Write a love song.' So this song is about, sorta 'bout Asbury Park, which is about an hour and a half away from here. Last year, before, before we had any jobs—we didn't get jobs, last year—I was just letting it be [*chuckles*], hanging around the boardwalk. I been trying to get CBS to put me on TV in the afternoon [*laughter*]. I want to . . . I wanna do a soap opera, right . . . for a week."

Certainly, Irwin Segelstein's son heard something of the sort, because the next day he phoned his father and said, "Dad, why does Bruce Springsteen hate you guys? And why isn't he a star? I saw him last night, and it was the best concert I've ever seen. You really need to take better care of this guy."

They certainly did.

> "He was just a warm-up act at this show. After watching him I remember thinking to myself that this was a guy that wasn't gonna be warming up the crowd for us—or for anybody—for very long."
>
> —Don Henley

Chapter Three

The Whole World Walking Pretty

"No matter where you sleep tonight or how far you run . . ."

THE BOTTOM LINE SEEMS SUCH a strange place to have witnessed rock and roll future. It was nothing like Liverpool's grimy Cavern Club: The Bottom Line was the first purpose-built rock club (even if the noiseless eating utensils turned out to be plastic forks), and with that awful name, harbinger of too much of rock and roll future at its worst.

In the five nights Bruce Springsteen and the E Street Band played there in 1975—August 13 to August 17—the Bottom Line heralded what was best and most promising about rock-and-roll future.

The Bottom Line held only 500 people. That means that only about 5,000 people—make it 5,500 with the standing-room patrons by the bar—saw those shows. There were probably twenty shows at Madison Square Garden that summer, and the flops drew at least twice as many as that, the sellouts four times as many in a single night.

But almost no one could tell you who played the Garden in August 1975. Whereas, 5,000 people might claim to have been there for the early show on August 15, the night that Springsteen rocked WNEW-FM live for two hours, and another couple of million envy those who really were. In short order, Bruce Springsteen at the Bottom Line became as legendary as the Rolling Stones at the Crawdaddy Club or Bob Dylan at the Newport Folk Festival.

There hadn't been this much excitement about a Jersey boy in Manhattan since Sinatra played the Paramount thirty years before. Waiting for the crowd to be let into the Bottom Line

The Bottom Line, August 1975

that first night, you felt you were about to attend some kind of coronation.

THE TALK ABOUT BRUCE Springsteen that summer concerned hype, as word got around that Columbia Records would roll out a $40,000 advertising budget for *Born to Run*. (The costliest items were full-page ads in *Billboard*, the trade paper, and *Rolling Stone*. Neither cost $5,000. There was no TV advertising in the budget and little radio.) The chatter about hype might have ended at the Bottom Line, three weeks before the album's release, since it established to anyone with ears to hear that Springsteen really was that good and that it really was true that he played a sweat-drenched epic of a show that told his version of the story of rock and roll up to that point.

That much you could tell from the radio broadcast, even if you heard it twenty-five years later on a cassette three generations from the original. There's more, just the kind of more that no tape—even videotape—can fully capture. The Bottom Line was the quintessential you-had-to-be-there experience.

I saw, if memory serves, three of those shows, the first one with my wife, Barbara Carr. That night, Barbara and I felt well-prepared for what we'd see. We'd seen Bruce three other times since my epiphany at Charlie's Bar. I'd missed the Harvard Square Theater show (a cold plus stupidity).

Barbara's initial Springsteen show was at the Bottom Line when Bruce played there for the first time, in July 1974. I heard "Born to Run" live for the first time that night.

We saw him again at Avery Fisher Hall, the night the stage caved in. The thing I remember about the stage collapsing was how appropriate it felt: The band bopping "Quarter to Three" with several dozen people dancing madly in front of the band and more pouring in from the seats by the minute—what else *could* happen?

And in February 1975, we saw him at Westbury Music Fair, a posh middle-class venue, perfect for Dionne Warwick but with a revolving stage designed to defeat Springsteen puncturing the fourth wall so he could crawl right in your face. (This was before wireless microphones, let alone wireless electric guitars.) He figured it out, sort of; got up on the grand piano and commanded the show from there. He also did Dylan's "I Want You" and sang it as the lithe rock and roll classic it is.

Sometime in that period, probably in summer 1974, we went to a party in California thrown by Michael Ochs, a big-league record collector. He put on a prerelease tape of "Born to Run."

My first reaction was cold shock. I thought, "This is some song I heard a long, long time ago. How could I have forgotten it? What *is* it?" It seemed like a search for this record had gotten me so involved with rock and roll in the first place—trying to find it again was the missing link in

Feb. 5, 1975 – Main Point, Bryn Mawr, PA
Bruce premieres "Thunder Road" (then known as "Wings for Wheels") at this show, which is broadcast locally on WMMR radio.

Feb. 18, 1975 – John Carroll University, Cleveland, OH
This show is arranged by 1972 John Carroll graduate Tim Russert, later host of NBC's *Meet the Press*.

Mar. 8 and 9, 1975 – Constitution Hall, Washington, DC
These are the last shows that feature Suki Lahav on violin and the last two nights of the *Wild and Innocent* tour. Miami Steve plays guitar at these shows dressed in a bright red suit and hat, but he does not officially join the band until July.

why and how I'd wound up working as a rock critic, hidden from even me until that moment.

It wasn't so mind altering that I didn't realize by the chorus that I'd heard the song in July at the Bottom Line. But then again, was it the same song? There were layers and layers of music here—half a dozen guitars, you could guess that on one listen—yet Bruce played the only guitar in the E Street Band. More likely, my reaction came from the way a record differs from a song heard played live—it's more permanent, meant to be reproduced many times in exactly this state, and live music can't be that way. It took many years and the addition of a third lead guitar player in the E Street Band before I felt that "Born to Run" onstage sounded anywhere near as great as it did on that record.

Crazy as it was, my reaction wasn't all that out of synch. A subterranean, homesick history of rock and roll was exactly what Bruce intended with "Born to Run." A lunatic ambition, but if you ask me, he pulled it off.

Anyway, I didn't have a copy of "Born to Run," and for about a year I couldn't get one. All that time, I imagined the music or heard part of it occasionally on WNEW-FM, or I heard the very different rendition in Bruce's shows. Just enough to whet my appetite, not enough to complete my sub-Stendahl experience in Los Angeles.

That completion would take place when the *Born to Run* album came out, I figured. But who knew when that would be? Westbury was one of the last shows Bruce played

before cloistering himself in the Record Plant studio. He was off the road from early March until late July. In those days, four months was a long time in the studio, a long time offstage.

I GOT AN ADVANCE COPY of the album as soon as there was one to be had—being a music editor at *Rolling Stone* isn't all drawbacks. But Columbia officially released *Born to Run* only in the first week of September, and there was almost as much paranoia in the seventies about leaks to radio as there is now about downloads, so I don't think I'd heard the record, certainly not more than once or twice, when the Bottom Line run started. So it's hard to say what I knew of the new songs—other than "Born to Run," "Thunder Road," and "Jungleland," which Bruce had been doing live for months. Whatever it was, it was more than most people had heard.

The furor changed the tone and the stakes of the Bottom Line event. The question about *Born to Run* wasn't whether the rest of it was as good as its title track. It was whether the rest of the album was as good as, captured the energy and full flavor of, Bruce Springsteen and the E Street Band live. (It certainly did not, because, as I once more must insist, that is not a realistic expectation. Don't get me wrong: It captured what it is possible to capture, and it is one of the greatest rock albums.)

July 20, 1975 – Palace Theater, Providence, RI
Opening night of the *Born to Run* tour and Miami Steve's first show as lead guitarist. "Tenth Avenue Freeze-Out" gets its live debut.

Aug. 8, 1975 – Civic Theater, Akron, OH
"Backstreets" is played for the first time.

August 13th-17th, 1975

by Dave Marsh
Not since Elton John's initial Troubadour appearances has an artist leapt so visibly and rapidly from cult fanaticism to mass acceptance as at Bruce Springsteen's ten Bottom Line shows. Hundreds of fans lined the Village streets outside the 450-seat club each night, hoping for a

life in the Jersey ba of them matured in Mighty Max Wei bassist Garry Talle comping to his ev sion and gesture; it ural but it's about a ous as Pearl Harb Clarence Clemons a Miami Steve Van Za fect foils for these ominous cool of Cle

At the Bottom Line, August 1975

The Bottom Line gigs featured many but not all of the album's eight songs. The WNEW broadcast is typical: "Tenth Avenue Freeze-Out" opened the show, and in the middle of the set, "She's the One," "Born to Run," and "Thunder Road" appeared. During the rest of his stand there, "Night" showed up at least once. He didn't play "Jungleland," "Backstreets," and, less surprisingly, "Meeting Across the River." Partly that's a reflection of the album not being out and Bruce trying to meet audience expectations. More important, it shows Bruce with a new E Street Band.

The band's personnel had changed by half since I'd seen that Max's show in 1973, and its musical personality had changed at least as much. Miami Steve (as Mr. Van Zandt then called himself) joined while they were in the studio, to play rhythm guitar and sing harmonies. Max Weinberg and Roy Bittan were still newcomers, having been added only a year before and having spent much of that year off the road. The songs left in the set from Bruce's first two albums were the ones that rocked—"Spirit in the Night," "Kitty's Back," "Rosalita"—or could be made sharper and harder, like "Growin' Up" and "The E Street Shuffle." R&B remained a prime influence in Bruce's singing, but the band's beat flattened out—no more skittering around the drum kit. This music rocked way more than it grooved. What little jazz influence survived felt wispy and vestigial. "Meeting Across the River," the one jazzy track on *Born to Run*, has hardly ever shown up in Bruce's show. That the band had gone from three African American members to one is not entirely coincidental.

Springsteen, freed of worries that he'd end his career playing Top 40 in New Jersey, added to these sets a batch of the rock and soul oldies he'd have had to play in those joints. One of the things I remember best about that first Bottom Line show is the band performing the Searchers' "When You Walk in the Room," and one of the highlights of the WNEW broadcast was a passionate rendition of the Crystals' Phil Spector classic, "And Then He Kissed Me." (Bruce sang "she.") With Gary Bonds's "Quarter to Three" closing the show (when the Beatles/Isley Brothers' "Twist and Shout" didn't), and "Born to Run"—itself at one level a pastiche of garage band, girl group, twangy guitar, and other rock and roll—you could come out of the show feeling like Bruce and the boys had plunked you down in an illustrated lecture-demonstration. But, as they knew even then, you could learn more from a three-minute record than you ever learned in school, and you could learn a lot more than that from a two-hour rock and roll show.

BRUCE ACTED LIKE A liberated man for those five nights. The Bottom Line's stage fronted on long tables maybe six inches shorter. He regularly danced on those table tops, and a mic with a long cord let him ramble further into the room on "Kitty's Back." His reunion with Van Zandt gave him a pair of foils, the Big Man to his right, Miami to his left.

Bruce has never seemed happier than when he is on stage making music, and if he felt any pressure then, he never showed it. He acted like what he is at his best: a naturally gifted stage performer. He could be sweet or serious when he spoke to the crowd, he could spin a tale that would have them laughing so hard they felt busted in two. The music burned with passion and jumped for joy. The Bottom Line shows felt like a celebration in large part because Springsteen treated them like one.

Maybe the most serious moment in the shows on that tour (not just at the Bottom Line, but later, too) came at the end of "The E Street Shuffle." Bruce introduced the song with a shaggy-dog story about the scuffling days in the Jersey circuit and how he and Steven met Clarence. Then he sang the song, its mood a little more blue than the bright colors of the record. At the end, he whispered into the mic, "And he slips on his jeans . . . he puts on his tube socks . . . and he puts on his sneakers . . . he walks outside, goes to get into his car, turns out that big light . . . and he moves on down to the scene."

HOW COULD BRUCE SPRINGSTEEN not become a darling of the rock press? His lyrics had many precedents but few parallels. His music had jelled into something accessible—"Born to Run" felt like a hit single, even if it never came nearer the top of the charts than number 23. His show challenged performer and audience, both in stamina and in its grasp of so many elements. There was a center in it waiting to be discovered, articulated, and analyzed. This wasn't just another "Johnny B. Goode" tale about the rise to fame and fortune. Springsteen's songs, especially the new ones, also addressed belief in your self and your community and the reality of love, what searching for it, let alone finding it, did to people—and what happened if you didn't make that search.

But not only rock writers, people who more-or-less shared Springsteen's background and values, wrote about him. The editors of some of America's most prominent publications decided that Springsteen was a story, and the easiest stories to tell involved hype: the raving conversion accounts of the writers, acting like nothing but a bunch of fans, not keeping a decent distance from their subject at all; the incredible amounts CBS Records reputedly spent (the $40,000 advertising budget was large for a record album, but for a movie, let alone a new toothpaste, it would have been a pittance); the live radio broadcast, which was unprecedented for an act who'd never had a hit. Behind all of it lay the idea that such unwashed trash

The Bottom Line, August 1975

At Hobart and William Smith College, Geneva, New York, December 7, 1974

wouldn't be popular in the first place if the process hadn't been tainted with payola or some other poison. Springsteen's very reputation for integrity could be turned against him—why would someone involved in the crass rock and roll business want to limit the size of his venues? Why would he lock himself away for months and emerge with merely a rock and roll band record, not something that alluded to respectable musical traditions? He played long, he played with rock history, but the music was not "sophisticated." His lyrics were "overblown," "romanticized," "sentimental"—that is, they used extravagant phrases to describe big ideas about love and life without much ironic distance.

The early part of the *Born to Run* tour played safe markets—the Northeast, Virginia, Texas—then spread out across the country. Bruce introduced material from the new album gradually—he didn't do as many as six of the album's songs in the same set until late September; he didn't play "Meeting Across the River" at all until September 27. (He opened a show with it in St. Louis.) He came up with a bunch more old songs, most notably, the "Detroit Medley," a tribute to Mitch Ryder and the Detroit Wheels, first of the blue-eyed soul bands. After playing Detroit on October 4, Bruce took his first week off since the recording sessions had shifted to the Record Plant.

On October 5, the *New York Times* Sunday Arts and Leisure section featured a piece called "If Bruce Springsteen Didn't Exist, Rock Critics Would Have Had to Make Him Up" by music writer Henry Edwards: "Springsteen's lyrics are an effusive jumble, his melodies either second-hand or undistinguished, and his performance tedious. Given such flaws, there has to be another important ingredient to the success of Bruce Springsteen: namely, vigorous promotion."

There are plenty of people who don't like Bruce Springsteen, though there are few souls so numb or square that they find rock and roll delirium merely tedious. The lyrics are not literature. But whatever Edwards believed about the quality of the work, his implication that the critical rapture had been purchased or fantasized to help CBS Records reflected things he knew weren't true. (It's like saying that he disparaged Springsteen only for the paycheck.)

Born to Run wasn't the biggest record of 1975, and it only made the top three in *Billboard's* album chart (although it spent more than two years on the chart). In the first year or so, the album sold a little more than one million copies, although by 2000, it had sold more than six million. Bruce went back about his business, with homecoming shows in Red Bank followed by a trip to the West Coast, where he did a four-night stint at the Roxy—Hollywood's Bottom Line—also accompanied by a live radio broadcast. The Roxy run finished October 19.

On October 20, *Time* and *Newsweek* hit newsstands. Both featured Bruce on the cover. The stories were polar. In *Time*, James Willwerth, who'd collaborated with Clive Davis on his autobiography, cele-

> "Springsteen's lyrics are an effusive jumble, his melodies either second-hand or undistinguished, and his performance tedious. Given such flaws, there has to be another important ingredient to the success of Bruce Springsteen: namely, vigorous promotion."
> —Henry Edwards, *The New York Times,* Oct. 5, 1975

brated Springsteen's success. *Newsweek*'s Maureen Orth offered a well-reported rendition of the *Times* article.

The contents mattered less than that the covers were simultaneous—that captured more media attention than either would have by itself. Which led, in a cycle now familiar but then fairly new, to articles analyzing the news magazines, articles saying all rock music was hype, articles saying that all news magazines were hype, articles about pundits as philistines and rock writing as a brothel, articles about the twin covers as the decline of Western civilization. *Time*'s editor-in-chief Henry Grunwald described the Springsteen cover as the most regrettable incident of his career. The whole furor piled absurdity upon absurdity, like a merger of *Bye Bye Birdie* and *Springtime for Hitler*.

Bruce continued to do what he'd always done: great shows. In Oakland, Bill Graham came out to tell the crowd the show was over and they began to leave. But half were still there when Bruce came back and plugged in for more, and the others returned when they heard the cheers. In Phoenix, Bruce worked the crowd into such a state that the balcony of Arizona State's Gammage Auditorium began to sway noticeably. (The subsequent engineering report revealed no damage.)

Bruce stopped doing interviews, but commentaries continued. On November 10, *St. Petersburg Times* music writer Bob Ross wrote a scathing analysis headlined "Miracle-child of Promotional Hype or Legitimate Heir to

Rock's Golden Throne." It offered Ross's "realistic assessment," concluding: "While Dylan's compositions offer timeless universality, Springsteen writes lyrics that flow gracefully but are hardly memorable. . . . [Springsteen's] backers are retreating from their high-pressure sales campaign in fear of a negative backlash reaction. . . . If one approaches tomorrow's concert with a desire to be entertained and not transformed, the event should be positive exposure to a burgeoning talent."

The next day Ross's review appeared under the headline "Bruce's Music Shatters Doubts." He concluded: "And all that shuck and jive about the Springsteen 'hype'—for once the record companies have put their money behind deserving talent. If you think that sentiment smells of bandwagon-hopping, you've never seen Springsteen in person."

Bruce took a week off, and on Thanksgiving, he and the band flew to London to make their international debut.

BRUCE'S FIRST LONDON SHOW, on November 18, was supposed to be broadcast live on the radio there. On the day of the show, Mike Appel backed out, saying he felt that Bruce's mood at the time "would not lead to a particularly good show."

Bruce's mood had everything to do with hype accusations. The charges followed him to London, where enthu-

Aug. 15, 1975 – Bottom Line, New York, NY
The first of two shows is broadcast by WNEW radio. It is the third night of a consecutive five-night stand, two shows each night.

Aug. 25, 1975
Born to Run is released by Columbia Records.

Aug. 29, 1975
"Born to Run"/"Meeting Across the River" is released as a single by Columbia Records.

At the Bottom Line, August 1975

**Sept. 23, 1975 –
University of Michigan,
Ann Arbor, MI**

Bruce's twenty-sixth birthday and the first time the "Detroit Medley" is played live.

Oct. 23, 1975 – Gerde's Folk City, New York, NY

Private birthday show for Mike Porco, owner of the club. Bruce and Bob Dylan meet for the first time and both join others onstage in singing "Happy Birthday" to Mike.

Nov. 18, 1975 – Hammersmith Odeon, London, England

This show is filmed and will be released thirty years later as part of the *Born to Run* thirteeth-anniversary package. It is the first gig on Bruce's debut overseas tour consisting of Amsterdam, Stockholm, and a second show in London on November 24.

At the Bottom Line, August 1975

At the Bottom Line, August 1975

siastic accounts of his live prowess had been appearing for months in *Melody Maker*, England's largest music weekly. CBS International plastered the city with "I saw rock and roll future and its name is Bruce Springsteen." Handbills pasted on the walls and laid on the seats of Hammersmith Odeon, the venue, read, "At Last! London Is Ready for Bruce Springsteen."

Bruce snapped. He went around the building tearing down posters, ripping up flyers. Then, the way Bruce told it, he went out and delivered one of his most lackluster performances.

The crowd thought he delivered. Peter Gabriel recalled leaving Hammersmith and finalizing his decision to leave Genesis to strike out on his own.

Fortunately, Appel did not fire the four-man camera crew he'd hired. But Bruce had no interest in the film of the event, and for the next twenty-nine years, it lay with his other masters in a storage vault.

In early 2005, Springsteen called Thom Zimny, director of *Wings for Wheels: The Making of Born to Run*, part of the album's thirtieth anniversary reissue. Bruce said he'd just seen a few seconds of black-and-white footage from the Hammersmith show and asked Zimny to take a look at what else had been shot.

The next day, sixteen boxes of film arrived at Zimny's editing room. None of them bore any identifying labels other than "Hammersmith 1975." The film cans had rusted. The accompanying audio tape had never been synched with the images. That is, the film was silent, out of sequence, and its physical condition was doubtful. Zimny decided he'd find out what it added up to. So he watched it, frame by frame, until he could figure out from some visual clue what song was being performed. (He was suited to the task, since he'd worked on several Springsteen concert films and had grown up down at the Shore.)

Months later, Zimny told Bruce, yes, they had the whole show. Yes, he could assemble it in time for the anniversary package.

Amen and hallelujah.

Now, I'm not taking back a word of what I said about how you have to be there to really know what it's like. I believe that totally. With any concert film, you're dealing with a shadow of a shadow. *Live at Hammersmith* presents almost a worst-case scenario, given the unfavorable camera positions (Bruce wanted nothing getting in his way onstage); Marc Brickman's lighting scheme, which involved a "blue curtain" around Bruce, a brilliant live effect that reproduces poorly; and the lack of any additional film lighting. It is the shadow of the shadow's shadow. Which means one thing: The actual shows were even better than this.

I wasn't at Hammersmith; Mike Appel saw me as some sort of Jon Landau appendage, at whom he was mad, so he said stay away.

But I saw the rough equivalent of the Hammersmith show many times. Looking now at Bruce then, I see Dylan, Van Morrison, Peter Wolf, soul men and blues singers, British Invasion bands. I hear all that and more: Roy Orbison, Dion, Ronnie Spector, Gene Pitney, Gary Bonds, Darlene Love, Sam and Dave. When Bruce slides off the stage during "Spirit in the Night," he's a nonmalignant—by which I do not at all mean benign—Iggy Pop. Swinging his arm to direct the band, he's Jack Nitzsche conducting the band in *The T.A.M.I. Show*.

Out of all that, I see a true original, a man who used his sources as tools to forge a version of himself that obeyed the prime injunction: connect.

At Hammersmith, Bruce's edginess shows in little ways: He mumbles his stories; swallows back spoken intros; gazes upward, seeming a little lost, during the exquisite opening "Thunder Road." Toward the end of the show, though, you can also see Bruce realizing that he's getting over, and that leads him back to his natural self. Then he's overjoyed to be doing this again, overjoyed to be doing it with his friends, overjoyed that you are overjoyed. I have never seen a performer who so consistently took so much pleasure in how much pleasure he gave.

At the Bottom Line, August 1975

This is the biggest reason those of us who experienced (still experience) Bruce's show as the exact opposite of tedium found ourselves lost in it. Unlike almost any other performer, Bruce becomes swept away with us without losing command of the moment. When that happens—as it does in the thunderous "She's the One," for instance—something else emerges with new clarity, which is why he does this at all, why we listen, why we and he feel so inspired, why we wind up doing whatever it is we may do with this inspiration. I cannot count the number of people who have told me that this guy's music changed their lives, but I know where to start the count: me.

BRUCE SPRINGSTEEN HAS SAID several times that *Born to Run* was an attempt to answer the question posed in its title track: "I want to know if love is real." Although his enduring, one might even say preternatural, optimism obscures it, Springsteen's answer is more than just ambiguous. There's a dark heart in *Born to Run*. How else to see the end, where the poets lie "wounded not even dead," and Magic Rat has been gunned down by his own dream—the struggle between "what's flesh and what's fantasy" has been a waste, although we're not told what that means in terms of who wins.

"Thunder Road" and "Born to Run" suggest that if you try hard enough to find yourself, you've already scored a triumph. "Backstreets" suggests struggle ain't that simple. "Jungleland," where kids "flash guitars just like switchblades," suggests that when you win your freedom, you still may find yourself lost.

So is love real?

"When you're that young, you're looking for some sort of assurance that those things not only exist but are in your grasp—that you're capable of that," Springsteen said in our October 2005 interview on Sirius Satellite Radio. "When you're young, sometimes you don't know . . . it's hard to know. . . . And the place we were, in the kinda political and cultural history of the country, you'd seen enough to be in doubt about whether that was true or not.

"The question I often get asked in relation to 'Thunder Road' is where did that line 'We're not that young anymore' come from, when you were twenty-four years old. I always say, 'Well, gee, in 1974, *nobody* was that young anymore, *anymore*.' It was that tremendous sense that the country had aged in a rather quick and a particularly violent fashion. That was just a part of your bones then. . . .

"The record is filled with hope. I was young and I was extremely excited about the music that I was just discovering—and the music that I was discovering had been popular only ten years before. . . . But when I went to build on those styles, my music was infused with its time, which is that sense of dread that sort of encompassed everything and everybody in 1974."

That year, while Bruce came up with "Born to Run," "Jungleland," and "Thunder Road," Richard Nixon fled the White House in the wake of the Watergate scandals, and that spring, as Bruce struggled to finish recording those songs, the Vietnamese recaptured Saigon and the last American troops fled.

"Lost in the Flood," a song Bruce revived in his shows as a direct response to the imperial wars of the turn of the century, serves at Hammersmith as a commentary on these huge political events and the way they affected young men. In "Jungleland," something different can be felt. "In the parking lot the visionaries dress in the latest rage / Inside the backstreet girls are dancing to the records that the D.J. plays / Lonely hearted lovers struggle in dark corners / Desperate as the night moves on." It's a Jersey teen club rendered as a Stephen King nightmare.

At Hammersmith, as he sings "Jungleland," Bruce toys incessantly with his green ski cap. He pulls it over his eyes, he pulls it on and off, he flicks at the tassle. A goofy, distracting thing to do—it ought to destroy the power of the moment. It doesn't.

"White Americans seem to feel that happy songs are *happy* and sad songs are *sad*, and that, God help us, is exactly the way most white Americans sing them," wrote James Baldwin. Saying that white singers lack sensuality, he adds: "To be sensual, I think, is to respect and rejoice in the force of life, of life itself,

Hammersmith Odeon, London, November 18, 1975

Hammersmith Odeon, London, November 18, 1975

and to be *present* in all that one does, from the effort of loving to the breaking of bread."

The E Street Band now played white, dead on the beat rather than behind or around it (poor "Kitty's Back," that's no way to do a shuffle), but Springsteen never sang white. Everything he chooses to sing, no matter who writes it, has the doubleness and contingency of which Baldwin speaks. You can't hear "The E Street Shuffle," or "Mountain of Love" or "Thunder Road" or "When You Walk in the Room," and make neat divisions between happy and sad, or even strong and weak. What exists in Bruce's renditions of these

Dec. 12, 1975 – C.W. Post College, Greenvale, NY
The first time Bruce plays the Animals' "It's My Life" onstage. "Santa Claus Is Coming to Town" is recorded at this show and is released ten years later as the B-side of the "My Hometown" single in 1985.

Dec. 27, 1975 – Tower Theater, Upper Darby, PA
"Lost in the Flood" is performed for the last time onstage until it surfaces again on July 1, 2000. This show is the first of a four-night stand that ends on New Year's Eve.

Apr. 4, 1976 – Michigan State University, East Lansing, MI
Live premiere of "Frankie"

songs is precisely sensual presence. So, this night, he undercuts his most bombastic and portentous song with the prop that's available: his hat.

"It's bigger than me," the hat says. "It's bigger than any of us up here. Bigger than you guys out there, too." Then the band erupts, spewing out the kind of chords that threaten with their darkness and lift with their intensity, and you get the idea: It ain't bigger than *all* of us. "The hungry and the hunted explode into rock and roll bands." Yes, just like that.

WHAT CAN BE SEEN, heard, and felt in the Hammersmith film—and all the shows on that tour—was the story of young men coming of age in a time and place where the world thought they were wrong, and they thought the world might be correct, and yet, every note and chord and beat of their music, a source of why they were despised, reinforced a feeling of being in the right. One of the things they're right about has to do with self-respect. Another involves what it means to be in a band, to do something *together*, not in the prescribed "individualistic" way (which usually leads to an apex of conformity).

They also know that their behavior has consequences and that some of those are beyond unpleasant. What ties together "Lost in the Flood" and "Thunder Road" is a single truth: You can die out there—and you can die hidden in yourself, too. In these shows is the beginning of an aesthetic, a philosophy, a way of living, that Bruce Springsteen spent the rest of his career defining and trying to live up to and sometimes just trying to figure out. It's there on the albums, too, but it is there most fully in the stage show, where he's looking his audience in the eye, where when he sings "Climb in!" everybody has the choice to stay or go.

Here's the hideous truth: Most people don't think they have that choice. Rock and roll is liberating because it insists that the choice is real and must be made. The price is you don't get to make it just once.

I knew all this. Hell, I walked into the rock and roll world with the MC5, and they not only knew it, they wanted to fight a war over it. What I saw, as rock and roll future became rock and roll present, was a guy—an artist, yes, for once that's appropriate—who wanted to live up to the spirit of it, and possessed such tremendous force that maybe he could make it all the way—and carry the rest of us through the breach.

At the Lenox Music Inn, Lenox, Massachusetts, July 23, 1975

Chapter Four

Rendezvous

"When the truth is spoken and it don't make no difference"

AFTER DOING SHOWS IN STOCKHOLM and Amsterdam, the brief European jaunt returned to Hammersmith for a show received with unquestionable ecstasy. Then home again, and back on the road. In December 1975, Bruce started singing "Santa Claus Is Coming to Town" using Phil Spector's arrangement, and during the holiday season, it's still in his shows. Appel got a recording truck out to C. W. Post College on Long Island to record it on December 12, though it wasn't released officially for several years.

That night at Post, Bruce did his first version of the Animals' "It's My Life," which he introduced with a lengthy introductory story about his teenage battles with his father. The song developed over the next year into the most epic number in his show, more dramatically and musically extended than even "Jungleland."

The *Born to Run* experience, its pleasures and its frustrations, cracked Bruce's future wide open ("like a '57 Chevy running on melted-down Crystals' records," in Greil Marcus's words). But it also set off darker things in Bruce, both professionally and personally.

A typical set in this period included six songs from *Born to Run* (everything but "Meeting Across the River" and "Night"), two or three from each of the other albums, and up to a half dozen older rock and R&B songs ("Pretty Flamingo," "Sha La La," "The Detroit Medley," "Quarter to Three," and "Twist and Shout" were all standard, and another would sometimes be slipped in).

To me, this seems the inevitable consequence of adding Max Weinberg, whose biggest influence was British Invasion music, and Steven Van Zandt, whose love for garage rock and its associated genres eventually led him to invent a radio format for it. At that time, Springsteen had few songs of his own that fit that model, so he filled in with cover material.

What made all the difference was that he reinvented those songs so radically. The paradigmatic example is the "Detroit Medley," which fused two Mitch Ryder hits, "Jenny Take a Ride" and "Devil with a Blue Dress On"/ "Good Golly Miss Molly," which were already medleys themselves. By the time he was done, Springsteen had so fully extended, revamped, and inhabited his version that Ryder's originals, both great records, had been virtually wiped out of memory altogether.

At the time, people were commenting on how success hadn't changed Bruce much. Change came, though, as it must.

THE ROAD CREW CALLED the shows that began on March 25 in Columbia, South Carolina, the Chicken Scratch tour, because if you mapped it out, there were so many doublings back and forth across the South and the Midwest: Charlotte, Atlanta, back to Charlotte and Durham, just to start.

The band's popularity had grown so much that colleges competed with one another for Bruce's shows, and when a general admission show was booked at Ohio University, a near calamity ensued, with doors torn from hinges and fans crowded up against walls, doors, and plate-glass display cases. There wasn't any teen-idol nonsense, no screaming girls, but there was a slightly more sophisticated variant of it.

Playing places they'd never been before, there was the occasional bust. In Chattanooga, only a thousand people came to an auditorium built for almost four thousand. Bruce's road crew came out before the show and nailed a board across the orchestra pit so that Bruce could reach the seats more easily. He spent an unusual amount of time in the audience, up in people's faces. He wasn't about to leave those who did come with any doubts, or let the word of mouth be anything but fabulous. After drawing only six hundred in Little Rock, Bruce allegedly vowed never to return, but anybody who knew him would have bet that the opposite would be true.

The highlight of the Chicken Scratch tour unquestionably came in Memphis, where the E Streeters played Ellis Auditorium. Soul singer Eddie Floyd joined them onstage at the end of the show for "Raise Your Hand" and "Knock on Wood," two of his bigger hits. ("Raise" made intermittent appearances in Bruce's show for years afterward.)

Afterward, still a little giddy (apparently), Bruce, Miami Steve, and publicist Glen Brunman decided to head over to

Apr. 10, 1976 – Choate School, Wallingford, CT
This show, a benefit for the Choate School, is played at the request of John Hammond.

Apr. 22, 1976 – Virginia Polytechnic Institute, Blacksburg, VA
Fans camped out for a week to buy tickets to this show, an early scenario that would later become de rigeur. Bruce falls into the orchestra pit during the show and climbs out unharmed. About one hundred people in the audience keep cheering long after the show is over. Twenty-five minutes after they leave the stage, Bruce and band come back and play "Twist and Shout." After the show, Bruce goes to the Town Hall Bar in Blacksburg, where he joins future E Street Band guitarist Nils Lofgren onstage.

Elvis Presley Boulevard and take a look at Graceland. Once there, Bruce had a further inspiration: He would meet Elvis. So he scaled the fence, dropped over to the other side, and headed to the house, maybe fifty yards straight ahead. But before he got that far, a security guard stopped him. Undoubtedly concluding that this character who claimed to have been on the cover of *Time* and *Newsweek* was a crackpot—that was the first and only time Bruce ever bragged about it, so desperate was he to at least leave a message for his original hero—the guard showed him to the gate. Bruce used to tell the story onstage sometimes, first as a funny yarn about his Elvis fanaticism, later as an example of how instant karma can be.

After a few more Southern shows, the *Born to Run* tour finally came to an end on home turf—sort of: The last two shows were in New York and Maryland, but they were back-to-back shows at the military academies in West Point and Annapolis.

ONE FINE AFTERNOON in the spring of 1976, I walked a few blocks from the offices of *Rolling Stone* in midtown Manhattan to the offices of Warner Bros. Records. Warner was throwing a party to celebrate a new Dion album, *Streetheart*. He'd always been a favorite; the only fifties rocker who stayed creative, wrote new songs, and sang them in new ways.

I wasn't surprised to see Miami Steve there in the early seventies—between stints with Bruce, he'd played guitar with Dion. I didn't recognize the guy he was with, though, 'til he said hello to me.

There was no mistaking that raspy voice or its high-pitched chuckle when I started at the sound of it. It was Bruce, all right, shaven and shorn, not particularly dressed up but certainly not wearing his old ragged jeans. He looked trim, handsome, and comfortable.

When we left the party, Bruce and I walked together awhile. He asked what I'd been up to; I asked what he'd been up to. I don't remember what I said—my kids, my work, whatever I'd been listening to that wasn't out in the shops yet. I won't forget what he said.

"I'm on my way to see this lawyer," he said, naming a firm I knew. "Mike and I are . . ." Having some trouble, is how he put it, I think.

Bruce knew I knew about it. I'd tried to write a book about him. The problem was, I wanted to quote some of his lyrics. Appel said no.

That was a mistake. Not because I had a right to the lyric permissions. It was a mistake because Bruce had no objection to the book including them. Now he wanted something else of his that Appel controlled.

He'd never realized that his contracts ceded control to Laurel Canyon, the company owned by Appel (and his ex-partner Jim Cretecos). There was a lot he didn't realize:

Apr. 29, 1976 – Ellis Auditorium, Memphis, TN

Eddie Floyd joins the band onstage for encores of his hits "Knock on Wood" and "Raise Your Hand." After the show, Bruce takes a cab to Graceland to try to meet Elvis and is stopped by security guards.

Aug. 1, 1976 – Monmouth Arts Center (formerly Carlton Theater), Red Bank, NJ

"Rendezvous" and "Something in the Night" receive their live premieres. The Miami Horns (Carlo Novi and Ed Manion on sax, Tony Palligrosi and Rick Gazda on trumpet) are added to the tour. They are recruited from the Jukes' horns during a break in Southside Johnny's touring schedule.

Aug. 3, 1976 – Monmouth Arts Center, Red Bank, NJ

"The Promise" is played live for the first time.

Bruce wasn't signed directly to CBS Records, for instance, so all money flowed through Laurel Canyon. The deal allowed Laurel Canyon to get paid twice in those areas: once as managers, once as the record company and/or music publisher. (That is, they'd take their share plus 20 percent of Bruce's.)

There were many other problems, all stemming from the fact that Bruce had signed the deal without benefit of a lawyer of his own; he used Laurel Canyon's and even then didn't bother to read the contract or pay attention if it was read to him. In one version he used to tell, he signed the papers on the hood of a car in a dark parking lot outside a Jersey club. If that isn't true, it might as well have been.

The strangest part of it all is that Bruce felt he had spent all the time up to then winning his creative freedom, even more than financial independence. The contracts told him otherwise. Appel's only sound move would have been to set things aright and renegotiate everything. But Appel preferred to fight for what he saw as his fair share.

So they sued one another, and Appel also sued Jon Landau, who continued to give Springsteen career advice. Laurel Canyon and Springsteen both laid claim to the royalties from *Born to Run*, a sum not inconsiderable to either of them. CBS held the money pending the outcome of the lawsuit.

Laurel Canyon did successfully obtain an injunction preventing Bruce from recording anything. Bruce said later that he wasn't ready to make a record anyway, having yet to digest what happened with *Born to Run*. But that wasn't how it seemed then—then, it seemed like the injunction was Appel showing Springsteen just how much control the management/production/publishing company had. It's hard to imagine a surer formula for a permanent breach.

Meantime, Bruce and his band needed to work to survive. They'd have needed that even with the royalties. So they had Barry Bell at the William Morris Agency book a tour, starting in early August, with six shows at the Monmouth Arts Center in Red Bank.

Appel's lawyers immediately filed for an injunction, claiming that Bruce working independently of his management and production company would permanently harm Laurel Canyon's interests. The injunction was denied and the tour began.

THE MOST STRIKING THING about those Red Bank shows was Bruce's look. He'd retained all his

Sept. 30, 1976 – Roxy, Los Angeles, CA (Dion)
Bruce and Miami Steve join Dion onstage for "A Teenager in Love" and are introduced as "honorary Belmonts."

Oct. 25, 1976 – Spectrum, Philadelphia, PA
The band's first arena show takes place at the same venue in which Bruce was booed when opening for Chicago three years earlier. It is the first of two shows, the second taking place on October 27.

Oct. 29, 1976 – Palladium, New York, NY
Gary "U.S." Bonds joins the band onstage for "Quarter to Three" on the second night of a six-night stand.

Oct. 30 and Nov. 3, 1976 – Palladium, New York, NY
Patti Smith is a guest during "Rosalita" on both nights.

At the Palladium, October 1976

Nov. 4, 1976 – Palladium, New York, NY

Ronnie Spector sings three Ronettes songs with Bruce during the encores.

Nov. 26, 1976 – Bottom Line, New York, NY

Patti Smith Group headlines and Bruce joins them onstage during two shows for "Gloria" and "My Generation."

At the Palladium, New York City, October 1976

intensity, but it seemed different coming from a guy with a shaven face, trim hair, better fitting clothes. Gone was the street urchin, replaced by the ruggedly handsome, assertively modest rock star. Meaning, he looked good, and he acted like he was somebody special only when it seemed essential to the task, which was putting on a great rock and roll show.

The E Street Band remained itself—with the addition of a horn section, the Miami Horns Quartet, two trumpets and two saxes. Every show on the tour featured a horn section, though its personnel changed after the first month, when the Miami Horns Quartet left to join Southside Johnny and the Asbury Jukes, from whence they came. (The Jukes had just finished an album for the CBS Records label Epic, produced by Miami Steve Van Zandt.)

The pace of the show hadn't slackened. It mostly rehashed the Chicken Scratch tour sets, with a handful of key additions. Three of those were new Bruce songs, "Rendezvous," "Something in the Night," and "The Promise." "Rendezvous" zinged straight out of the British Invasion, Bruce singing in the mode of Manfred Mann lead singer Paul Jones, Steven and he carrying the tune with spitfire guitar. To that point, "Rendezvous" represented Bruce's most clearly and simply articulated melodic rock song—a sure hit, one would have thought.

"Something in the Night" went in the opposite direction, a stark piece of singer-songwriter music that acquired a jazz edge when arranged to feature trumpet, sliding back toward when the arrangement centered around the E Street keyboards. Like "Rendezvous," "Something" appeared in virtually all the shows in the first half of what inevitably became known as the Lawsuit tour, and intermittently thereafter. By the last couple of weeks, Bruce had arranged it as on the subsequent album.

The third of these new songs, "The Promise," appeared less frequently. It turned up in the third Red Bank show, disappeared until the end of September, and showed up infrequently thereafter.

"The Promise" ranks with "Jungleland," "Incident on 57th Street," and "New York City Serenade" among Springsteen's early efforts at writing epic-length narrative ballads, clocking in at between five and six carefully sung minutes. (The breakneck "She's the One" could go longer and seem shorter.) Clearly, it represented a major statement, but Bruce never made much of it—didn't introduce it with a story, for instance, or elaborate on it at all, just gave the lyrics (which had a couple of minor variations but not enough to suggest that it was a work in progress, like "Something") a very stark and emotive reading. One night in New York City, he did begin by saying, "If you ever wanted something you could never have . . . this is called 'The Promise.'"

This song needed to speak for itself, because it metaphorically addressed the breakup with Mike Appel. Ostensibly the lyrics concern four friends—a factory worker, a guy with a job "downtown," a rock musician, and the protagonist, who has "a little job" but focuses his attention on building a hot rod called the Challenger.

"Well now I built that Challenger by myself," begins the second verse, "But I needed money and so I sold it / I lived a secret I should'a kept to myself / But I got drunk one night and I told it."

The final verse barely bothers to pretend that it's metaphor: "I won big once. . . . But somehow I paid the big cost. . . . When the promise is broken you go on living / But it steals something from down in your soul." It's a song about betrayal but with an interesting twist: The betrayer is the protagonist himself, who has to learn to live with the fact that he sold his dream and bared his secrets. "The Promise" has always been taken to be a song about the Springsteen-Appel lawsuit, but it is most certainly not a song about Bruce's ex-manager. It's a song about Bruce.

From left: Danny, Bruce, Steven Van Zandt, Garry Tallent at the Music Inn, Lenox, Massachusetts, July 23, 1975

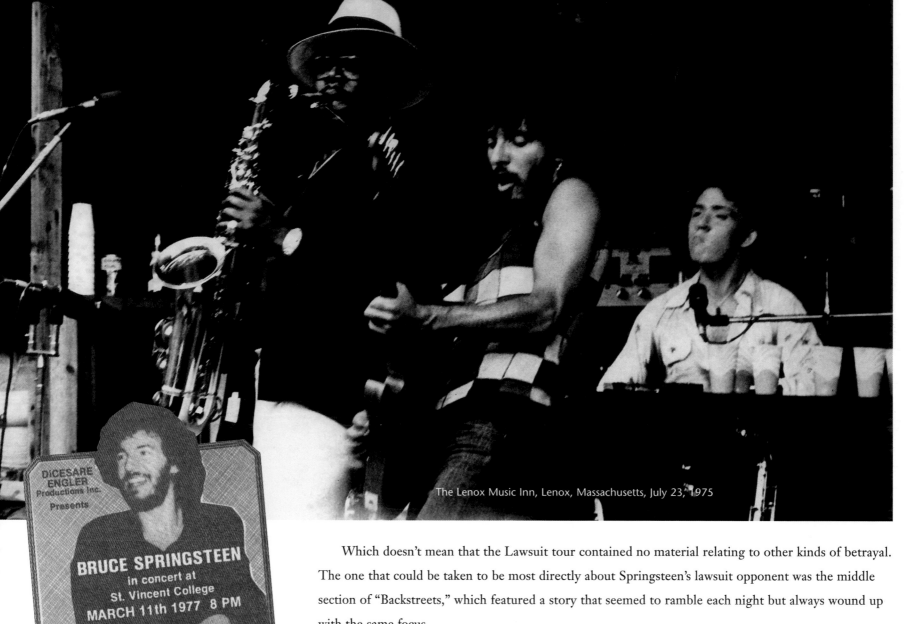

The Lenox Music Inn, Lenox, Massachusetts, July 23, 1975

DiCESARE ENGLER Productions Inc. Presents

BRUCE SPRINGSTEEN
in concert at
St. Vincent College
MARCH 11th 1977 8 PM

BACKSTAGE

Which doesn't mean that the Lawsuit tour contained no material relating to other kinds of betrayal. The one that could be taken to be most directly about Springsteen's lawsuit opponent was the middle section of "Backstreets," which featured a story that seemed to ramble each night but always wound up with the same focus.

Like many of Bruce's stories, it grew more and more elaborate as time went on. Most of the time, the story wound up with Bruce fulminating, "You LIED, you LIED, you LIED" until your own throat hurt from hearing it. But it evolved until by the end of the tour in Boston the next March it went more or less like this:

Feb. 8, 1977 – Auditorium Theater, Rochester, NY
For the first time, Bruce inserts a long monologue during the middle of a song— "Backstreets."

Feb. 17, 1977 – Richfield Coliseum, Cleveland, OH
Bruce is joined onstage by Ronnie Spector, who sings three Ronettes songs with him as well as the Billy Joel song "Say Goodbye to Hollywood, " later released as a promo single (produced by Miami Steve), accompanied by the E Street Band, for an album that is never completed.

Mar. 25, 1977 – Music Hall, Boston, MA
Final night of the *Born to Run* tour and the last night of a spectacular four-night stand at the Music Hall.

**BRUCE SPRINGS
AND THE E STREET**

Sunday
March 20, 1977
8 p.m.
Providence
College
Alumni
Hall
$7.00 & $7.50

"Let the rain fall down . . . and wash your tears away . . . open your eyes," he sang, "because it's branded in your heart, and it'll be a part of you now. So, baby . . . little girl, don't cry . . . little girl, don't cry, it's all over now . . . tonight . . . tonight . . . fall into my arms . . . and we will go away. . . . Me and you, baby . . . me and you, girl. . . ."

He began speaking now, in his most dramatic voice.

"Well, I remember running back . . . I remember this guy abandoned this car in this field 'bout a mile and a half outside of town, and at night me and her and Billy used to hitchhike out there. . . . I remember the kids, they stripped down the outside of it 'til there was almost nothing left but the interior, but the insides were still all right. And we'd ride—way down by the railroad tracks. We'd go riding in the backseat."

He sings as much as speaks now, staring into the black beyond the stage like it's his meditative universe, the perfect platform for pointed, vengeful free association: "Baby, take me riding in the backseat . . . in the backseat . . . in the backseat . . . in the backseat of that old Cadillac. Billy's got cleats on his boots, oh, her heels are stacked. . . . Yeah, in the backseat. . . . Oh, take me down. . . . Hey, Terry, take me down . . . and the world and this madness 'round and 'round and 'round and down and down and down and 'round and 'round and 'round we go and down and down and down. . . ."

He speaks again, with lots of little pauses, like he's catching his breath from the torment of remembering, like he's fighting to remember or maybe to forget, although by the end he's singing, first in a passionate voice he learned from all those old girl-group records, then in his most stentorian rock-and-roll shout: "I remember these kids that night, they set fire to this abandoned farmhouse that was about a half a mile up the tracks, and they had these machines down there, and they had these engines down there. We'd see the flames shooting out across the sky 'til they caught the field. We set up on the hood and watched it rushing toward us, watching the flames rushing toward, watching 'em rushing toward us across the field 'til we ran back on the tracks and started heading back into town . . . and then . . . and then . . . then she kissed me . . . then she kissed me . . . then she kissed me . . . then she kissed me . . . oh, oh. And then she promised . . . and then she promised . . . and then she promised. . . . And then she lied . . . and then she lied . . . and then she lied . . . and then she lied . . . she lied . . . she lied . . . she lied. . . . Pretty li-li-li-lies . . . pretty li-li-li-lies. . . .

"And I was just wishing . . . I remember praying that God would send some angels and blow this whole damn town right into the sea. I remember wishing that God would send some angels and blow this whole fucking town right into the sea . . . just wishing that God would send some angels and blow this whole damn town right into the sea . . . just blow this whole . . . just blow it into the sea . . . just

At the Academy of Music, New York, 1976

Here and opposite: Academy of Music, New York, 1976

blow it all away . . . just blow it all away . . . just blow it all away . . . BLOW IT ALL AWAY . . . BLOW IT ALL AWAY . . . MAKE IT GO AWAY . . . BLOW IT ALL AWAY . . . JUST BLOW IT ALL AWAY . . . JUST BLOW IT ALL AWAY . . . JUST BLOW IT ALL AWAY . . . JUST BLOW IT ALL AWAY . . ."

It wasn't going away, not right away. The process of suing someone isn't quite as depleting as Dickens made it in *Bleak House*, but it's way too close. Anyway, this suit wasn't just about the irreducible fact that money changes everything—that really is easy enough to put in the past.

Bruce began now to deal with some of the consuming themes of his career, stuff he'd been alluding to since his first album (with "Growin' Up" in particular) and that he'd begun grappling with in earnest when he added "It's My Life" to his set toward the end of the *Born to Run* tour.

He sang "It's My Life" at every single show, and he went at it with a vengeance—eight, ten, twelve minutes, one version went on for almost fourteen. This was a whole other kind of exorcism, and it had little to do with Mike Appel. It had to do with Bruce's relationship with his father, Douglas.

This was rock and roll future come home.

AT THE END OF OCTOBER and early November, Bruce did a six-night stand at the Palladium Theater, the old Academy of Music, the city's original opera house on Fourteenth Street in the East Village. It held about 2,500 people, so Bruce played to about thirty times as many people as he had at the Bottom Line. Those shows aren't nearly so famous. But they were better shows.

I think I saw five of those shows; I know I skipped out to watch election results on November 2. Some of the most exhilarating and some of the scariest moments I've ever experienced in rock and roll came on those nights. The rhythm of those sets can still be felt by those who were there. Bruce's look might start out sober—he sometimes wore a three-piece suit—but when the time for release came at the end, the script always felt torn up and tossed in the air. Those shows are seamless in memory, but they peaked when Bruce tore more deeply than ever into himself for "It's My Life," then followed with the affirmation of "Thunder Road."

The "It's My Life" Bruce did in those shows had only the barest relationship to the "It's My Life" that was a hit for the Animals in late 1965. Not even one of their biggest hits, one of the ones their producer Mickie Most probably nicked out of some excursion to the hacks in the Brill Building, certainly the only important song written by its composers, Carl D'Errico and Roger Atkins, an invitation to the most maudlin self-pity, rendered transcendent because Eric Burdon's gruff, bullying vocal is perfectly balanced by the virtual rock and roll pointillism of Hilton Valentine's guitar and Chas Chandler's bass. It's callow, of course, but in 1965, rock and roll's glory was its callowness.

Patti Smith joins Bruce onstage at the Palladium in New York City, October 30, 1976.

The version I love best, listening back to those old bootlegged tapes, starts in a way that's reminiscent of nothing else the E Street Band ever did. Clarence on soprano sax, playing as close as he ever did to free jazz, though the overall effect's really more like an ominous movie score. The rest of the band comes in, but gently, and the sax beats them back, and beats them back, and beats them back again—that cry won't be denied, it won't even be modified, it hurts too bad, and it has waited too long to say so.

And then it drops back behind Bruce's voice and is stilled by it, as he begins to spin his own tale, which is my tale, which is the tale of way too many and not just if you happened to be a teenager in the middle of the sixties, either.

"I grew up in this small town, was about ten thousand people," he said one of those nights at the Palladium. "I lived in this two-family house next to this Sinclair station.

"I used to have this roof right out my bedroom window, my bedroom was facing the main highway. In the summertime when it used to get real hot, I used to climb out the window, drag my mattress out there, sleep outside. They used to shut the gas-station around one o'clock, and all night long there'd be different guys pulling in, meeting somebody there, pulling out onto the highway, trucks rolling through town.

"And I remember as soon as I got old enough, I used to come up to the city as much as I could, I'd stay with some friends here, I'd stay down at the beach.

"My pop . . . well, he was, he worked in this plastics factory, and he was a guard down at the jail. He spent most of his nights at home, and I remember every night he used to shut off all the lights in the house at nine o'clock. The only light in the house would be the TV, my mother'd be sitting in the front room watching the TV—'til she fell asleep in the chair, get up to go to work the next morning. And my father, he'd be sitting in the kitchen, drinking a six-pack, smoking cigarettes . . . just waiting for me and my sister to come back home.

"The older I got, the more I stayed away . . . but I always knew I'd always have to come back, and when I did, he'd be sitting there at that kitchen table in the dark, just waiting to hear my footsteps coming up on that porch. And I used to stand in the driveway, 'cause he used to lock up the front door so I couldn't get in that way, and I used to stand in the driveway, look through the screen door, and see the

May 12–13, 1977 – Monmouth Arts Centre, Red Bank, NJ

Southside Johnny and the Asbury Jukes' homecoming shows (after their first European tour) are scheduled on these dates. The shows are nearly cancelled when Southside becomes ill, but proceed, billed as the Asbury All-Star Revue. Miami Steve sings lead on the songs, Bruce plays guitar and contributes backing vocals for most of the show, and Ronnie Spector plays four numbers (joined by Bruce on "You Mean So Much to Me"). The E Street Band performs with Bruce for the encores both nights.

Dec. 2, 1977 – NYU Loeb Student Center, New York, NY

Bruce joins Robert Gordon and Link Wray for "Heartbreak Hotel."

Dec. 30, 1977 – CBGB, New York, NY

At this Patti Smith show, Bruce joins her onstage for his song "Because the Night," which will be included on her 1978 album *Easter* and released as a single. This is the only time Bruce performs live at CBGB's.

light—see the light of his cigarette, see the blue light of the TV on in the living room, thinking about when I was gonna be old enough. . . .

"I'd end up slicking my hair back real tight so he couldn't tell how long it was, trying to make it through the kitchen. But soon as I hit that bottom step of the stairs, he'd be calling me to come back and sit down in the dark. And we'd be sitting there in the kitchen . . . and in the wintertime he used to turn the gas jets on in the stove so it got real hot in there, he'd close the kitchen door, and we'd sit there and he . . . I remember I could always hear his voice telling me . . . telling me . . . just telling me . . . but I could never . . . I could never see his face."

Bruce says almost all of this in a flat voice, almost a Joe Friday just-the-facts monotone. But as he gets to the next part, tension leaps into his voice, his cadences grow more abrupt, you can feel anger and fear, and most of all, violence.

"Then he'd start talking about nothing too much . . . how it was going, how things were going. Pretty soon he'd be asking me what I thought I was doing with myself. Where I was getting my money from. We'd end up screaming at each other, and my mother'd end up running in from the front room trying to, trying to pull him off me, trying to keep us from fighting with each other.

"I'd end up running out the back door telling him . . . telling him, telling him . . . that it was my life and I was gonna do whatever I wanted to do."

Then the band crashed into the song. It's a song of rage and courage—odd combination, they almost never come together, but Bruce made you see how he could be both furious and brave at once. "It's My Life" reaches its pinnacle in the chorus: "Show me I'm wrong, hurt me sometime / But someday I'll treat you real fine."

The perfect song for the image Bruce Springsteen was carving for himself. A vengeance song that ends with the threat of . . . kindness.

THAT WAS THE CORE of those shows. Along the way, Bruce premiered two more songs, "Don't Look Back" and "Action in the Streets," both showing the British Invasion influence very strongly. I remember seeing a magisterial show in Detroit, where he revived the dormant "Detroit Medley" because Mitch Ryder and two of the Wheels, Johnny Badanjek and Jim McCarty, were in the house, and dedicated "Born to Run," now the show's finale, to Bob Seger, who'd just broken through with "Night Moves," a hit inspired by "Born to Run."

It went on like that for about nine months, and then, after the shows at the Boston Music Hall toward the end of March, the tour ended as unexpectedly as it had begun. The lawsuit settled, Bruce left the stage and headed back to the windowless rooms where records are made.

Chapter Five

From the Dark Heart of a Dream

"Let them melt, let them fire, let them burn"

S HEA'S THEATER IN BUFFALO, New York, looked much the same on May 23, 1978, as it probably had when it was built fifty years before. The beautiful Beaux Arts movie palace, with its Tiffany interior, held a little more than three thousand people. Rabid fans of Bruce Springsteen and the E Street Band filled it to see Springsteen's first show in more than a year. His new album, *Darkness on the Edge of Town*, wasn't due in the stores for a week but the track list was known. Almost nothing Bruce had ever performed live was on it: Of the four new songs he'd done the previous year, only "Something in the Night" appeared.

It seemed a lot longer than fourteen months since Springsteen and the band had toured. *Born to Run*, the *Time* and *Newsweek* cover controversy, the accusations of "hype" were almost three years distant. Three years was a risky wait for an artist whose breakthrough album had sold "only" a little more than a million copies.

During these years, the talk about Springsteen revolved around his lawsuit with manager-producer Mike Appel. That suit also dragged Jon Landau and CBS Records into the mire. Appel had gone from crusader to combatant in the twinkling of an eye, but there wasn't much advantage to him in publicizing the one-sided ways in which he benefited from that crusade. Bruce proved to be among the most private public persons of our time. So the buzz was confused and contradictory. Presumably, the new songs would be filled with clues about what it all meant to Bruce.

At the Spectrum, Philadelphia, Pennsylvania, 1978

After the settlement of the lawsuit, Bruce controlled his music. He was free to work with whomever he chose—producer Jon Landau, engineer Jimmy Iovine, and the E Street Band stayed; Appel went. Although he told the *Washington Post* that the legal fees left him in debt, a new record contract allowed him to spend extended time in the studio. He'd used that time right up until the tour began.

What had this ugly business done to the zealous rock and roll idealism that made his early music so compelling? Would the new songs be bitter portrayals of betrayal, a rejection of life in the big time, or perhaps a coming to terms with compromise? Maybe the music would speak for itself, but in that case, it *had* been a very long time since he'd been heard.

I went to Buffalo as a *Rolling Stone* writer and editor. Also on hand were John Rockwell of the *New York Times*, Robert Hilburn of the *Los Angeles Times*, and Lisa Robinson of the *New York Post*. We sat in the orchestra, a few rows back.

About half an hour after the time on the ticket, the house lights dropped. Bruce and the band took their places amid expectant shouts and cries.

Bruce boldly counted off, and for the first time, "Badlands" ripped out of a PA system. It's a song about freedom and its price. That night, and as far as I'm concerned for as many times as he's played it since, the song

felt to me like the sound of a caged man carving out free space in his life, in the world.

I can still remember both first times I heard "Badlands"—the recording and the live version. When I heard it on Jon Landau's stereo, a week or so before the Buffalo show, I remember thinking, "This is exactly the record I needed to hear." I didn't mean it was better for understanding Bruce's life; I was thinking how much better it let me understand mine.

Onstage, "Badlands" didn't portray one man against a corrupt world. It created a guitar army come to clear the air. The live "Badlands" creates a sense of liberation that climaxes in its beautiful vocal break, Bruce and the band (and now, however many tens of thousands are in the crowd singing the same) chanting "*ooo-ooo, ooo-ooo, ooo-ooo ooh*" until you feel your heart begin to burst as Bruce steps up to sing some of his greatest lines: "For the ones who had a notion, a notion deep inside / That it ain't no sin to be glad you're alive."

That was the rock and roll concept at its core: Elvis, James Brown, Little Richard, Bob Dylan, the Stones, Otis Redding, the Beatles, Jimi Hendrix, and ten thousand more all found a way to say it. Now Bruce picked up the idea—this grandiose "notion"—and flung it back as a statement and as a challenge. "I wanna find one face that ain't lookin' through me," he shouted, and there was in the air that

May 23, 1978 – Shea's Theater, Buffalo, NY
The opening night of the *Darkness* tour. The show is so long that it now includes an intermission, the second set starting with an instrumental called "Paradise by the 'C.'"

June 2, 1978
Darkness on the Edge of Town is released.

night the feeling that it was not just up to Bruce Springsteen or even Bruce and the E Street Band but to everybody in the room to present that face. And there was the feeling that we could.

Yet much of the material that followed reflected a new and darker self-scrutiny. The ten songs on *Darkness* tell a story that begins with the hopes of "Badlands" and ends with a victory that leaves the hero looking down at the wreckage of his world. It was impossible to separate this very dark ride to the heights from the journey Bruce Springsteen had been through—from his boyhood poverty to the scars acquired along the way to that liberated zone the music provided.

BRUCE DIDN'T SHY AWAY from playing unfamiliar material. At that opening show there couldn't have been a dozen people outside his band who knew the new songs. He still played all but one song from *Darkness* ("Factory" was the orphan). For the only time ever, he played a full band arrangement of "The Promise," ordinarily a solo piano piece. He romped midset through an unreleased instrumental, "Paradise by the 'C'," and sang "Fire," a little-known gem that had been recorded by punkabilly Robert Gordon. He played "For You," which he'd never done with the band in its twin-keyboard, twin-guitar for-

mation. Bo Diddley's "Mona" now segued into "She's the One." The night ended not with "Quarter to Three" but with a rave-up rendition of the Dovells' "You Can't Sit Down."

That is, of the twenty-three songs the E Street Band played that night, twelve—almost exactly half—were either brand new or radically altered.

The show took the idea of a rock and roll concert into a place of self-revelation and communal ecstasy. This was the promise not betrayed but fulfilled.

Bruce's songs affirmed the idea of rock and roll as an inchoate set of principles that made life worthwhile. You could look at his concerts as the continuation of that idea. Bruce's show clearly left the band, as exhausted as they were by the intensity of the two hour workout, more exhilarated than tired. Bruce seemed desperately joyous at the chance for physical release. The audience neared mass delirium.

Psychic and dramatic tension filled the set. Even at the start, he sang, "I wanna spit in the face of these badlands." "Something in the Night" explores despair; "Streets of Fire" and "Adam Raised a Cain" instill despair with rage; and "Darkness," though it climbs the mountaintop, spends

June 9, 1978
"Prove It All Night"/"Factory" is released as a single.

July 7, 1978 – Roxy, Los Angeles, CA
FM Broadcast and the live premiere of "Point Blank."

July 8, 1978 – Memorial Coliseum, Phoenix, AR
The live "Rosalita" music video is filmed at this show.

July 19, 1978 – Auditorium, Memphis, TN
Live premiere of "Factory," the final song from the *Darkness* album to be played live.

Cleveland, Ohio, Richfield Coliseum, January 1, 1979,
the final night of a 118-date tour

most of its time in the lonely valley. Even "The Promised Land," whose exuberance matches "Badlands," begins with "Driving all night, chasing some mirage."

So the ugly truths were never out of sight. Bruce used the struggle as a way of validating the release.

There's barely a glint of humor in those *Darkness* songs—no, that's too mild. Every joke has its throat slashed by the line that follows: "If dreams came true, oh, wouldn't that be nice / But this ain't no dream we're living through tonight." That's about as close as these songs come to a smile. Bruce called the album "a relentless barrage of the particular thing." Thankfully, there was lots in the show that wasn't on the record.

The entire *Darkness on the Edge of Town* tour could be boiled down to a message: If you're able, committed, find a community you can call your own, and willing to take life and love on their own terms—wild and real—then you can "Prove It All Night." You can make your own face shine, and when you do, other faces will shine, too.

BRUCE CONDUCTED THE *Darkness on the Edge of Town* tour as a crusade—a crusade for the values he felt rock and roll represented and a crusade to keep himself an honest man.

Rock and roll didn't start out as something you could crusade about, but it evolved in that direction as artists like John Lennon, Pete Townshend and the Who, and the MC5, followed by a horde of rock writers, articulated how and why the music changed their lives. For such performers, rock and roll represented something "that won't solve your problems but it will let you dance all over them," to use Townshend's phrase.

AN EVENING WITH
BRUCE SPRINGSTEEN

Tuesday, June 13
8:30 p.m.
Hancher Auditorium
Iowa City

Reserved Seats:
$7.50 students
$8.00 others
Mail & phone orders
accepted

For Bruce Springsteen, to champion this simple but effective musical art implied a certain egalitarianism, honoring the working class and African-American roots of rock's 1950s pioneers. It implied a commitment to peace, justice, and that elusive state labeled freedom, the values of the great social movements of the 1960s. It meant doing your best to look your audience in the eye—to pay attention to the way your fans listened to you. It involved challenging everybody's preconceptions, starting with your own, and risking the favor of the public by standing up for what is right. It required seeing the music for its value in people's lives and rejecting the idea that it was a superficial toy, a mere consumer product or fit only for adolescents.

About this time, Bruce began decrying stardom as "the booby prize" of success. Nevertheless, he was a rock star now. Strangers recognized him, his presence at a social event would be boldfaced in the gossip columns. He went to damn few events, and he mostly ran into strangers at the movies, but the recognition was real. He was a star, sure enough.

He wrapped himself in his musical world to compensate. His fanatic urge for control of all detail extended past the recording studio into the arenas he and the band played on the *Darkness* tour. He spent hours every day at sound checks that involved him taking a seat in every section of the building to make sure the sound was clear there. "And if it isn't right, even in the last row, I hear about it and we make changes. I mean every date, too," said Bruce Jackson, his chief sound engineer.

"Anyone who works for me, the first thing you better know is I'm gonna drive you crazy," said Springsteen at the time. "Because I don't compromise in certain areas. So if you're gonna be in, you better be ready for that." Marc Brickman had already given him a fascinating and dramatic (sometimes, distracting) lighting design. Other elements of the backstage load, though, were still being carried by guys left over from the New Jersey band circuit.

In Los Angeles and New York, particularly, the lack of professionalism told in terms of crew tensions and jobs that didn't get done or didn't get done correctly. Only rarely was the problem evident to the audience, but when it was, Bruce melted down. A special club show at the Roxy sold out in minutes, leaving hundreds of fans who'd spent the night in line ticketless. Bruce reacted offstage as if personally stung and delivered a lengthy apology for the show, even though all there could have heard every word on a live broadcast.

There were a half-dozen incidents of that kind early in the tour, and for Bruce, changing the situation became an open matter of principle. "Every person, every individual in the crowd counts—to me. I see it both ways. There's a crowd reaction. But then I also think very, very personally, one-to-one, with the kids. 'Cause you put out the effort, and then if it doesn't come through, it's a . . . it's a breakdown. What I always feel is that I don't like to let people that have supported me down. I don't like to let myself down. . . . I don't wanna try to get by." He spoke like a man who'd learned the lesson of his first teacher: Elvis Presley, the paragon of just getting by, who—it could be argued—died from that very ailment.

The haphazard behind-the-scenes situation began to change with the promotion to de facto tour manager of George Travis, who had been chief rigger (the guy who leads the part of the crew that works with the sound and light equipment suspended over the stage).

Travis, the same age as Bruce and most of the band, at first paid no particular attention to Bruce's show; it was just another band to work with. Then, at the promoter's suggestion, he went out to watch the Shea Theater show as it began. He at once recognized a kindred spirit. Travis's own attention to detail, sense of caution, avoidance of conflict, and insistence on integrity remains one of the concert industry's most durable stories. He played a large role in professionalizing the concert-touring business, which had become sophisticated in terms of technology and marketing but lagged in terms of the structure of the workplace and expectations from and treatment of backstage workers. Just as booking agent Frank Barsalona played the key role in creating a group of concert promoters who treated rock artists with respect, George Travis trained a generation of road crews about how to go about making the business of rock shows run more efficiently and how to make accountings, for instance, less fly-by-night. The legend began with the *Darkness* tour.

It fit Springsteen's vision. "Every time I read stuff that I say, like in the papers, I always think I come off sounding like some kind of crazed fanatic," he told me in our *Rolling Stone* interviews that summer. "It's like you have to go the whole way because . . . that's what keeps everything *real*. It all ties in with the records and the values, the morality of the records. There's a certain morality of the show and it's very strict."

That morality leaked out all over the place, most explicitly in long, roaming rants in the middle of

At the Spectrum, Philadelphia, 1978

Bruce's mother requests another encore at Madison Square Garden, August 23, 1978.

"Backstreets." He did an elaborate version of it in Miami that August, the band comping behind his rhythmic spiel, which became a statement, a chant, a croon, 'til it was hard to know which parts were spoken, which sung:

"Hey there baby . . . hey there, little girl . . . it's good, it's good to see you back again. . . . It's good, it's good to see you back again . . . and you know, honey, you're still looking *fiii-ii-iine*. But, baby, I remember you. Baby, I remember you standing on the corner of Richmond Avenue, with your hair rolled up, with your high heels on. And back then . . . I remember back then I swore . . . I swore I'd drive all night . . . I'd drive all night—anytime,

anyplace, anywhere—baby, I'd drive all night . . . just to buy you some shoes, and to taste . . . and to taste your tender charms, to have you hold me in your arms. And girl, for just one kiss . . . baby, just one kiss and a look, and a look from your sad eyes . . . you had such lonely, sad eyes, you had such lonely, sad eyes. Oh, they cry and cry and cry and cry, they cry and cry and cry and cry.

"And me, I was your fool. I thought that maybe I could stop your crying, that maybe I could stop your crying. . . . I thought that I could stop your crying . . . I thought that I could stop your crying . . . you knew I couldn't stop you . . . 'cause baby, you were lying . . . baby, you were lying . . . baby'd been lying . . . baby'd been lying . . . telling such, telling such pretty lies—you were young, you could tell such pretty lies, you were young and you could tell such pretty lies . . . you were young and you could tell such pretty lies, you could tell such pretty lies, you could tell such pretty lies . . . you could tell such pretty lies. . . . And now you're back . . . and now you're back . . . and now you're back . . . but baby, I'm back too . . . little girl, I'm back too . . . and I've been out . . . and I've seen some things . . . about me, about you . . . I want you . . . LOOK INTO MY FACE . . . LOOK INTO MY FACE . . . STOP . . . LOOK INTO MY FACE . . . STOP . . . LOOK INTO MY FACE . . . STOP, STOP, STOP, STOP, STOP, STOP, STOP!"

There's nothing there that fans of gospel preaching or

July 28, 1978 – Jai Alai Fronton, Miami, FL
The show includes Bruce's first known version of "Summertime Blues."

Aug. 14, 1978
"Badlands"/"Streets of Fire" is released as a single by Columbia Records.

Aug. 23, 1978 – Madison Square Garden, New York, NY
On the final night of a spectacular three-night stand, Bruce's mother comes onstage at the end of the show to demand a final encore.

Van Morrison won't recognize in structure. But gospel preachers weren't sermonizing to their lovers, and Morrison's dreamy digressions didn't end in explosions. It's the combination of the two that marked the "raps" Springsteen did in the midst of his songs on the *Darkness* tour—and which became one of his signatures—leading him eventually to a new group of songs ("Drive All Night" and "Fade Away" in particular) that related, more verbally than sonically, to his jazzy past. Bruce has mellowed some, but nobody who watched him do ten years of "Light of Day" a la Jimmy Swaggart followed by ten years of "Tenth Avenue Freeze-Out" in the same mode could deny the connection.

THE TOUR TOOK OFF when Springsteen went west, starting with two torrid shows at the smallish Berkeley Community Theater that found Bruce spending a good bit of the night in the aisles, followed by his arrival in Hollywood as an arena rock icon at the Forum; the Roxy show, which introduced two significant new songs, "Independence Day" and "Point Blank"; and finally, a wild night at the Phoenix Coliseum, memorialized in the famous video clip of "Rosalita," which ends with him flat on his back in the embrace of a gaggle of teenage girls. I was there, and that finale felt as inevitable as the collapsed stage at Lincoln Center four years earlier.

Kindling such ecstasy came out of the same commitment—the same "morality"—that generated the introspection and the fanatic attention to detail. Really, what happened in Phoenix was the more pertinent part—there was a grueling aspect to those marathon shows, with the half-hour break between sets seeming to me as much to let the audience collect its wits as to freshen up the band, but being at them was as much fun as I've ever had, legally or otherwise.

Nor was it a drag offstage. There was, for instance, the night before the Forum show when Bruce, Steven, Clarence, Garry, and several crew members climbed to the top of the billboard advertising *Darkness* over on the Sunset Strip in Los Angeles, and "made some artistic improvements," as Bruce noted at the show, with twenty cans of spray paint. (He couldn't reach his nose, which he found way too big for comfort, but he did manage to scrawl "E Street" and "Prove It All Night" up there.)

It was a teenage prank, but then, isn't that always lurking somewhere at the heart of rock and roll? Trusting that instinct—more precisely, knowing when to trust yourself to indulge it—might be a key to this whole rock and roll morality thing.

Yet always, always, came the other side. Introducing one of his consummate statements of freedom, Bruce told a story every night, about a drive he'd taken with Steven and a couple of other friends out through the desert in a junker

Aug. 25, 1978 – Toad's Place, New Haven, CT
After a sold-out show at the Veterans Memorial Coliseum, Bruce and Clarence join Rhode Island band Beaver Brown onstage for three encores ("Rosalita," "Double Shot of My Baby's Love," "You Can't Sit Down"). The place goes wild. This is the first of many times Bruce will join Beaver Brown onstage at a club gig.

Aug. 31, 1978 – The Agora, Cleveland, OH
After a sold-out show at the Coliseum, Bruce joins Southside Johnny and the Asbury Jukes onstage during their second set. The show starts late to give Miami Steve, then lead guitarist for the Jukes as well as the E Street Band, time to travel between shows.

CELLAR DOOR
PRESENTS
RUCE SPRINGSTEEN
★ ★ ★ ★ ★ ★ ★ ★ ★ ★ ★ ★ ★ ★
MIAMI JAI-ALAI FRONTON
MIAMI, FLORIDA
28 1
9
7
8
FRIDAY
8:00 P.M.
TAX INCLUDED

$7·50

New Year's Eve, 1978, post-firecracker, Richfield Coliseum, Cleveland, Ohio

car during a break in the recording sessions the summer before. "When we were driving through the desert, we came upon this house this Indian had built out of, sculpted outta the stuff he'd scavenged off the desert. And I remember out in front it had a sign, it said, 'This is the land of peace, love, justice, and no mercy.' And at the bottom of the sign, it pointed down this little dirt road that said 'Thunder Road.'..."

The *Darkness* tour followed that route, wherever it happened to lead.

ODDLY, IT DIDN'T LEAD them that long or that far. They never left North America, and for that matter, they barely left 1978. It took Bruce until July 21 to do a live version of "Factory," but for the most part, the nightly surprise was that rock and roll could be this consistently good, that a performer was willing to continually stretch himself so strenuously, that commitment and conviction could come in such an attractive package.

Somewhere in the midst of it all, Jon Landau officially became the manager, a position he'd held in fact since the split with Appel became final. A series of regional live radio broadcasts of club shows (from Los Angeles, New Jersey, Cleveland, Atlanta, San Francisco) on FM album rock stations helped make up for the lack of a hit single—"Prove It All Night" flopped at number thirty-three on the *Billboard* chart, ten places lower than "Born to Run." Jukebox hits of the past came and went in the show—half of Buddy Holly's hits, Dion's "Runaround Sue," "The Last Time"—and occasionally, one of Bruce's own old tunes got a workout, usually due to incessant fan requests: "Kitty's Back" at a September return to the Palladium in New York, for instance. He sang "Santa Claus Is Coming to Town" for the first time that year at Boston Garden on September 25, on the theory, he told the crowd, that he wouldn't make it back to town before Christmas. (He was right, by almost three Christmases.)

He'd whipped the Cleveland crowd into a New Year's Eve lather when some moron tossed a firecracker almost at the stroke of twelve. The crowd had been admonished about fireworks several times, and this one nearly hit Springsteen himself. He spent several minutes collecting himself, a few seconds letting the idiot

"**Well, I almost lost my eye thanks to some asshole . . . but that ain't gonna ruin my New Year and I hope it don't ruin yours . . . best of 1979 to all you guys."**
—BS

Nov. 1, 1978 – Princeton University, Princeton, NJ
Live premiere of "The Ties That Bind."

Dec. 28, 1978 – Stanley Theater, Pittsburgh, PA
"Ramrod" is played at this show for the first time, with a different arrangement than later versions.

Dec. 31, 1978 – Richfield Coliseum, Cleveland, OH
At midnight, Bruce invites all the band members' girlfriends onstage. There is general chaos for a few moments, and someone from the audience throws a firecracker that hits Bruce under the eye. After a few frenzied minutes, the show goes on as planned.

New Year's Eve '78 BACK STAGE

have it—"Well, I almost lost my eye thanks to some asshole . . . but that ain't gonna ruin my New Year and I hope it don't ruin yours . . . best of 1979 to all you guys." Then he thanked the audience for being so great, strapped his guitar back on, rocked into Holly's "Rave On," and played another hour or so.

Crowds took to lingering longer and longer in the aisles. Several times they were rewarded when Bruce and the band retook the stage, up to a half hour after they'd been presumed to be gone. So the faithful lingered. It was good practice for what came next—or for the longest time, did not.

It was just the next stage of a very long journey. Bruce Springsteen had made up his mind: It was not enough to just be a rock star, and it wasn't even enough to be the best rocker anyone had seen in years. He was in it for the long haul.

Jan. 1, 1979 — Richfield Coliseum, Cleveland, OH
Last night of the *Darkness* tour. Between "Backstreets" and "Rosalita" (the usual show closers prior to the encores) a cover of the Rolling Stones' "The Last Time" is played. Jon Landau joins the band onstage for the final encores.

June 3, 1979 — The Whiskey, Los Angeles, CA
At the wedding of lighting designer Marc Brickman, Bruce and E Street Band members join Boz Scaggs and Rickie Lee Jones for a multisong set that includes "Hava Nagila" and "Mother-in-Law."

The *River* tour, 1981

Chapter Six

Not Fade Away

"To settle back is to settle without knowing."

I T LOOKED LIKE IT WOULD be pretty simple, pretty fast, no drawn-out agonies or long nights of nitpicking.

Bruce, the band, and producers Jon Landau and Chuck Plotkin, who'd worked on the mix of *Darkness*, began recording his fifth album in early 1979. He had "Independence Day" and "Point Blank," and since then had written several more good songs.

In May, a group of mainly West Coast stars, led by Jackson Browne and Bonnie Raitt, asked Bruce to play two concerts, the final pair of five, at Madison Square Garden for their political group, Musicians United for Safe Energy (MUSE). He said yes relatively quickly.

The concerts, on September 21 and September 22 (the night before Bruce's thirtieth birthday) would be priced at a premium—$18.50—and Bruce would come on after several other acts to close both nights with a shortened edition of his show.

The presence of rock's most reclusive contemporary personality doubled media interest. Skeptics felt that Bruce, apolitical as far as they could see, since he didn't make the usual rounds of demonstrations and fundraisers, had simply seized an opportunity to promote his upcoming album. (CBS Records had let it be known that Landau had let it be known that Bruce was getting very close.) His more political admirers fretted that Bruce the Outsider was finally cozying up to the Rock Establishment.

Bruce let his music talk. The Garden shook on its suspension foundation as the E Street

On the *River* tour, 1981

Band took the stage each night and ripped into a super-condensed version of its standard set. "Prove It All Night," "Badlands," and "The Promised Land" landed like cudgel blows after the soft rock that preceded them. Bruce quieted the house, announced a new song, and tore into "The River," a statement of working-class despair that pushed the same political buttons as "Factory," but with greater eloquence, more melodic grace, and one of the finest arrangements he's ever come up with. Then another new one, the slight frat-rocker "Sherry Darling," before ending with patented bravado: "Thunder Road," "Jungleland," "Rosalita," "Born to Run," a quick romp through the Zodiacs' "Stay" with Jackson Browne, and the unstoppable, all-but-unending "Detroit Medley."

The MUSE shows were as pulse pounding as anything Springsteen's ever done, all white heat. Not better than his usual concerts, for they lacked most of the pensive, dreamy moments. But hotter and fiercer, as fierce as he knows how to play and without surcease. (A portion of the experience can be seen and heard on the MUSE records and video.)

The E Street–starved crowd lowed "*Broooce*" throughout everyone else's set, an obnoxious but unpreventable practice. Some of the other acts thought they were being booed until set straight by Bonnie Raitt, who'd heard it as the headliner when Bruce was her opening act. Tom Petty, Raitt, and Browne did go over well.

But the final night had a sour aspect. Bruce wasn't thrilled to be turning thirty. Someone handed up a birthday cake to the stage. He threw it into the front rows, splattering icing all over the fans, then snapped, "Send me the cleaning bill." It wasn't funny.

Bruce saw something he didn't like down front: his ex-girlfriend, Lynn Goldsmith, a professional photographer. He'd expressly requested she not be given a press pass; she didn't have one but snapped away anyhow. During "Rosalita," Bruce called for security; the security guards didn't see a problem. He called them back. They still couldn't figure it out. So he jumped into the crowd and dragged an unwilling Goldsmith behind him to the stage. "This is my *ex*-girlfriend," he said. Then he picked Lynn up, carried her to the back of the stage, and dumped her on his road crew, who quickly saw her out of the building.

What the hell was that?

Maybe it was Bruce Springsteen feeling superstar power. The whole point of being publicity shy meant that no one could interpret his relationship with his girlfriend—any of his girlfriends and for that matter, later on, his wife.

As it turned out, Bruce shortly thereafter blew up the album the scuttlebutt claimed he'd almost finished and faded from view for another year. He kept a few of the old parts and tinkered himself another.

I'm not saying that the recording tension caused Springsteen to act so miserably. All that's sure, to me, is that after watching him for more than three decades, I've never seen him ever behave anywhere near so rudely or with such needless belligerence. Not to mention, anywhere near that self-destructively. But he did it, and another thing a writer knows is that no one acts out of character. It

mightn't be anybody's business, except that then and there, it happened to mar everybody's experience.

WHEN BRUCE NEXT STEPPED out to do a show, on October 3, 1980, in Ann Arbor, Michigan, karma hit him with an instant dose. He'd finally finished his album, now called *The River*, although it was still a few weeks away from the shops.

He stepped out that night all duded up and with a huge grin on his face, loving being on stage, and loving the adulation, too, no doubt, with Bossmaniacs from all over the United States gathered to celebrate. The band blasted into "Born to Run."

Bruce couldn't remember the words.

He just couldn't get going. He stumbled through a few lines, then looked around desperately. Behind him, the band cracked up but kept playing. Finally, he looked down at the fans in the front row. They fed him the next line, and his memory resumed.

They were repaid in full and with interest.

Bruce started with three older songs, but the fourth was "Wreck on the Highway" (which would be the last song on the new album), and for the rest of the first set every other song was brand new. (The sequence was "Darkness on the Edge of Town," "Jackson Cage," "The Promised Land," "Out in the Street," "Racing in the Street," "The River,"

Sept. 21, 22, 1979 – MUSE concerts, Madison Square Garden, New York, NY
At the final two shows of five successive nights of concerts to raise awareness about the dangers of nuclear energy, Bruce plays ninety-minute sets. This is the first time that he allows his music to be part of an overtly political agenda. On the second night, he spots ex-girlfriend Lynn Goldsmith in the crowd and throws her out of the building. Earlier, playing on the eve of his thirtieth birthday, he throws a birthday cake handed up from the audience back into the crowd. Film footage from these shows later turns up in the 1980 theatrical release *No Nukes*.

Dec. 1979
No Nukes–The MUSE Concerts for a Non-Nuclear Future, released on Elektra/Asylum Records, includes Bruce's "Stay," with Jackson Browne, and "Devil With the Blue Dress Medley." These are the first live recordings of Bruce to be officially released.

At the Spectrum in Philadlephia, December 1980

Jan. 9, 1980 – Fast Lane, Asbury Park, NJ

Bruce joins Jon Bon Jovi's band Atlantic City Expressway onstage for two songs, "Prove It All Night" and "Promised Land." The band's set consists entirely of Springsteen and Asbury Jukes cover songs.

Oct. 3, 1980 – Chrysler Arena, Ann Arbor, MI

Opening night of the *River* tour. "Born to Run" opens the show; Bruce forgets the words and the audience sings them to him. "Thunder Road" is played twice, the second time with guest Bob Seger joining the band onstage. "Jungleland" is an unplanned encore, and Bruce sits on the stage reading the lyrics from a sheet.

Oct. 6, 1980 – Richfield Coliseum, Cleveland, OH

Live premiere of "Two Hearts"

"Thunder Road.") The second set began with "Badlands," but then they ripped off seven from *The River* plus "Fire" and "Backstreets," neither of which he'd released. "Detroit Medley" seemed to end it, until Bruce popped back up for a reprise of "Thunder Road," with local hero Bob Seger as his duet partner.

The set could be so boldly constructed because *The River*, two vinyl discs long, contains so much material suited for the stage. Among its twenty songs, the album contains every kind of musical performance Springsteen had done or alluded to since *Greetings*: the flowing Van Morrison influence of "Fade Away" and "Drive All Night," versions of fifties rock and roll ("Cadillac Ranch," "Hungry Heart"), frat rock ("Sherry Darling," "Crush on You"), the singer-songwriter confessional ("Stolen Car"), the British Invasion ("The Ties That Bind"), folk-rock ("The Price You Pay"), soul music ("Two Hearts"), and even country with "Wreck on the Highway," based on Roy Acuff's title. Narratives, jokes, introspection and exhibitionism, careful lyricism, and verbal hijinks jostled one another throughout. Many of the characters reflected a more adult worldview, but then, there was that guy in "Ramrod" who had to have a pack of Luckys rolled up in his sleeve. Bruce less often played older rock songs on the *River* tour because now he had songs of his own.

Even so, he'd not used some of his most potent rock

Oct. 7, 1980 – Richfield Coliseum, Cleveland, OH
Live premiere of "You Can Look (But You Better Not Touch)"

Oct. 10, 1980
The River is released by Columbia Records.

Oct. 18, 1980
"Hungry Heart"/"Held Up Without a Gun" is released as a single by Columbia Records.

Oct. 18, 1980 – Kiel Opera House, St. Louis, MO
"Hungry Heart," "Drive All Night," and "I'm a Rocker" make their live debuts.

Bruce audtions Kiss rejects for possible inclusion in his new band, 1979.

numbers—"Loose Ends," "Restless Nights," "Take 'Em As They Come." Few if any other performers had such a wealth of original songs.

Bruce modified much but discarded very little in his stage raps: The yarn he used to introduce "Pretty Flamingo" mutated into an opening for "I Wanna Marry You"; the stories about his conflict with his father led to "Independence Day" (or to "Factory," played much more often than it had been on the *Darkness* tour). The stories involving Clarence's cosmic stature, witches, genies, fairies, dark forests, and busted cars with broken radios varied to suit the season or the place or just his mood that evening, turning "Growin' Up" into a reflection of innocence retained.

Oct. 31, 1980 – Sports Arena, Los Angeles, CA

Bruce emerges from a coffin at the start of the show and then launches into Jumpin' Gene Simmons's "Haunted House." Live premiere of "The Price You Pay."

Nov. 1, 1980 – Sports Arena, Los Angeles, CA

"Fade Away" is played live for the first time.

Dec. 9, 1980 – Spectrum, Philadelphia, PA

John Lennon had been killed the night before. Bruce opens the show with the following words: "I'd just like to say one thing . . . it's a hard night to come out and play tonight when so much has been lost. The first record that I ever learned was a record called 'Twist and Shout,' and if it wasn't for John Lennon, we'd all be in some place very different tonight. It's an unreasonable world, and you have to live with a lot of things that are just unlivable, and it's a hard thing to come out and play, but there's just nothing else you can do."

Fans, not Bruce, generated the one important piece of new stage business. Live, "Hungry Heart" began with an instrumental-only verse. In Chicago, a week into the tour and with "Hungry Heart" all over the radio, the crowd sang the missing lyrics. Bruce stuck out his mic to amplify them, and a ritual was born. It soon took place every night. The point was the turning of the spotlight from stage to crowd. Like any group of performers, the crowds responded in various ways, many nowhere near the song's pitch, others faltering, and the most rabid reacting as if this were the very reason they'd bought tickets.

The encores extended deeper and deeper past midnight, usually ending with the "Detroit Medley," into which Bruce interpolated soul songs, from the familiar "The Midnight Hour" to the obscure "Raise Your Hand." An added untitled section that fans called "I Hear a Train" developed. Bruce called out the tour stops like a crazed conductor.

Some nights, even not counting the half-hour break, the E Streeters spent four hours, even a little more, on that stage. Bruce had an athlete's stamina and seemed determined to spend all the energy pent up by the two years off the road—spend it in as few evenings as possible. He looked inexhaustible right to the end, every time.

By the end of any given show, the band looked as weary as a football team at the end of a tough game—especially Max Weinberg, trapped in the most physically demanding role on literally every single song, with barely time to wipe himself off during the raps, since he had to punctuate those with fills and rimshots. Max told me in 1978 that being in the E Street Band was his dream job, exactly what he'd fantasized doing for the rest of his life when he saw the Beatles on *Ed Sullivan*. Now he showed incredible stamina, a match for Bruce's, especially in his ability to stay focused on Bruce's movements so he could accent them. Or maybe what strikes me as most powerful was the huge grin he gave every night as the group took its final bows.

On *The River* tour, Bruce Springsteen acted the part of a man holding a million-volt electrical wire. He couldn't let go, even when it seemed like the audience might mostly be ready to quit. There were always those eager to carry on before getting back to whatever mundane reality awaited them in daylight. While they were happening, those shows seemed miraculous—even more than the "fanatical" (by his own measure) pronouncements about musical "morality"—but a little lunatic. Well, it's rock and roll, it's supposed to be at least a little lunatic.

Trouble often starts right there. What was Bruce trying to outlast with those marathons? What was he trying to purge? His own loneliness and sense of isolation, he said later. That's not all there was to those shows by any means, of course. The band played great shows that felt like the once-in-a-lifetime experiences they were. Bruce made sure

Dec. 28, 1980 – Nassau Coliseum, Uniondale, NY
The first time "Merry Christmas, Baby" and "This Land Is Your Land" are played in concert

Dec. 31, 1980 – Nassau Coliseum, Uniondale, NY
One of the longest ever Springsteen shows—thirty-eight songs over a four-hour period. "Held Up Without A Gun" is played live for the first time, because a short song is needed before the countdown to midnight.

After Show Only
BRUCE SPRINGSTEEN TOUR '81
MEMPHIS, TENNESSEE
MID-SOUTH COLISEUM   FEBRUARY 25, 1981

Apr. 7, 1981 – Congress Centrum, Hamburg, West Germany
First show in Europe since 1975 and the start of Bruce's first real European tour

Cadillac Ranch, Amarillo, Texas

The Forum, Copenhagen, Denmark, May 1, 1981

Palais des Sports, Lyon, France, April 24, 1981

Festalle, Frankfurt, Germany, April 14, 1981

nobody felt cheated. If there was a soul to be moved, he didn't stop 'til he'd reached it.

He could do this. Nobody else could. Maybe the Grateful Dead played for just as many hours, but their pulses never raced, and they never leapt off the tops of pianos and skidded forty feet across the front of the stage on their knees. If you're a show-off, and no performer isn't one, the fact that you've performed such feats creates a demand, some of it in your own head, to do them again. So he did. And did. And did.

BRUCE SPRINGSTEEN AND THE E Street Band ranked with the world's top concert attractions. In the last three months of 1980, they played forty-eight shows, virtually all in sports arenas, including five dates at Madison Square Garden and another five at the Los Angeles Sports Arena.

In early 1981, Bruce toured what were for him secondary markets, in eastern Canada, the South, and Midwest. The response was often just as rapturous as in places where his prowess was known. One fan recalled the crowd at the Ames, Iowa, show running in circles around the upper level of Iowa University's Hilton Coliseum while Bruce chanted "I see a train" during the "Detroit Medley."

Bruce finally had a real hit, "Hungry Heart," which even John Lennon called a great rock single in his last

interviews. "Hungry Heart" peaked at number five and created enough steam to tow the less likely "Fade Away" to number twenty as its follow-up. *The River* spent four weeks at number one on the album chart. Concerts sold out rapidly, at prices mostly between $10.00 and $12.50. (Tickets for the *Darkness* tour cost $8.00 or $8.50 in most places. *Born to Run* tickets were around $6.00, with the Bottom Line a five-buck bargain.)

Travis continued to professionalize the work offstage. Barry Bell, Springsteen's booking agent since Bruce signed with William Morris, had moved with him to Frank Barsalona's Premier Talent, which far better understood what Bruce was about. Jon Landau proved a very effective manager, as committed as Appel without being as alienating. They priced Bruce's work at the premium he deserved, but within limits set by Bruce's determination not to exploit his fans. Thus, the price of seeing him generally remained one tier below the established superstar limit. So if the Rolling Stones and the Eagles were going out at a fifteen-dollar ticket price, Bruce ducats might sell for twelve.

Almost everywhere, Bruce, band, and crew found promoters and building staff eager to work with them. Many concert professionals entered the business for love of the music, and they responded to Bruce's shows, his commitment to quality, the basic honesty of the whole thing. Those hard bargains were no fun, but the shows sure were, which

May 13, 1981 – Apollo, Manchester, England
Debut of "Johnny Bye-Bye"

May 29, 1981 – Wembley Arena, London, England
The first time "Trapped" is played live

June 7, 1981 – Birmingham International Arena, Birmingham, England
Pete Townshend joins the band onstage for the final two encores.

Festalle, Frankfurt, Germany, April 14, 1981

Palais des Sports, Paris, France, April 18, 1981

was almost as good as the other way around.

Anyway, if Springsteen was crazy enough to play two hours into union overtime, the bill went to him, not them.

Bruce enjoyed playing arenas, once he knew for sure that the sound could be good everywhere. Marc Brickman became the most innovative lighting designer in arena rock, dealing skillfully with the difficulties and opportunities afforded by larger venues. Bruce still refused to consider playing stadiums, though. He believed that a stadium would be too impersonal to convey what he wanted his shows to get across. He thought that move smacked of greed.

There was another kind of greed out there, though: the lust of fans eager to see a Bruce Springsteen and the E Street Band concert. In New York, Philadelphia, Boston, and Los Angeles, Bruce was popular enough to play long runs at arenas, but those buildings, stuffed with hockey and basketball games, only had so many dates available. He was offered a million dollars to play a Philadelphia stadium. He turned it down without hesitation.

There were other mountains to climb, anyway: Europe, Asia, the whole rest of the world. A tour of England, Germany, France, Spain, Holland, Belgium, and Scandinavia was arranged for late March through mid-May 1981. He would play a few theaters and a batch of arenas and similar buildings. Bruce was up for that.

In early February, he took sick and couldn't take the stage for a few days, condemned to bed rest and silence. The symptoms may have looked like the flu or a throat infection or whatever diagnosis was given, but he'd flat knocked himself out to the point of exhaustion.

Bell arranged to move two U.S. dates from mid-February to the end of March. That meant moving the European tour, so that England, where the band expected to start, flipped to journey's end. He'd open in Hamburg, Germany, the first Continental abode of the Beatles, who'd honed their act in dives along the whorehouse strip called the Reeperbahn. The Congress Centrum, where they'd play, was nothing like that.

What was it like? Nobody in the band had a clue.

AROUND 11:00 P.M. ON April 7, 1981, my home phone rang. Steven Van Zandt was on the line from Hamburg, a couple hours after the band finished its first European show.

"Where *were* you?" Steven chastised me. "This was history tonight!"

There was no way I could've made it. (The manager who kept me home this time was Landau's new partner, Barbara Carr. I needed to stay with our kids until Easter vacation started.)

Van Zandt called from another world. The E Streeters were both taken aback and infatuated with the whole idea of Europe: the unintelligible languages, the unfamiliar food (or familiar food with unfamiliar ingredients—fried egg on the burgers), the whole set of unknown customs. Out on the road in North America, the South could throw you some curves, and Canadians had strange money and talked funny, but you still got your Cokes cold without asking for ice.

More than that, when North American audiences were excited, they responded right away. That wasn't how it worked in London, so the band prepared for a delayed reaction. But instant party *really* wasn't how it went down in Hamburg.

Festalle, Frankfurt, Germany, April 14, 1981

In the States, a show that began with "Prove It All Night," "Out in the Street," and "Tenth Avenue Freeze-Out" would have had Bruce breathlessly reminding the aroused fans jumping up and down before him that they could sit down, that the night would be long, and they would need their energy.

In Hamburg, the crowd sat on its hands even after the reeling duet with Steven climaxed in "Out in the Street."

Which left it up to "Tenth Avenue Freeze-Out." On that one, Bruce typically slipped to his knees, crept to the edge of the stage, and dropped into the audience. There he would be instantly engulfed, struggling up the aisle, microphone in hand, letting himself be touched, groped, pulled at, worshipped, potentially endangered. There didn't seem to be any real danger: He usually was lifted to shoulders, or given a seat on the aisle on which to stand and sing. But after John Lennon's assassination the previous December, who could be sure?

It wasn't really a test of courage, but it was an act of faith. Bruce's dive into the crowd became the central physical expression of the show's attempt to create an eye-to-eye relationship with the audience, the ultimate test of the show's "morality" in his unreserved trust of the fan response.

But that was a dive into the midst of commotion. What would leaving the stage for the audience mean in Hamburg? He dropped down to find out.

"People didn't really get it," Jon Landau admitted, "but it was great, anyway." Some people did get it, not least the guys back up on the stage, who were encouraged that Bruce remained Bruce no matter what. But not only them. The rest of the set got a much less restrained, noticeably louder response. Lowering himself from the pedestal, Bruce lowered the threshold of the audience's inhibition.

For the last song of the first set, Roy Bittan played an introduction they'd been working on: A quiet but stirring theme from Ennio Morricone's score for the film *Once Upon a Time in the West*.

What the band couldn't have predicted was that this met the Hamburg crowd more than halfway. Morricone's "Once Upon a Time in the West" theme was a European jukebox hit. So when Roy finished and "Badlands" erupted into its march-time rock beat, it was lights *on* tonight, trouble in the heartland—but none at all here in Hamburg.

Little by little, one section after another, the crowd rose to its feet, until finally all of them were roused and dancing, fists pumping the air.

I shoulda been there.

They came back out for the second set, and four songs in, hit "Hungry Heart." In Germany, the single wasn't a hit, but in the morality of the show, why should that matter? They played the instrumental verse, as always, and as always, Bruce stuck out his mic. By now, the Hamburg fans had a handle on what to do. The crowd began singing, even those who didn't know the words. Some sang the

Roy Bittan in Stockholm, 1981

verse, some the chorus, some sang in English, some sang in German. Jon Landau remembered seeing Bruce "overwhelmed with the moment. . . . There it was, you could see it. It was just . . . international."

I *really* shoulda been there.

The crowd remained in pandemonium right up to the last encore, when Bruce debuted a new cover song: John Fogerty's "Rockin' All Over the World." Then he left the stage, the crowd still clamoring for more.

As the frenzy dimmed, Fritz Rau, the very dignified German promoter who, Bruce would say during his last German encore, "treated us like sons," stopped the sweat-sopped star and asked, "What have you done to my Germans?"

I *really*, *really* shoulda been there.

A WEEK LATER, I WAS, and the next three weeks changed my life, too. Not because of the museums, the food, the atmosphere, the light in Paris, the architecture in Barcelona, the discussions with Europeans far more sophisticated about America than almost anyone back in the United States was about them, the hospitality everywhere. Not just because of that.

In the dark, in the midst of a crowd with one purpose, unique lessons are learned. Speaking of common humanity, art that crosses borders and barriers doesn't come close to

July 2, 1981 – Meadowlands Arena, East Rutherford, NJ
The first event scheduled for the newly built Meadowlands Arena. Tom Waits's "Jersey Girl" is played for the first time.

July 11, 1981 – Big Man's West, Red Bank, NJ
The E Street Band plays a six-song set at the opening night of Clarence's nightclub. The show is cut short because there is absolutely no air circulation. "Game called on account of heat!" Bruce yells at the end of the set.

Aug. 6, 1981 – Bayou Club, Washington, DC
On an off night during shows at the Capitol Center, Bruce joins ex–Steel Mill singer Robbin Thompson onstage for an eight-minute version of Chuck Berry's "Carol."

the heart of what happens, because it isn't something about the world you are learning, it is something about yourself, how you fit into the world and how the world now fits into you.

Such lessons often terrify. In that focused dark lurks the capacity for lust to turn to riot, or even to hate, for empowerment to become thuggery. But the passions there sometimes offer something simple and beautiful, the power of personal connection arising in the midst of anonymity.

One moment I remember is sitting in the front row of the back section of the Forest National Stadium (an arena) in Brussels, listening to people who knew English translating Bruce's stage raps for their companions. Doing it in a whisper, unnoticeable except that all those European shows were so quiet. Whenever Bruce spoke, he received a deep, attentive silence that America doesn't know.

In Brussels, he was introducing the sixth song of the set after opening with his gentle rewrite of "Follow That Dream," making mean with a hoary Elvis program number, then the usual trilogy of rockers and using "Darkness on the Edge of Town" to steer the energy back within manageable levels.

Bruce talked a great deal to his European audiences, something he has continued to do over the years. When he had become virtually mute at American shows, he remained the narrator of his shows on the Continent. Some of it, that first time, had to do with seeing just how

far the universality of the show went. Some of it had to do with the chance for reflection presented by the depth of the quiet.

"This is 'Independence Day,'" Bruce began that night, then asked, as he did every night in Europe, for "a little quiet for this," and, as always, said thanks when he got it. As the music started, he resumed:

"I grew up in this little town. There was a rug mill that in the fifties and the sixties most everybody worked there. And I went to high school, and when I was fifteen or sixteen, I looked around. And I saw all my friends, all the people that I'd grown up with, and it didn't seem like they were going anywhere or they had anything that they could do to make them feel strong inside. And I looked back at my father, and he was working in a plastics factory, and his father before him worked in the rug mill and . . .

"And I tried to think what it was that we had in common and how it was that generation after generation, we'd end up doing the same kind of work, living in the same houses. And I thought . . . and I thought . . . and I found out that the one thing that we had in common is that we didn't know enough—we didn't know enough to understand the forces that were working on our lives. Enough to be able to change them or to get out of that same old pattern every day.

"And later I was reading this book, it was called *The*

Steven Van Zandt, 1981

Aug. 12, 1981 – Joe Louis Arena, Detroit, MI
Mitch Ryder joins Bruce onstage for the "Detroit Medley."

Aug. 20, 1981 – Sports Arena, Los Angeles, CA
A benefit for the Vietnam Veterans of America. "Who'll Stop the Rain" and "The Ballad of Easy Rider" are played.

At the Los Angeles Sports Arena, October 31, 1980

History of the United States, and in it you find out, I found out how I ended up where I was and how the chances of me breaking out of that kind of life—or anybody, anybody breaking out of that kind of life get slimmer and slimmer every day. But if you don't find out about yourself, if you don't find out about where you come from and how you got to be who you are today. . . . If you don't find out how, you end up a victim and you don't even know it. 'Cause there's a lot of people that I grew up with back home, people with good hearts and strong inside that are gonna die because. . . . Because they never found out and they were never able to pull up . . . the strength that they had inside of them . . . and be able to live just like . . . just like decent people should be able to live everywhere in the world. . . ."

Who was Bruce talking to? He'd never told American audiences how he thought about the American class system or about his allegiance to the class he came from. He did talk a little bit about reading Joe Klein's *Woody Guthrie: A Life*, and why he'd begun singing "This Land Is Your Land," expounding on his fascination with finding in Woody's words anger as well as the soporific "wheat fields waving and dust clouds rolling."

Not that he was acting out of character. Beginning with the *Darkness* songs, and even more so in "Independence Day," "Point Blank," and "The River," Bruce began to identify himself with his working-class background. So maybe he rehearsed these arguments for the future, maybe he said those lines for himself, maybe he'd been struggling to find them for months, and they came to him only through reading that paperback history. Anyway, he kept on in the half twang of his Jersey accent, rooting out of himself some of the most intimate insights he'd ever articulate. It didn't hurt the music, and it intensified what the shows meant.

The pinnacle came in Barcelona on April 21.

Spain had nominally been democratic since the death of its fascist dictator Francisco Franco in 1975, yet no American rock star had ever come to Barcelona. It would be Bruce's only show in the country.

Backstage at the bullfight ring where it was held, I came upon the emergency medical personnel

standing beside their ambulance, a common sight at any show. The show-stopper was that these paramedics wore military-style uniforms and carried sidearms.

Barcelona's beauty already entranced me—its gorgeous Mediterranean air and light, the colorful architecture capped by the surreal Gaudi park and cathedral, its intense spirit of creative possibility.

The paramilitary paramedics showed me that I had seen what I was meant to see but hardly what there was to know. Barcelona's spirit of possibility felt so intense because it had been so oppressed.

Bruce had been warned not to expect much initial rap-

Palais des Sports, Paris, France, April 18, 1981

port with the crowd, and the fans stayed still through "Factory." But then came the first notes of "Prove It All Night." The crowd leaped up as one and began raving, waving, shouting, stomping, pressing forward as if every one of their lives depended on every note. By the time Bruce hit "Badlands," at the end of the set, the night was a froth of something well beyond simple rock and roll joy.

It wasn't just the waves created by Bruce's short, hard rockers, either. There were dimensions in songs like "Point Blank," "Because the Night," and "The River" I never fathomed at all until I heard those alongside these Catalonian ecstatics. You could smell freedom busting loose in the air, scent above the bullshit the yearning the Barcelonans had for what Americans took for granted, feel the desire out there to win something I'd have a hard time defining because I never spent my life being denied it. There was an overpowering atmosphere that night, but it didn't scare me. It was too filled with love.

The record company threw a party, so we got back to the band's hotel very late. Nevertheless, a mob remained outside—the kind of thing that virtually never happened to the E Streeters in those years. As we prepared for bed, a noise rose up from the sidewalks.

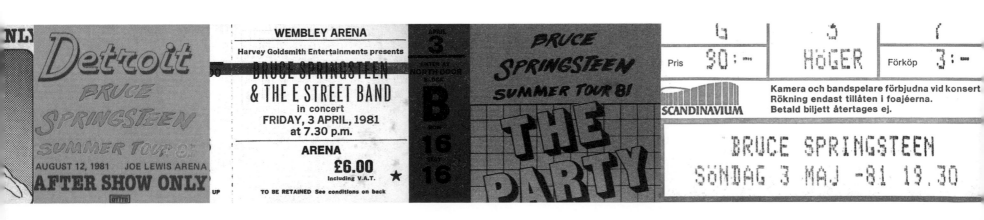

It was the crowd. Past the dawn, they serenaded us with "Hungry Heart"—and every other anthem in Bruce's catalog.

Every time Bruce plays Barcelona, he gets some variation of this reaction, as can be seen from the live DVD of his 2002 show there. They still serenade him, too. But no crowd I've ever been around has proved it all night the way that that one in 1981 did. Not in Barcelona, and not anywhere else. It was the greatest concert I've ever attended.

Rock and roll as a metaphor for freedom may be bullshit 99 percent of the time. But it wasn't bullshit to those Barcelonans. They spit in the face of their badlands, captured their glee at being alive, and fed it back to one another, the band, all who could hear. It wasn't freedom, it was liberation.

Do I romanticize? Many years later, I did an interview with Sal Trepat, the editor of the Barcelona-based Springsteen fanzine *Point Blank*. He asked me to tell him about the best concert I ever saw. I told him it had been the '81 show in Barcelona, that no other, by Bruce or anyone else, even came very close. I said that the reason was the sense of freedom I found there, that the magnitude of it came both from the stage and from the audience, that being caught in the flow of it had changed me for good. Sal had

been there, of course. He didn't disagree.

BRUCE SPRINGSTEEN AND the E Street Band returned to the United States June 9, after just over two months in Europe, having finished up with a triumphant six nights at Wembley Arena, London's principal large venue, and icing the cake with another pair up in Birmingham. It wasn't a long tour, but it altered Springsteen's perspective permanently, from what I could see. He knew a lot more about how his ideas worked. He also knew a lot more about how small his world had been.

In early July, the state of New Jersey opened the Meadowlands Arena in its new sports and entertainment complex in what had been swampland right off the Turnpike's Exit 16W. Bruce Springsteen headlining its initial event seemed an inevitability, but the scale of it wasn't: a six-night run, playing to more than a hundred thousand people. Though hardly historic in one way, unless you count the number of promoters and politicians jockeying for quantity and quality of tickets, the Meadowlands stand reflected how the E Street Band had grown musically during the *River* tour. On opening night, July 2, Bruce introduced a new song in the encores, a rewrite of "Jersey Girl," a Tom Waits original, and brought the

---

Sept. 5, 1981 – Perkin's Palace, Pasadena, CA
Bruce joins the Pretenders onstage for Jackie Wilson's "Higher and Higher."

Sept. 14, 1981 – Riverfront Coliseum, Cincinnati, OH
Last night of the *River* tour. Final show with Steven Van Zandt as lead guitarist; he will not return to the band until March 1999.

Jan. 12, 1982 – Royal Manor North, New Brunswick, NJ
Bruce joins future E Street Band member Nils Lofgren onstage for two encores, Chuck Berry's "Lucille" and "Carol."

Jersey-bred audience to the edge of its wits. He sang "I Don't Wanna Go Home," the song Steven had written for Ben E. King, which became the title track to the debut album Van Zandt produced for their old pal Southside Johnny and his Asbury Jukes. Steven had also produced an album for "Quarter to Three" maestro Gary "U.S." Bonds, who showed up to sing "This Little Girl," an R&B trifle that Bruce had written for him, then riding the charts. (The run was recorded, and several tracks from the last two nights were used on the *Live/1975-85* box set, with "Jersey Girl" also appearing as the B-side of "Cover Me" in 1984.)

Bruce spent the rest of the tour doing multiple-date arena stands in the cities where he was most popular: Philadelphia, Boston, Detroit, Cleveland, Los Angeles (six more sellouts), Denver, Baltimore, Washington (where he sat in with Robbin Thompson at a club one night).

The most important date of this last leg of the tour undoubtedly came on August 20, 1981, at the Los Angeles Sports Arena, from which Bruce donated all the profits as a benefit for the Vietnam Veterans of America and Los Angeles–area vets centers.

Bruce's involvement with the Vietnam Veterans reflects his intensified interest in the American working class and his own background. He had known well two young Jersey musicians killed in Vietnam: Bart Haynes from the Castiles

and Walter Cichon from the Motifs, who would be mentioned onstage as late as 2005 as one of his important early influences. (Bruce had by then written "The Wall," a song about the war's waste of Cichon's life.)

That summer, Jon Landau had called Bob Muller, leader of the VVA, in Washington, D.C. Muller, paralyzed since being shot during combat in 1969, a major figure in Vietnam Veterans Against the War (VVAW), and a lawyer, had formed VVA in 1978 as an advocacy group. VVA lobbied for military personnel who'd come home from Vietnam, walking or wounded, to be neglected, denied, and forgotten by the political and corporate interests that had sent them off to fight.

Muller understood that this stemmed from the U.S. military and political defeat, but he didn't believe that both politicians and corporate leaders would abandon the men who'd fought. Both the politicians and the executives gradually convinced him that they would. Even after Muller's lobbying generated thirty-five *Washington Post* editorials and his own inclusion among fifty future leaders of America in the *New York Times*, Muller got the same message. From former Defense Secretary Robert McNamara to *Time*'s Henry Grunwald (so embarrassed by the Springsteen cover story), "They all told me to go away." The week that he got the call from Landau, Muller told

Sept. 20, 1982
Nebraska is released by Columbia Records.

Dec. 22, 1982
World Premiere of the "Atlantic City" music video on MTV. This is Bruce's first music video. He does not appear in it.

Dec. 31, 1982 – Harkness House, New York, NY
Bruce and the band play at the party following Steven Van Zandt's wedding.

Palais des Sports, Lyon, France, April 24, 1981

his staff that they were dead broke and the organization would soon have to fold.

Landau stunned Muller by reporting Bruce's interest in exploring ways to help VVA. Muller met with Bruce after one of the Meadowlands gigs. They talked for forty-five minutes and became friends, agreeing to work together. The first step would be dedicating the first night of Springsteen's six shows at L.A.'s Sports Arena to a benefit for VVA.

By the week of that August 20 show, Muller had lined up additional benefit commitments from power pop singer Pat Benatar and country-rocker Charlie Daniels. The three shows netted about $250,000. Muller still says that the only reason that Vietnam veterans have been visible in America since the 1980s is rock and roll, and especially Bruce Springsteen.

Bruce didn't just play a show, he visited vets centers the day before the concert, meeting men all but ruined in body or mind, and yet, the kind of people he recognized. Just before they went onstage the next night, Bruce told Muller he'd barely slept. "He said he was petrified, that when he walked onstage without the guitar, he felt naked," said Muller.

Muller sympathized. He'd never spoken to twenty thousand people waiting for the guitar.

That night, Travis and his crew built a gallery along the side of the stage, so that several dozen paraplegic and quadriplegic vets could be at the show. And, no doubt, so that there was a visible representation of the problem.

Bruce appeared, barren of guitar, to introduce the show. He talked about meeting the vets, feeling a little embarrassed, and then said why. "It's like when you feel like you're walking down a dark street at night, and out of the corner of your eye you see somebody getting hurt or somebody getting hit in the dark alley, but you keep walkin' on because you think it don't have nothin' to do with you, and you just want to get home. Vietnam turned this whole country into that dark street. And unless we're able to walk down those dark alleys and look into the eyes of the men and the women that are down there and the things that happened, we're never gonna be able to get home. . . ."

Muller spoke even more directly: "Tonight is the first step in ending the silence that has surrounded Vietnam. It is the beginning of taking all the people that have worked so hard for these years all over the country . . . and it's bringin' us together."

To conclude, he gave the band maybe the most rousing send-off it ever got.

"The last thing I gotta say: It's a little bit ironic that for the years that we've been tryin', when the businesses haven't come behind us and the political leaders have failed to rally behind us that, when you remember the divisions within our own generation about the war, it ultimately turns out to be the very symbol of our generation—rock and roll!—that brings us together. And it is rock and roll that is going to

> **"Tonight is the first step in ending the silence that has surrounded Vietnam. It is the beginning of taking all the people that have worked so hard for these years all over the country . . . and it's bringin' us together."**
> **—Bobby Muller**

From the MUSE concert, Madison Square Garden, New York City, September 1979

Palais des Sports, Paris, France, April 18, 1981

provide the healing process that everybody needs."

He shifted into rabble-rousing mode, campaign shouting like a Southern diplomat: "So let's not talk about it, let's get down to it, let's rock and roll it!"

The band cracked into a song it hadn't played live before, Creedence Clearwater Revival's "Who'll Stop the Rain," a song taken by the vets as an anthem. Bruce later told Muller that after the song, he already felt like he'd played an entire show, and indeed, the music came in at the energy level usually found in the encores. Yet he sang the song gently, tenderly, letting the fury rise from Max's beat, and Steven's harmony vocal and the storm surge out of Clarence's saxophone. He saved his own heat—passion not rage—for a coda he'd added to CCR's recorded arrangement: "Well, I wanna know! Well, I wanna know! Well, I wanna *knoooow*! Baby, I wanna know. Well, I wanna know! I wanna *knooow*!"

They played for another couple hours, as on every night, including a beautiful one-off rendition of the Byrds' "Ballad of Easy Rider," another that the vets claimed for their own, and "This Land Is Your Land," which didn't speak any more eloquently than Bruce's own songs as they snapped into a different focus on a night when he'd turned them to such pointed purpose.

To my mind, anyhow, no other social effect that Bruce Springsteen has had is quite so remarkable as lifting the discarded remnants of his nation's shame and showing their dignity. Undeniably, as benefits improved, the veterans movement became infected with an even worse kind of deceit (as evidenced in attacks during the 2004 Presidential campaign against another VVAW leader, John Kerry). Even Muller finally shifted focus from the rights of his comrades to developing the International Campaign to Ban Landmines, which continue to kill long after wars end. That project succeeded so well that in 1997, Muller and his group won the Nobel Peace Prize.

Bruce Springsteen was beginning to know the real potential of being a rock and roll star. Not just affecting policy and big shots, either. Barbara Carr said afterward that in the gallery by the stage that night, she saw men twitch muscles that hadn't moved in years. For a man who based his entire approach on the premise that "every person, every individual in the crowd counts," that mattered most.

THE *RIVER* TOUR ENDED three weeks later at Cincinnati's Riverfront Stadium, the E Streeters ripping up "Quarter to Three." The band, the crew, and a couple dozen visitors retired to the hotel for an all-night revel, drinking the barely sublethal Kahuna Punch mixed by Clarence and dancing to Dave Clark Five records. Bruce danced them all off to bed, the last man standing, acting like a guy who wouldn't have this much time again for quite a while.

But three years?

Chapter Seven

A Dangerous Thing

"Lost souls callin' long distance salvation"

THE EARLY 1980S BURIED the egalitarian pop culture dream that Best might also be Biggest. That happy notion gave way to the equation that made such distinctions beside the point: Biggest is Best, don't bother us with the details.

Bruce Springsteen worked from a different concept: Be at your best, and biggest will take care of itself. Operating under his own rules took a great deal of luck, a large portion of talent, an unyielding faith in a set of long-nurtured ideals, and an exploitation of a major loophole in biggest-is-best ideology, which required maintaining a veil of authenticity. Bruce got away with it all, and, with *Born in the U.S.A.*, scored the kind of public success that makes a thirty-six-year-old man who's been playing arena concerts for six years into a household word "overnight."

Oh, and one more thing: He got out of his own way. CBS Records spent a huge amount of money promoting his seventh album—but Springsteen had been marketed avidly since his first record. It's just that on *Born in the U.S.A.*, the most commercial tracks he'd made for an album actually wound up on the released version. Instead of selling one or two million copies, almost all in the United States, CBS wound up selling more than forty million worldwide.

In a way, the most fascinating part is the haphazard nature of that success, the way what looked like trouble on the horizon turned out to be Springsteen's ship coming in. At one point, Bruce dead-ended in recording some homemade demos without his band. He loved the sound of

Sydney, Australia, March 1985

Dec. 28, 1983 – Monmouth Arts Center, Red Bank, NJ
Bruce performs "From Small Things," "Santa Claus Is Coming to Town," and "Twist and Shout" at the end of a show called "La Bamba's Holiday Hurrah," which also features Nils Lofgren.

May 15, 1984
"Dancing in the Dark"/"Pink Cadillac" is released as a single.

May 26, 1984 – Xanadu, Asbury Park, NJ
Bruce performs "Dancing in the Dark" live for the first time with local Jersey band Bystander.

From a photo shoot with Annie Leibovitz for the cover of *Born in the U.S.A.*

the demos, so he put them out as the solo album, *Nebraska*.

The album offered nothing especially appetizing, its music lean to the point of emaciation, its lyrics and narratives less stark than ravaged, and its conclusion, "Reason to Believe," nihilistic, a set of verses portraying both reason and belief as pointless.

In a declining market, *Nebraska* arrived on the album chart at number three, and sold almost a million copies. Overseas it did better. Everywhere, its naked alienation earned Springsteen greater credibility, its isolated agonies taken for an attack on Reaganism. (I can't say that I didn't hear it that way myself.) That these songs were also the product of enormous personal despair and spiritual disconnect made virtually no impression.

Not only that: One song from the *Nebraska* demos did result in a successful band track. So Bruce didn't tour with *Nebraska* but spent the next year crafting an album built around that song—which was, of course, "Born in the U.S.A."

Giving the game something to play with gave Bruce a series of hit singles—seven of the album's twelve tracks reached the Top Ten. He played stadiums. He made successful music videos (starting with a black-and-white one from *Nebraska* in which he didn't even appear). He sold as many records as the biggest artists in the world—not only of *Born in the U.S.A.* but also five million copies of a five-CD live set mostly based on the *Born in the U.S.A.* tour. He made a vast amount of money.

At the end, though, his peculiar vision of the morality of his music remained intact. Then again, not offering that for sale served as the predicate of all the rest of it. It was like the Zen route to rock and roll stardom. If Zen were an exit off the New Jersey Turnpike.

BORN IN THE U.S.A. made everything different, because it made the stakes higher, because it made him and his process more visible, because times had changed and Bruce both had and hadn't changed with them.

He had a superstar record contract. He held ticket prices below what the traffic would bear. He displayed a casual indifference to tour merchandise. (Maybe not so much indifference as indecision: He

June 4, 1984
Born in the U.S.A. is released by Columbia Records.

June 8, 1984 – Stone Pony, Asbury Park, NJ
Bruce and the band play the entire second set at a John Eddie gig. This is Nils Lofgren's first appearance onstage with the E Street Band.

Here and opposite: Born in the U.S.A. hijinks, 1986

sweated weeks over a record cover, so forget about asking him to make decisions on five different T-shirts and a couple of sweatshirts.) He paid his band very well. He paid his crew well (though the least competent would swear otherwise when he "only" gave them six-figure severance, almost certainly the highest in guitar-tech history). He'd only owned his own home for a year or two (another complicated decision-making process), but the one he bought had been built for a banker. He lived the New Jersey version of the rock and roll high life, out in the clubs at the Shore all weekend, but emerged from the studio pumped up from a serious workout regimen.

On the road, he'd moved from clubs and theaters to arenas, because otherwise it would have taken him two years to fill the demand in the major markets. Demand again forced his hand when he began doing multiple arena dates in many cities.

The demand reflected not only more Springsteen fans but also the eagerness of Springsteen initiates to get to see all possible shows, because Bruce made each concert so different. He always figured out two or three, sometimes more, different songs to slot in; if there were an occasion, from an upcoming holiday to a band member's birthday, he'd celebrate it; if he had a new song or thought of a new way to perform an old one, you'd be likely to hear it. A cult of Springsteen fans thrived on all that.

So in markets where he played several shows in a row, the turnover from night to night was nowhere near 100 percent. Sometimes, in New Jersey, New York, and Philadelphia, particularly, it seemed like about half the crowd consisted of people who'd seen all the shows there. The real number probably never amounted to more than about 20 percent or so, but four hundred people out of two thousand, and four thousand people out of twenty thousand can make a lot of difference in tutoring the rest of the crowd in how the ritual's supposed to run. Although *Born in the U.S.A.* didn't necessarily add a lot of troops to the hardcore, it moved millions to want to see him at least once. Suddenly, it might have taken the E Streeters a year just to slake the appetites of their fans in the Northeast with arena dates.

Bruce had three choices:

He could frustrate the majority of people who wanted to see him, which wasn't at all Bruce-like.

He could tour for the next three or four years, rather than the next one or two, which would—and everybody knew this, starting with Bruce—give him one hell of a warped life, because the "normal" of living on the road has little relationship to how even a superstar spends his time off tour. (For instance, it's far from the best way to meet women, especially if you don't mean "girls.")

Or, he could give in and play stadiums, reaching the maximum number of people with the minimum number of shows, which was not at all, as everyone around him kept saying, the same thing as the minimum amount of effort.

Besides that, if Bruce wanted to play Europe and Asia, he needed to play stadiums. There simply weren't many ten- or twenty-thousand-seat sports arenas to play over there.

THE MORNING FLIGHT to Syracuse, New York, on January 26, 1985, was so full of Springsteen fans that the pilot joked about us before takeoff. Even booking agent Barry Bell was aboard. A lot of fans knew each other; a few recognized me as Bruce's biographer. Hardly anyone knew Bell, though he'd later become notorious, albeit anonymously, as the first of Springsteen's "men in black," Springsteen personnel who roamed the farthest seats before shows, selecting a couple or two to exchange tickets and move all the way to the front rows. (One strategy for foiling scalpers who made their killings off the best seats.)

Barry had worked with Bruce longer than anybody on the business side; they were also good friends. He spent the flight explaining where the tour was headed and I felt lucky to hear an account I could trust.

The first six months of the *Born in the U.S.A.* tour had gone all but perfectly, selling out almost every date, the already great demand stoked by the hit singles, press and TV coverage of the "new" superstar, and most important, word of mouth that Bruce's show remained as exciting and inspiring as ever.

The closest Bruce came to a false move was at a concert in St. Paul, Minnesota, on June 29. Director Brian De Palma filmed much of the "Dancing in the Dark" video during that show, and Bruce agreed to do back-to-back versions of "Dancing" for the shoot, which felt awkward and out of place.

Bruce had more than two dozen new songs—ten from *Nebraska*, the twelve on *Born in the U.S.A.*, plus assorted others, like "Pink Cadillac." That first show had thirteen new originals, plus "Street Fighting Man" as an encore. Only "Rosalita" survived from the pre–*Born to Run* records, and the next night, not even "Rosie" appeared. As the tour went on, Bruce worked in a great many other original songs, some well-known, others as yet unreleased, but the music from the first two albums stayed on the bench. He now played to crowds in which almost no one knew anything about his early songs, and the extravaganzas of "Rosalita" and "Growin' Up" felt shopworn even to many veteran fans.

The E Street Band changed more than its music had. Steven Van Zandt quit during the album sessions, determined to pursue a solo career and his interest in radical politics. During the remainder of the sessions, Bruce covered all the guitar parts himself. For the tour, though, he needed a second guitar. He chose Nils Lofgren.

A Neil Young accompanist at nineteen, a major-label recording artist a year later, considered for the Rolling Stones when Mick Taylor left, Lofgren's solo career also

June 29, 1984 – Civic Center, St. Paul, MN
Opening night of the *Born in the U.S.A.* tour and Patti Scialfa's first show with the band. The "Dancing in the Dark" video is filmed during the show.

July 2, 1984
Bruce's first 12-inch single is released by Columbia Records: "Dancing in the Dark" (blaster mix)/"Dancing in the Dark" (radio)/"Dancing in the Dark" (dub).

July 25, 1984
The "Dancing in the Dark" music video premieres on MTV.

began in the early seventies. But none of his fine records sold well, and he mainly played clubs or toured as a Young sideman.

Springsteen and Lofgren had long been friends. When Nils heard that Steven was leaving the E Street Band, he called to volunteer. In May 1984, about six weeks before the tour began, Bruce invited him to rehearse, and Nils quickly fit in.

Bruce the procrastinator waited longer than that to implement his idea of adding a female singer to the group. Patti Scialfa got the call on June 24. She had four days to rehearse, pack, and hit the stage in St. Paul. Patti knew many of the band members—she'd gone to Asbury Park High School and later sang with the Asbury Jukes and other area groups. But the E Street arrangements didn't have parts for a full-time backup singer, let alone a female voice. Patti later said she felt like she ought to tell Bruce she couldn't go because she had to wash her hair.

Although it took several weeks for Patti's voice to find its place in the mix, Bruce pronounced himself well satisfied in an interview the night of that first show: "It's kinda like, 'Yeah, everybody join in.' She's a local person and it just feels like a bunch of people up there. It has a little of that community thing to it."

Bruce had changed, too, at least in appearance. His restless energy, bottled up for all those months offstage, lent itself to a dedication to gym workouts. He emerged with an upper body cut without seeming artificially sculpted. Below the waist, he had enough muscle tone that the cover of *Born in the U.S.A.* featured his back to the camera because, he claimed, "the picture of my ass looked better than the pictures of my face." He'd had his teeth capped. If he was still worried about the look of his nose, no one else was. Springsteen no longer looked the scruffy Jersey urchin but instead came across as a ruggedly handsome man.

All that summer, the unlikely idol and his traveling-band community rolled on through America. The ten-night homestand at the Meadowlands arena in August proved the highlight. On the last night, guest Steven Van Zandt and Bruce did a heated duet on Dobie Gray's "Drift Away": "Gimme that beat, boys, and free my soul / I want to get lost in your rock and roll. . . ." That was the way the whole tour felt.

It was the era of the pop superstar: Michael Jackson on the road with his brothers in the heavy wake of *Thriller*; Prince and the Revolution celebrating the success of his film and soundtrack album *Purple Rain*; U2 ushering in a new generation of Anglo-Irish contenders; Madonna moving from the dance clubs to the arenas. A funny time to hold back on becoming a "stadium act."

The Syracuse shows, to be held in the 38,000-seat Carrier Dome, constituted a test run of the larger stage, bigger light and sound setups, video screens and other accoutrements of a stadium show. But this was the only stadium in

July 31, 1984
"Cover Me"/"Jersey Girl" (live from July 9, 1981) is released as a single by Columbia Records.

Aug. 11, 1984 – Meadowlands Arena, East Rutherford, NJ
John Entwistle joins the band onstage for "Twist and Shout."

Aug. 20, 1984 – Meadowlands Arena, East Rutherford, NJ
This is the last of a ten-night sold-out stand. Little Steven joins Bruce onstage for "Two Hearts" and "Drift Away."

the Northeast with a dome, which made it feel like a much bigger arena. George Travis had even figured out a way to put reserved seats on the floor, to avoid the perils of general-admission crowds crushing one another, an issue that Bruce took very seriously.

Until then, there hadn't been much at stake on the *Born in the U.S.A.* tour. Bruce quickly knew which songs deserved a regular place in the set and how to use Nils and Patti. That part of the tour tasted like a victory lap. They did some great shows—it was especially interesting to hear *Nebraska*'s "Atlantic City" with Lofgren's electric guitar and to watch reactions to the stirring ambiguities of "Born in the U.S.A.," to see Bruce pull off a solo acoustic number or two in such large spaces. But on the many nights whose encores featured the old Motown hit "Do You Love Me?" the answer could never have been doubted. It couldn't have been doubted if he'd begun with that question.

The stadium venture presented risk, at least in Springsteen's own mind. Oh, he'd still get over just by taking the stage. The cheers would come, the excitement would mount. The challenge didn't lie there—the challenge lay in constructing an event that remained musical and involved everyone in those back-row seats. To make a stadium show that amounted to more than a spectacle, one that still counted the way rock and roll counted to the kids—and the bands—at the Hullabaloo Club and the Upstage.

STADIUM CONCERTS OBVIOUSLY have more requirements than arena shows; less obviously, they also have different ones. The larger space offers a bigger stage, with more chance to roam, but the greater distances require broader gestures, the creation of tableaus whose meaning can be perceived from their physical appearance. Some of Springsteen's indoor shows had had video screens over the years, though he dealt with them warily. But video, a necessity in stadiums, wasn't any real problem. The camera loved Bruce and offered a perfect extension of the joyous mugging that made up so much of his show.

But could he do his whole show, including the quiet parts, the ones meant to make you ponder, not just the ones that set everyone boogying? Could he keep the morality of the show, make his point felt, be heard as someone who had found the key to the universe in learning how to make his guitar talk?

Every other band's stadium show had been a cash-in, a hollow hunk of entertainment, a way of meeting "demand" without ever fulfilling any higher expectation, a pretext for fireworks, props, everything *but* music making meaning. Bruce wondered if he could do better than that.

Bell, Landau, Travis—all his key advisers—believed he could do it and that he could do it in any space he was provided.

But they didn't have to do the work. They didn't have to construct a show that tested the possibilities of the stadium format.

Greetings from the *Born in the U.S.A.* tour. *From top left:* Max Weinberg; Danny Federici and Patti Scialfa, the new kid on the block; Roy Bittan. *At right:* Patti Scialfa; tour manager George Travis with Jon Landau; Clarence goes disco. *Above:* An everlasting kiss.

At the first Syracuse sound check, Bruce started "Working on the Highway," and the sound system responded with the biggest blast of feedback he'd ever heard. But that was a cosmic giggle, not an omen. If the artist was willing to spend the money to hunt out the best PA equipment, there wasn't any technical reason not to play stadiums. Nils Lofgren actually believed it was possible to sound better in stadiums, because the absence of a roof presented fewer acoustic complications.

Of course, the Carrier Dome had a roof. But anyway . . .

Nebraska increased the number of dark, moody songs in Bruce's repertoire, and they made a lot of his more casual fans restless. So he'd been steadily minimizing their presence in his sets. But in Syracuse, four songs into the first set, he strung together five slow examples of *Nebraska*-style fatalism: "Johnny 99," "Atlantic City," "Reason to Believe," "Shut Out the Light," and "Johnny Bye-Bye."

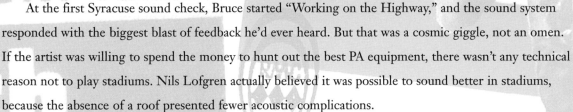

Glory days at Wembley Arena, July 1985

It felt like what it was—a test of the artist's passion versus the audience's patience, a measure of whether this kind of setting contained that much freedom of action, of whether Bruce could use a stadium encounter to his purpose, whether the increased physical separation outstripped a chance to create the deep rapport that, to him, represented the best he had to offer, that constituted the show's morality.

By the time he came out of the second "Johnny" into the sternly rocking "Prove It All Night," he knew the answer. Yes, he could. He just had. There was more to-and-fro in the audience than during the anthems, but that happened on slow songs in theaters. Those five long songs held the greatest part of the crowd, and the response told him the meaning of them had held, too.

When the spotlight hit Bruce alone at center stage for "Reason to Believe," the sense of intimacy did not diminish from previous shows. If anything, because Bruce reached so deep, the frightened loneliness might have increased a hair.

After that, he was ready to handle anything the stadiums could throw at him.

WHEN BRUCE HEARD THAT Ronald Reagan, campaigning for his second term as President, had expropriated the lyrics of "Born in the U.S.A."—and Bruce himself—in a New Jersey speech that September, he laughed out loud.

Bruce trusted his audience to get his message from his songs and stories. Their cheers said he'd connected. But what was the connection this time? While everybody loved him for his message as much as his music, there was more than one way to read that message.

In a community the size of a rock band, everyone knows everyone else and easily figures out the meaning of one another's behavior. Even in a subculture big enough to fill sports arenas worldwide, shared standards abound.

In the truly mass audience gathered around *Born in the U.S.A.*, you didn't even need to know the music to feel part of it. You could see Bruce the way he and his older fans understood him—working-class boy uneasy that he'd made good. Or, you could look at Springsteen, strutting on stage in his bulked-up body and his dress-denim rags, carrying his guitar like a cross between a caveman cudgel and an imperial

Oct. 19, 1984 – Tacoma Dome, Tacoma, WA
For the first time in ten years, "Rosalita" is not played. "Born To Run" is the last song of the show prior to the encores.

Oct. 22, 1984 – Coliseum, Oakland, CA
Live debut of "Shut Out the Light"

Oct. 30, 1984
"Born in the U.S.A."/"Shut Out the Light" single is released

scepter, and figure you'd located rock's Rambo. The American-flag backdrop on his album cover, the enormous Stars and Stripes draped across the back of his stadium stage reinforced the impression. If you did listen, the bellowing, "*Baaaawn* in the U.S.A. / I was *bawwwwn* in the U.S.A.*" did nothing to dissuade you. The verses . . . there were verses?

At his November 5, 1980, show at Arizona State University, just a few hours after Reagan's victory, Bruce introduced "Badlands" by saying, "I don't know what you guys think about what happened last night, but I think it's pretty frightening." Understanding *Nebraska* as a portrait of the poor Reagan had abandoned and vilified got a lot of it right. From the beginning, Bruce's songs questioned the conservative presentation of America as the land of unbounded fairness, prosperity, and harmony.

As closely as he protected those songs, Bruce didn't seem to grasp right away how their meaning could be hijacked. He didn't seem to understand, yet, the superficial reading of *Born in the U.S.A.* that heard support of the veterans as support of war, understood the love of home as chauvinism, that looked at protagonists handcuffed to the bumper of a cop car as a gag. He couldn't see that Ronald Reagan and Bruce Springsteen standing in front of the Stars and Stripes sent a lot of people the same message: It's morning in America and all's swell because we're on top.

Left-wing European intellectuals often heard the song and interpreted Bruce's poses the same way as American conservatives, especially since Springsteen's popularity grew in synch with the acceleration of U.S. military aggression and attacks on the social infrastructure.

The president's speechwriters sought to exploit the connection, not because the election ever stood in doubt, but because they deemed the whole wide world at their disposal. So one afternoon in mid-September, Reagan made a stop at Hammonton, New Jersey, and said, "America's future rests in a thousand dreams inside your hearts; it rests in the message of hope in songs so many young Americans admire: New Jersey's own Bruce Springsteen. And helping you make those dreams come true is what this job of mine is all about."

A conventional celebrity might respond to falsification and distortion by, for instance, issuing a press release or holding a press conference. Or maybe going on a TV talk show or calling up a friendly radio personality.

> **"Well, the president was mentioning my name in his speech the other day and I kind of got to wondering, you know, what his favorite album of mine must've been. I don't think it was the *Nebraska* album, I don't think he's been listening to this one. . . ."**
>
> **—BS**

Oct. 31, 1984 – Sports Arena, Los Angeles, CA
The show opens with Bruce lying on a table in the center of the stage as smoke swirls around him and eerie music plays. He narrates the story of "Dr. Frankensteen," who cannot be awoken from his trance until Clarence brings him his guitar. When Clarence appears, ax in hand, Bruce jumps up and starts the show with "High School Confidential."

Nov. 4, 1984 – Sports Arena, Los Angeles, CA
The "Born in the U.S.A." music video is filmed at this show.

Nov. 16, 1984 – State University, Ames, IA
"Sugarland" is played live for the first time.

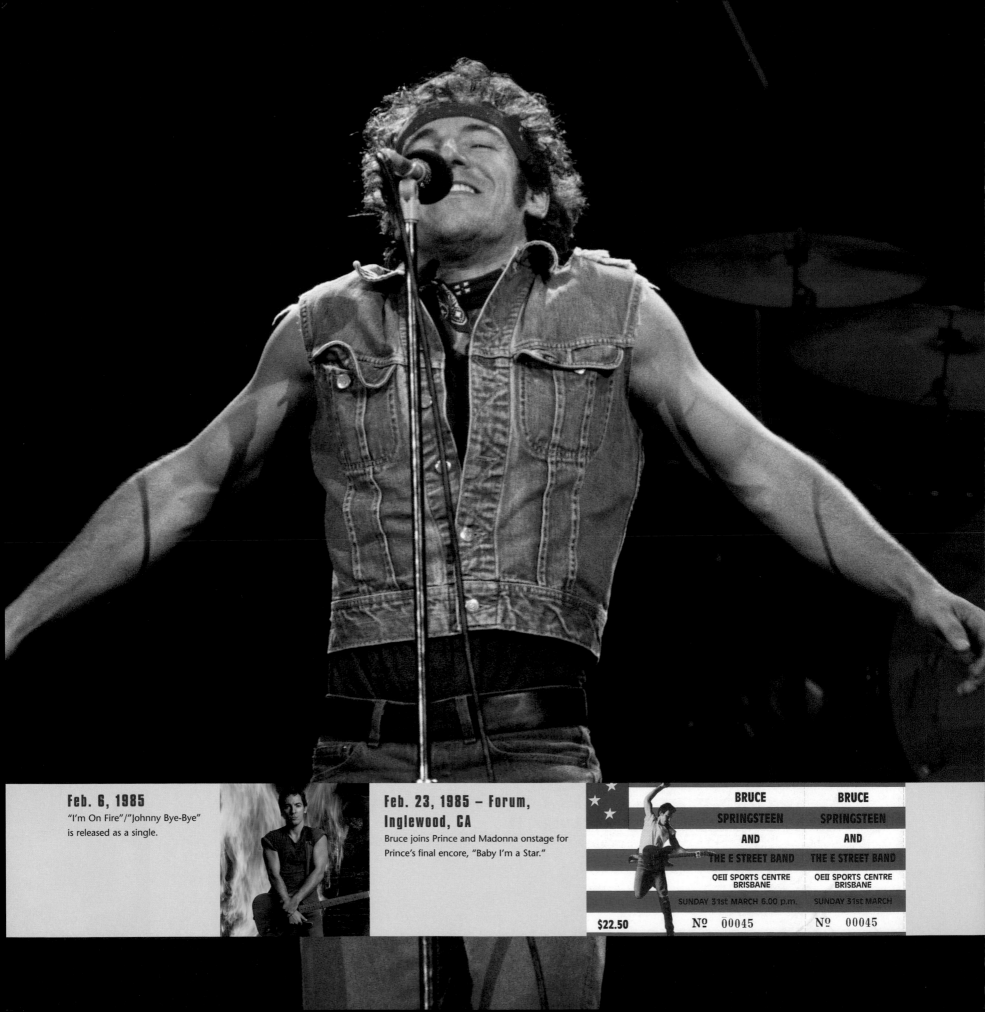

Feb. 6, 1985
"I'm On Fire"/"Johnny Bye-Bye" is released as a single.

Feb. 23, 1985 – Forum, Inglewood, CA
Bruce joins Prince and Madonna onstage for Prince's final encore, "Baby I'm a Star."

BRUCE SPRINGSTEEN AND THE E STREET BAND

BRUCE SPRINGSTEEN AND THE E STREET BAND

QEII SPORTS CENTRE BRISBANE

QEII SPORTS CENTRE BRISBANE

SUNDAY 31st MARCH 6.00 p.m.

SUNDAY 31st MARCH

$22.50

№ 00045

№ 00045

May 13, 1985
Bruce marries Julianne Phillips in Lake Oswego, Oregon.

May 22, 1985
"Glory Days"/"Stand on It" is released as a single.

June 1, 1985 – Slane Castle, Dublin, Ireland
The Beach Boys song "When I Grow Up to Be a Man" is performed at this show for the only time.

RUCE SPRINGST
ND THE E. STREET

SLANE CASTLE Saturday 1st June
Gates open 3-00pm   Concert from 5-
TICKETS £15.00 No Refunds, No Exch
No Bottles, Cans, Tape Recorders, C
ling Chairs, or Umbrellas. CONCERT R
ONE SEEKING TO GAIN ADMISSION USING A COUN
WILL BE PROSECUTED

Bruce Springsteen used his show. Two nights later, on September 21, he played a concert in Pittsburgh, the city most devastated by Reaganomics. After four songs, Bruce said, "Well, the president was mentioning my name in his speech the other day and I kind of got to wondering, you know, what his favorite album of mine must've been. I don't think it was the *Nebraska* album, I don't think he's been listening to this one. . . ."

Then he played "Johnny 99," in which he portrays the homicidal urges of a laid-off autoworker.

Springsteen continued talking back the next night: "There's something really dangerous happening to us out there now," he told the crowd. "We're slowly getting split up into two different Americas. Things are getting taken away from the people that need 'em and given to the people that don't need 'em . . . and there's a promise getting broken. I think that in the beginning the idea was we all live here a little bit like a family where the strong can help the weak ones, the rich can help the poor ones, and, you know, the American Dream. I don't think it was that everybody was gonna make it or everybody was gonna make a billion dollars, but it was that everybody was gonna have the opportunity and a chance to live a life with some decency and some dignity and a chance for some self-respect. And I know you gotta be feeling the pinch here where the rivers meet, so. . . ." He went into "The River," a song that said it more tellingly.

Responding that way, rather than with a press release, didn't reach as many people as Reagan's comment. Those who weren't at the show wouldn't hear what Bruce said.

But press releases are only partial responses, too. The real test of what Reagan said was how he and his government acted. And the real test of Bruce's meaning was what he did next.

BRUCE SPENT THE NEXT three weeks on a break. During the layoff, he asked Barbara Carr to locate charitable organizations operating in the next set of cities he'd play. He wanted groups that worked with hungry and homeless people, striking and unemployed workers, and people trying to change laws about the environment and other social conditions. Those organizations could put up information tables at the shows, talk to fans, distribute literature, and collect donations.

During the show, Bruce endorsed the groups Carr found. In Tacoma, Washington, on October 17, the first time he tried it, he introduced "My Hometown" by saying, "I guess I originally started to write this song about the town where I grew up. In the end, I guess, it's really a song about responsibility to the place that you live. Right here in Washington, you got a group called Washington Fair Share, and they're trying to live up to that responsibility. They're a coalition of church and labor and community organizations that are working together trying to make this a better place for you. . . . They're a group, you could say, that believes that the people should come before profit and it should be the community before the corporation. . . . If you need any information, you can find the address and phone numbers of Washington Fair Share in intermission time out where the concessions are. This is your hometown, so do something about it. . . ."

Since that night, Springsteen has made such presentations about hundreds of groups, at least one, sometimes several, at virtually every show he's done for the past twenty years. He got better at making that speech, acting more confident and feeling less awkward. The food banks, homeless shelters, and other groups he endorsed saw some donations and, sometimes, an increase in volunteers. (Bruce makes his own financial donation to each of them.)

That was his real response to Ronald Reagan: finding a way to extend his idea of rock and roll as a vehicle for community. Helping realize the dreams of an America that took care of its most powerless—that's what the job of being Bruce Springsteen is all about. As far as he was concerned, he wasn't in it alone. "They're out there trying to make the place you live a better place to live," he often said during the encores. "It's possible, it can be done, but you gotta fight for it."

That didn't change the trajectory of the *Born in the U.S.A.* tour at all. From opening night, Bruce

Aug. 31, 1985 – Giants Stadium, E. Rutherford, NJ
Live debut of "Stand on It"

Sept. 27, 1985 – Coliseum, Los Angeles, CA
"Janey Don't You Lose Heart" and "War" are performed for the first time.

Oct. 2, 1985 – Coliseum, Los Angeles, CA
Final show of the *Born in the U.S.A.* tour. Jon Landau plays guitar during the last song, "Glory Days."

DIMANCHE 23 JUIN
MONTPELLIER - Sta

BRUCE SPRINGSTEEN
MONTPELLIER
Stade Richter
Dimanche 23 Juin 1985
Ouverture des portes 17H
Invitation

drummed the same theme. But Reagan's speech did change how Springsteen spoke out. Before Pittsburgh, he made his case in moral and historical terms, even when he did comedic intros to "Pink Cadillac." He still didn't want to alienate anyone who might hear his core message, which he truly meant for everyone. But starting in Pittsburgh, Bruce made many more expressly political comments.

In Lincoln, Nebraska, introducing "Reason to Believe," he commented, "Now, this is a song about blind faith. They say the safeguard of democracy is an educated citizenry, and if I was you, I'd watch what was going on down in Central America right now. Because last time it was my generation and this time it could be your generation . . . and just plain blind faith is a dangerous thing. . . ." Before singing "Nebraska" in Kansas City, he said, "I guess this is a song about what happens when the ties that bind don't bind no more and people start feeling isolated from their families and their friends . . . from their government. . . ."

He reacted permanently to what Reagan said, I believe, because the president perverted a premise he sang about in "Follow That Dream," the Elvis movie song he rewrote. Bruce's version ended by declaring that every man has "the right to fight for the things he believes, the things that come to him in dreams."

The dream—the rock and roll dream, whatever part that was of the overall American Dream—still resided at the heart of his vision. "I guess, then, a dream, a dream that comes true, can be a dangerous thing," he mused one night as he prepared to sing about Elvis. Bruce Springsteen did not intend to surrender to that danger on any terms at all. He intended to do what he sometimes said at the end of "Racing in the Street": "Sometimes it seems like time gets running so short on you—like it's running out on you—and that so much gets left behind, so much gets lost some-where, that there's not much you can do . . . but keep going and keep searching . . . and keep going and keep going and keep going and keep going. . . ."

THE TOUR OF AUSTRALIA, where they played five indoor shows in Sydney and stadium shows in Brisbane and Melbourne, and in Japan, all the shows, beginning with five in Tokyo and carrying on to Kyoto and Osaka, felt as much like tourism as work. Bruce connected with Australian Vietnam veterans in Melbourne. In Japan, where community can be construed as identity but remains very closed and private for that very reason, his wide-open vision met tremendous enthusiasm, but it was hard to tell how it connected. Japanese music culture had never created its own Elvis, let alone its own John Lennon. Rock stars in Japan were still nouns, not verbs. There, though, it was probably the music more than the ideas that sank home.

The other significant thing that happened in Japan was the arrival of actress Julianne Phillips, his new girlfriend.

Jan. 19, 1986 – Stone Pony, Asbury Park, NJ
Benefit for the 3M Plant workers in Freehold, New Jersey. The E Street Band (minus Nils and Roy) joins Bruce for seven songs.

Oct. 13, 1986 – Bridge School Benefit / Shoreline Amphitheatre, Mountain View, CA
Bruce joins Neil Young for one song, "Helpless." He plays a short acoustic set with Nils and Danny, performs "Hungry Heart" with Crosby, Stills, Nash, and Young, and joins in on the encore ("Teach Your Children") with all the artists. His acoustic performance of "Fire" will be released as a music video in 1987.

Nov. 3, 1986
"War" (live from Sept. 30, 1985)/"War" (radio edit, Sept. 30, 1985) is released as a single.

Slane Castle, Dublin, Ireland, June 1, 1985

Bruce and Patti Scialfa seemed on the edge of becoming an item all through the U.S. tour, but Bruce became smitten with Philips, ten years younger than he was, after meeting her through Barry Bell. Juli stayed with Bruce for the whole Japanese run. A month after coming back to the States, they got married near her home in Portland, Oregon.

Six weeks later, on June 1, 1985, Bruce Springsteen and the E Street Band played on the grounds of Slane Castle, thirty miles north of Dublin. Slane accommodated more than a hundred thousand fans, and it was packed that day. Bruce, the only act, went on after a large amount of beer had been sold and while the day was still hot.

Without fixed seating, the key to crowd safety is a flexible barrier before the stage. Otherwise as the fans surge forward, the ones in the front can be crushed, the smaller, weaker ones driven under, injured, even killed.

The Springsteen show at Slane had such a barrier fence. But the combination of sunburn, drink, and crush gave many fans in the front a scare and they were necessarily handled brusquely as they were whisked over the barricade, thence to paramedics if they needed more help, or back into a safer part of the crowd if they wished to go.

Most of the fans "rescued" from the crush got a quick glimpse of backstage, then went right back out to see the show, and before the day was done, some found themselves hoisted over the fence again. The few who went to the medical tent were mostly cases of inebriation and sun-sickness.

To Bruce, onstage, this registered as a chaotic distraction. "What you gotta do down here is if you can . . . push back a little bit from the barrier so the people that are crushed up against the barrier here won't hurt themselves . . . make sure everybody's up on their feet there," he exhorted after "Out in the Street." "And if you can, try and stay in one place and not sway around. If anybody needs help to get out of there, raise your hand, and somebody will pull you out." He laughed his hoarse, nervous laugh. "What you gotta do is you gotta stop that swaying back and forth 'cause it's knocking people down, okay?"

He did "Johnny 99," not a song you can do much swaying to. But three songs later, they played "Working on the Highway," whose beat is a call to swayers everywhere.

By the time the first set ended, Bruce was furious. You could practically hear him thinking, "*This* is what stadium shows are going to be like?" A few minutes after the final note, Jon Landau joined Bruce and Juli on a helicopter ride back to Dublin. Several hours worth of traffic formed outside the castle, but nobody left on the ground envied Jon his seat.

Afterwards, Travis and crew did make a few adjustments to the barriers and the safety procedures, and probably more important, took steps to control how drunk the fans were by the time the show started. In addition, it was

Nov. 26, 1986
"My Hometown"/"Santa Claus Is Coming to Town" is released as a single.

Jan. 20, 1987
"Fire"/"Incident on 57th Street" (live from Dec. 16, 1978) is released as a single.

firmly decided that the U.S. tour would be all reserved seating—chairs on the stadium carpets. Nobody had tried that before.

As it turned out, Slane was the only moment in the entire European tour when failure ever loomed. Three days after Slane, at his second European show, held at St. James Park in rowdy Newcastle, Bruce was adjusted to the crowd conditions. Sunshine greeted every show, which is the crucial thing outdoors, and from Gothenburg to Frankfurt, Milan to Paris, the E Streeters rolled on, leaving happy crowds in their wake and, for those who had a mind for more, something to ponder, too.

The big party came in London, with three shows at 100,000-seat Wembley Stadium, the middle one held on the Fourth of July. Every celebrity in town, from the Wimbeldon tennis players and the Australian cricket team to assorted pop and movie stars, found their way to those shows. On the Fourth, Little Steven even turned up for the encores, and he reappeared at the final show of the tour, at Roundhay Park in Leeds, on July 7.

Then it was home for a three-week break before trying out stadiums in the States.

BRUCE SPRINGSTEEN AND THE E Street Band just kept on going and kept on going and kept on going that summer. Whatever they searched for, they found.

The only hitch came backstage at Pittsburgh's Three

Rivers Stadium. A ping-pong table was provided next to the dressing room and Roy Bittan and Nils Lofgren were in the midst of a furious match when the door burst open and they heard "Born in the U.S.A" . . . *being played onstage!*

From that show onward, Bruce initiated a head count before they went on—and has kept it up ever since.

In mid-August, the E Streeters played four shows at Giants Stadium in the New Jersey Meadowlands complex. All sold out. A fifth went on sale. All seventy thousand seats sold out in minutes. They wound up doing a sixth show, too. They played to over four hundred thousand fans at the stadium, more than twice as many as in their ten nights at the next-door arena in 1984.

They could have sold out the stadium at least once more.

When you're in the midst of a once-in-a-lifetime experience, you have two feelings: This can't be happening. This will never end.

But it always does end. If the ending is scheduled, you're luckier than most, because you've got the chance to make sure it's special, something that will keep the flavor in your mouth.

The final four dates at Los Angeles Coliseum were perfect. Another 100,000-seat stadium, crammed. Weather beautiful. Bruce and the E Street Band coming on each night just as the sun set behind them, so they entered looking like so many gunslingers.

Jan. 21, 1987 – Waldorf Astoria Hotel, New York, NY
Bruce inducts Roy Orbison into the Rock and Roll Hall of Fame and joins him onstage for two songs, "Stand By Me" and "Pretty Woman."

Apr. 12, 1987 – Stone Pony, Asbury Park, NJ
Bruce and some members of the E Street Band play a full set that includes the first live performance of "Light of Day."

July 29, 1987 – Key Largo, Belmar, NJ
Bruce performs reggae versions of "Born in the U.S.A." and "My Hometown" with local band Jah Love.

Aug. 2, 1987 – Stone Pony, Asbury Park, NJ
The full E Street Band with everyone present except for Nils performs a fourteen-song set.

All night, the emotional pitch rose and rose, every show just a notch more than the one before. Bruce pulled it back to Earth sometimes, with a sober story or a *Nebraska* song. But emotions soon soared again. It felt more like the middle of a dream than the end of a journey.

It was both, the youthful Bruce Springsteen in a realm that might sustain him for the rest of his life. All the old stories got told but the angle changed. Douglas Springsteen still sat in that overheated Freehold kitchen, with his beer growing stale as he sucked incessantly on his cigarettes. But now, the story turned out different. Now it was about how incapable either of them was of imagining the dreams of the other, and how important it was to reach out across that barrier simply to survive.

"When I was growing up, my dad used to play this trick on me," Springsteen began on one of those nights. "He used to lock up the front door, so I used to have to come through the side, and he'd sit in the kitchen waiting on me, smoking a cigarette.

"I'd stand out there in the driveway. And I used to have real long hair, like way down to my shoulders, and he used to hate it, you know, we used to fight about it all the time. I'd stand there and I'd get my collar up and I'd tuck it back as tight as I could, trying to make it look as short as it would, and I'd get up my nerve and I'd get up on the porch.

"He'd always let me get through the kitchen . . . and

he'd always let me get through the living room—my mom'd be sleeping on the couch in front of the TV—and then, just as I got my foot on that bottom step, thinking like, 'I made it, I'm gonna get to my room,' from the kitchen I'd hear '*Bruuuuce.*'"

The crowd lowed "*Bruuuuce*" back at him.

"It didn't sound that nice, though, at the time," he said and let go of one of his hoarse, ambiguous chuckles.

"He used to call me back, and I'd come in the kitchen and I'd sit down with him, and we'd be sitting in the dark and I remember the thing that used to bother me was that I could never see him. And he wouldn't say nothing for the next ten or fifteen minutes . . . and then he'd ask me, like, the same old question, what I thought I was doing with myself. . . .

"I guess the worst part about it was that I was never able to explain it to him, I couldn't explain to him why I looked the way I did. It was like that old song . . . about trying to tell a stranger about rock and roll. . . .

"But that's kind of a two-way street, because I didn't know what he was doing with himself, either. I didn't understand—at the time, I guess, I was about seventeen or eighteen and he was probably only about a year or two older than I am right now, and I couldn't understand the pressure of trying to raise a family, looking for work, and feeling like . . . feeling like you were failing at it.

"We came down through the Monongahela Valley in

Sept. 25, 1987 – J.F.K. Stadium, Philadelphia, PA
Bruce joins U2 onstage for "Stand By Me."

Sept. 30, 1987 – Coconut Grove, Los Angeles, CA
As part of an all-star band with Roy Orbison for a Showtime concert special, Bruce plays guitar and sings backing vocals. Musicians include Jackson Browne, Elvis Costello, T-Bone Burnett, J. D. Souther, Jennifer Warnes, K. D. Lang, Bonnie Raitt, and Tom Waits.

NOV. 24, 1987
"Tunnel of Love"/"Two for the Road" is released as a single.

From left: Clarence Clemons, Max Weinberg, Bruce Springsteen, Nils Lofgren, Garry Tallent, Roy Bittan, Patti Scialfa, Danny Federici

Pittsburgh at the beginning of this tour, where they're shutting all the steel mills down, like they're doing here in East Los Angeles. What do you do when the jobs go away but the people remain? When communities begin to disappear, and families fall apart, and you end up living in the shadow of a dream? That's what this song is about."

The music resolved into a melody and a beat and he began to sing, this time the one about the world where "they bring you up to do like your daddy done."

Another night, he wrapped the same incident into a package with his version of Edwin Starr's "War"—a screaming, blue-eyed soul refusal to give up his dream or your dream or anyone else's dream. But he made sure that the punch line included the fact that in that hot kitchen, the man drawing on his smokes and trying to figure out why the hell his son looked and acted like such a freak—a World War II veteran who'd always said that a stint in the Army would straighten his son out in no time flat—had pronounced just two words when he learned that Bruce had been rejected for the draft. "That's good," said Douglas Springsteen.

Even if you had seen Bruce's show a hundred times, he kept it fresh, kept it new, made it into something so immediate you couldn't turn away from it. He had to. The time had come.

So *Born in the U.S.A.* would draw to its close on October 2, 1985. No surprise. It was written right there on the schedule.

The way it's supposed to work is that Bruce Springsteen comes to a close, too. He never again sells forty million records. He can't make that marriage last. He has fewer and fewer hit singles, and less and less play on the radio. He is frustrated, gives up on himself—you can see the burnt-out results in a hundred hackneyed screenplays and novels.

In real life, Bruce Springsteen kept going, kept searching. . . .

Chapter Eight

Mystery Ride

"And it's a thin, thin line . . ."

THIS IS A DARK RIDE," read the sign over the booth where Terry Magovern sat and
accepted each band member's ticket as the *Tunnel of Love Express* tour began.

Nothing about *Tunnel* contradicted that atmosphere. The album that initiated it,
Tunnel of Love, was, from beginning to end, concerned with aspects of intimate relationships that weren't even on the horizon of any of Springsteen's previous albums.

As a tour, *Tunnel of Love Express* presents the great puzzle of Springsteen's career. You couldn't
call it half-hearted; every performance was up to his and the band's creative standard. But the
Express started late—the album came out in October 1987, the first show wasn't until February 25,
1988—and finished soon thereafter on August 3. Six months in, they would have been just hitting
their stride on any previous tour.

The *Express* extended its route at the end, when Bruce surprised everyone by announcing that
he would participate as one of several acts on Amnesty International's Human Rights Now tour,
celebrating the fortieth anniversary of the Universal Declaration of Human Rights. But that
excursion lasted only six weeks.

By October 16, 1988, Bruce Springsteen and the E Street Band were flying home.

At the Omni, Atlanta, Georgia, March 23, 1988

From the *Tunnel of Love* tour book

BRUCE SPENT A CONSIDERABLE amount of time after the *Born in the U.S.A.* tour reviewing live tapes from the previous decade for the album released in 1986 as *Bruce Springsteen and the E Street Band/Live 1975-85*, the first Springsteen album on which the band got title billing.

Soon afterward, he came up with a batch of songs and recorded them in a studio set up in the carriage house at his Rumson home. He cut all the parts himself, then brought in the E Street band members to overdub their instruments and some backing vocals. This might have reflected a certain ambivalence about whether to do a solo album. The tour strategy compounded that ambivalence: The record came out in October 1987, sold well, with "Brilliant Disguise" becoming a hit single, yet the tour did not begin until late February 1988.

After having the band spruce up the album, Springsteen had the band spruced up. Sartorially, the E Streeters had always been a motley crew, each dressed to suit his own mind's eye. For the *Tunnel of Love* tour, they got a little coordination from a professional costumer. Nothing extreme—a lot of fans might never notice it—but it gave the show a more consistent look. A more adult look.

Bruce spruced up, too, wearing quietly fashionable coats, shirts, and trousers rather than decking

Clarence takes a chance.

Max Weinberg

With LaBamba on the *Tunnel of Love* tour

Bruce and the Miami Horns

himself in denim, chambray, and bandanas. Beardless, still pumped from the gym, he presented a clear-eyed, square-jawed pose. Of course, once he got onstage, he revealed that there was still a lot of kid in him. But the new material he'd made for *Tunnel of Love* didn't offer much of a vehicle for horsing around.

A few of the songs offered dense, brooding rock—the title song, "Brilliant Disguise," and the moral fable "Spare Parts" in particular—and there was a nicely done nick of the Yardbirds' version of Billy Boy Arnold's "Ain't Got You" that wryly commented on Bruce's wealth and fame. But the bulk of the record consisted of country-infected rock and stern ballads. It wasn't ideal stage material.

Bruce supplemented the *Tunnel* songs with a handful of other unfamiliar numbers: "Roulette," the screaming antinuke rocker written during the *River* sessions but unheard live until now; "Be True," a light pop B-side; "Seeds," the heavy metal–like song about homelessness from the *Born in the U.S.A.* tour; "Part Man, Part Monkey," a swirling reggae-accented tune; and "I'm a Coward (When It Comes to Love)," a rewrite of Gino Washington's Motor City R&B antique, "Gino Is a Coward."

He supplemented the band with a full horn section led by Richie "La Bamba" Rosenberg; basically it consisted of guys who'd played behind Southside Johnny and the Asbury Jukes for years. This emphasized the strong suit of Bruce's writing about sex and romance, which was its link to soul music. At last, he could afford to carry a ten-piece band.

On that tour, Bruce played the most rigidly constructed sets of his career. For the first few weeks, only one song in each show varied. (He actually did the exact same setlist on two consecutive nights at the Philadelphia Spectrum, and I don't think he'd ever done that at *any* arena, let alone during a virtual home stand.) The shows clocked in at a little under three hours—thirty to sixty minutes less than the extravaganzas he had been doing. Bruce also discarded several warhorses: "Badlands" and "Thunder Road" didn't get played at all on the U.S. leg of the tour. "Racing in the Street" didn't even get played in Europe or on the Amnesty tour. "Out in the Street" appeared only in a show in East Berlin, one of the few shows done there by an American rock artist during the Communist regime. For the first ninety minutes, only "Adam Raised a Cain" was held over from the pre–*Born in the U.S.A.* albums. The rousing climax of that first set was not an affirmation but an ambiguity: "War" segued into "Born in the U.S.A."

The second set might have been lighter; it included "She's the One" and "Dancing in the Dark."

"And I realized that those two people were out there looking, looking for some connection, which is mainly what I'm doing here tonight. They were looking for connection and some place that maybe they could stand and make their own and call home. . . ."

—BS

Oct. 22, 1987 – St. Peter's Church, New York, NY
Bruce performs a solo acoustic version of Bob Dylan's "Forever Young" at John Hammond's memorial service.

Oct. 31, 1987 – McLoone's Rum Runner, Sea Bright, NJ
Bruce performs a complete set with the E Street Band minus Nils and Clarence. Live premieres of "Brilliant Disguise," "Tougher Than the Rest," "Two Faces," and the first acoustic live version of "Born to Run."

Dec. 7, 1987 – Harry Chapin Tribute / Carnegie Hall, New York, NY
Bruce performs "Remember When the Music" at this show.

Dec. 13, 1987 – All-Star Benefit for the Homeless / Madison Square Garden, New York, NY
Bruce performs "A Teenager in Love" with Dion and three more songs backed by David Letterman's band.

The potentially humorous "Part Man, Part Monkey," a discourse on evolution, and "I'm a Coward When It Comes to Love," a twist on the *Tunnel of Love* theme (the complications of mature love), were given introductions that reflected more of what Reaganism had wrought. "Part Man" deliberately confronted creationism, and "Coward" went further, lambasting the television evangelists who served as the shock-troop commanders of the right-wing assault on popular culture.

The introduction to "Coward" was a full bore antisermon. It went the same way almost every night of the tour, evolving very little, yet enough so that by the time the *Express* landed in Europe, Bruce abandoned it, because there was just no context for televised evangelism in which to receive it.

"Are there any brave men out there tonight?" Bruce began, and no matter how many cheers came back to him, he went on: "Are there any brave men out in the audience tonight? Are there any macho men? Because I've seen men that would climb mountains. That would swim rivers. That would get down on their knees and wrestle with a grizzly bear. But there's one thing that they was afraid of. Just one thing that scared them to death. Just one thing that frightened the hell out of them, and I'm gonna tell you what that one thing was." He had those cadences down pat after hours of fixating on the crazed Pentecostalists who mounted their most lunatic campaigns on cable TV (alongside the professional wrestlers he'd apparently also been observing).

"What I'm talking about is L . . . U . . . V . . . . *love*, do you hear me? Love scared 'em. Scared 'em to death. Now, women . . . I'm talking to you, too. Girls, I'm talking to you too. I've known women that would get into a canoe and go down the Amazon River. That would fight off alligators, crocodiles—they wasn't scared. They'd jump out of an airplane at thirty thousand feet. I know women that would even date the horn section in this band. But there was one thing that they was afraid of. And that one thing was *love*, *love*, *love*.

"Now, I'm down here tonight because I've got a confession to make, I've got something I've got to get off my shoulders, I've got to lay my burden down, and what I wanna say is, *I have sinned!*

"That's right!

"And I don't need no Jimmy Swaggart to forgive me, baby. He can kiss my *ass*! And that Pat Robertson and Jerry Falwell can kiss my ass twice, baby. Because I'm a brave man. Yes I am! Yes I am!

Backstage with Jon Landau at the Omni, Atlanta, Georgia, March 23, 1988

Jan. 20, 1988 – Waldorf Astoria Hotel, New York, NY
Bruce inducts Bob Dylan into the Rock and Roll Hall of Fame and performs at the jam session at the end of the evening.

Feb. 25, 1988 – The Centrum, Worcester, MA
Opening night of the *Tunnel of Love* tour

June 13, 1988 – Piazza di Spagna, Rome, Italy
During the European leg of the *Tunnel of Love* tour, Bruce joins Italian street musicians for "I'm on Fire," "The River," and "Dancing in the Dark" in front of fifteen onlookers.

"I don't care who you bring down here, baby. You can bring down Hulk Hogan, you can bring down the Road Warriors, you can bring down George "The Animal" Steele, you can bring down Andre the Giant, I'll take 'em on, I'm not afraid. But there's one thing I'm afraid of. And there's one thing I've got to say. I ain't scared of those kinds of things. But . . . I'm a coward when it comes to love! Save me, boys!"

Three other songs, two in the first set and one more in the second, got an introduction most every night. "You Can Look (But You Better Not Touch)," a slight rocker from *The River*, immediately preceded "Coward," and its surface joviality concealed sharper teeth.

"Here's a song dedicated to window shopping. I went down to the mall to buy one of those little beat boxes before I came out on the road. A woman come up to me. 'You wanna buy that thing?'

"Then she looked at me and she said, 'Ain't you, uh . . . ain't you that rock and roll singer?'

"Then she looked at me again and said, 'You wanna buy that thing, son?'" Bruce had lapsed into the depths of the central New Jersey accent, which vectors in somewhere between Brooklyn and Dixie.

"She said, 'Oh, I like, uh. . . .' She says, 'You know, I like your videos. You know that one where you dance with the girl?'" A long pause. "'Did you pay her? Did you pay her or was she really in the audience?'

"Then she says, 'You wanna buy that thing?'

"I said, 'Lady, I wanna bust this fucking thing right now.'"

A fitting moment for the song's rockabilly beat to begin. Almost an Elvis moment, if you're thinking of the one where he shot up the TV set every time Robert Goulet's face appeared.

Bruce used the stories in the first set to anchor the evening's theme. After four or five songs, when he'd done "Tunnel," John Lee Hooker's "Boom Boom," "Be True," "Adam Raised a Cain," and "Two Faces," he meanderd to a park bench on Clarence's side of the stage and took a seat. Clarence plopped down beside him.

He began a one-sided dialogue. Clarence occasionally mimed a response but only Bruce spoke, seeming to ramble a bit but sticking close to the same script night after night.

"Hey man . . . how you been doing? Ain't seen you in a little while. . . . About the last time I seen you was your anniversary.

"Yeah. Man, what you been up to? Uh-oh, here come the baby pictures." He chuckles as he looks through the photos that Clarence pretends to flash. "That's a good one. We've got a little Big Man out there now. He's three years old, right? Three? He's almost as big as me already . . . he's got a little saxophone, he looks good.

"I can remember we used to sit on this bench in 1975, and we used to watch the girls go by at lunchtime. Right about now, they'd come by out of that big office building on the corner. Check the one in the red dress, red skirt, here she comes." He chuckled some more.

Brilliant disguise, 1988

"Man, I . . . I remember I was with you, I was with you the night you met your wife. We were overseas and she came into the room."

Now he addressed the audience.

"Clarence came running back to my room that night and he said, 'Man, I met the girl I'm gonna marry!' But he used to say that after every girl that he used to meet . . . he used to mean it, it wasn't. . . . But he really meant it that time." More hoarse laughter.

"You know, that's nice, it was nice. Remember how it was like when . . . the first time that that person comes walking in the room and you're checking 'em out and you're waiting to see if they're, like, looking at you." He gestures over his shoulder at La Bamba, the trombone player, who's also a fine doo-wop harmonizer. "Hey, Richie, sing about it, man." La Bamba sings a little doo-wop refrain, some number everyone knows.

"Feels kind of like this, you know. Straight out of New Jersey, right? That was it, man."

He returns his attention to Clarence. "Well, I gotta get home, buddy, dinnertime now. I'll check you later, all right. . . . I'm in bed at like eleven o'clock now, you wouldn't believe it."

The band swung into "All That Heaven Will Allow," the story of a working man, broke on Friday night, desperately trying to get into the club where he's supposed to meet the girl of his dreams, who winds up telling us the true secret of his heart:

> Now some may wanna die young, man
> Young and gloriously
> Get it straight now, mister
> Hey buddy, that ain't me

It wasn't "Thunder Road," an argument that romantic connection could save your life and fire you off into eternity, all for the better. There's an acknowledgment in "Heaven" that you're gonna die, it's just a matter of when, and that you had better fill up the days with the best you have to offer—and you're not going to be able to do that alone.

Springsteen presented the other side in "Spare Parts," which concerns Janey—a name whose associations tumbled all the way back to "Spirit in the Night"—a single mother abandoned by her lover and so desperate to figure out what to do with the child born just about the time its father disappeared that she takes it not just down to the river but deep enough into the stream to drown.

It could have been taken, I guess, as the ultimate statement about a woman's right to choice. In his introduction, though, Bruce made it personal.

"Whenever we're about to get out on tour, there always seems to be a night when we sit around after rehearsals and we start telling old stories from the early days. I get to tell 'em. I've told 'em all about a

A rare stage appearance for the multi-talented Terry Magovern on the *Tunnel of Love* tour, 1988

hundred times but the band acts like they don't notice." He laughs at himself. "But it seems like even though we've all heard 'em a lot, there's something in telling 'em that brings us close together again after we've been apart.

"The past is a funny thing because the past does bind us all together. But it's also dangerous because you can end up living there if you're not careful—and then it just holds you down. You can't go on and change and face what tomorrow brings. This next song, this is a song about a woman struggling to free herself from the part of her past that is holding her back. From old dreams that allow the world to keep breaking her heart over and over again. She's struggling to understand the importance of her own individual existence, and the importance of the life of her child. It seems no matter where we go or what we become, the value of our own lives slips away from us from time to time. Maybe we wonder what we're doing here. You know, I struggle with it all the time, I would guess that most people do. So this is a song about a woman fighting that fight."

Bruce kept on talking into the encores. "Just Around the Corner to the Light of Day" had become the night's climactic moment, successor to "Rosalita," played deep into the encore set. It was an obscure choice, a song Bruce had given to Paul Schrader for *Light of Day*, Schrader's movie about a Midwestern rocker trying to make sense of his passion for music and his working-class reality. Joan Jett did the original version in her punkish rave-up style. Bruce drew out the soul undertones, setting up the band introductions delivered with evangelistic overtones, but when Max's drums came crashing through, the sound went right back to rock and roll nirvana—the most exciting song of the night, bathed in white light and glistening with the sweat of thousands.

The encores began on a quieter note—with "Born to Run," done by Bruce with just an acoustic guitar. He made a similar statement every night before he played it, demonstrating both his conflict about the *Express* tour and his purpose in being out there.

"Before we came out on tour, I was sitting around home trying to decide what we were gonna be doing out here this time. What I felt I wanted to sing and say to you. I was looking through a bunch of my

June 18, 1988 – SOS Racism Concert / Chateau de Vincennes, Paris, France
Bruce and Clarence perform acoustic versions of "Promised Land," "My Hometown," "Blowin' in the Wind," and "Bad Moon Rising." The concert is broadcast on French television.

July 19, 1988 – Radrennbahn Weissensee, Berlin, East Germany
The promoters call the show "A Concert for Nicaragua," which inspires Bruce to give a speech in German about the fact that he is not there "for or against any certain government, but to play rock and roll for East Berliners in the hope that one day all barriers will be torn down." The concert is broadcast in part on East German radio and television without the speech.

Aug. 3, 1988 – Nou Camp, Barcelona, Spain
Final night of the *Tunnel of Love* tour

songs and this is a song that I've sung I guess every night since I first wrote it.

"I'd been sitting around in my bedroom and I'd pick up my guitar and I'd sing it like this. It's a song I wrote fifteen years ago. I was twenty-four, I was living in New Jersey, Long Branch, New Jersey . . . and my parents had moved out to California a few years earlier.

"I think back on this song and it surprises me about how much I knew about what I wanted when I was so young. 'Cause the questions that I asked myself in this song, I've been trying to chase down them answers ever since. When I wrote it, I thought I was writing about a guy and a girl who wanted to get in the car and run and keep on running. That was a nice romantic idea. But as I got older, I realized, 'Gee, I put all these people in these cars. I'm gonna have to find some place for 'em to go.'

"And I realized that those two people were out there looking, looking for some connection, which is mainly what I'm doing here tonight. They were looking for connection and some place that maybe they could stand and make their own and call home. I realized later that home really wasn't out there but that it was buried deep inside of me someplace. And that if I fought for it and if I struggled for it enough and if I tried to keep my eye as true as possible, I might be able to get a little piece of it sometime.

"Anyway, I wanna do this song tonight for all of you, wishing with all my heart that you have a safe trip to home."

Nobody's ever found a better reason to go out and play some music. For Bruce Springsteen, the morality of his show remained intact.

Patti Scialfa, 1988

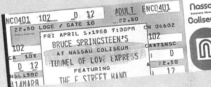

THOSE THINGS WERE WHAT the *Tunnel of Love* tour was all about, or at least what it was supposed to be about. There was another thread, though, that couldn't get talked about in words, but came across unmistakably in the music.

Sept. 2, 1988 – Wembley Stadium, London, England
First night of the Amnesty International Human Rights Now World Tour. Besides Bruce Springsteen and the E Street Band, the other artists are Sting, Peter Gabriel, Youssou N'Dour, and Tracy Chapman.

Oct. 15, 1988 – River Plate Stadium, Buenos Aires, Argentina
Final show of the Amnesty Tour, which is broadcast live on the radio worldwide. Part of the show is also shown on television later in the year.

Feb. 16, 1988
"One Step Up"/"Roulette" is released as a single.

The *Tunnel of Love* tour band. *From left:* Nils, Roy, Patti, Max, Bruce, Clarence, Garry, Danny, Richie "La Bamba" Rosenberg, Ed Manion, Mark Pender, Mike Spangler. At the Omni, Atlanta, Georgia, March 23, 1988.

Patti Scialfa had developed into Bruce's principal vocal duet partner. Each night, when they sang together, especially kicking off the show with "Tunnel of Love," sparks flew. You could have written it off just to musical magic . . . if you were dumb as a doorstop.

Even a doorstop might not have missed the drama in their singing together on "One Step Up." The lyric concerns a man who is failing to keep love alive in his marriage and confesses to not being all that sure he wants to. The furnace has gone out in the first verse of the song and no sparks flew on the recording. But between Bruce and Patti, not just in the way they sang but in the way they approached the mic, the way they held their bodies as they sang, some banked fire could not be concealed. Even a couple weeks into the tour, their byplay became the center of the show.

In early May, while they were on the last, West Coast leg of the tour, Bruce and Julianne Phillips separated. He and Patti immediately became a couple openly within the world of the tour but nowhere else.

Juli's divorce lawyer announced the split a few weeks later, but before that, Italian paparazzi caught Bruce and Patti in dishabille, necking on a balcony. There was probably no preventing it—you can announce your divorce, but not even the most press-hungry celebrities announce their new love affairs—but the tabloid tempest those photos stirred hurt all three of them. Bruce looked like a heartless man cheating on a wife halfway around the globe, Juli looked and probably felt humiliated, Patti came off as the "other woman" in a tawdry scenario.

Thinking back to the early days of the *Born in the U.S.A.* tour—and looking at the couple now that they've spent more than twenty years together and raised three kids— Patti and Bruce getting together kind of seems inevitable. But *Tunnel of Love* is constructed to imply a different story, ending as it does with "Valentine's Day," the promise of children and love eternal with his current wife.

The best sort of reason to prefer the reality of the road to the fantasy land of records.

On July 4, 1988, Bruce played a stadium in Stockholm, Sweden. Part of the show was broadcast worldwide. Bruce began the second set with a speech: "Earlier today Amnesty International announced a worldwide tour to celebrate the fortieth anniversary of the Declaration of Human Rights. The Declaration of Human Rights is a document that was signed by every government in the world forty years ago, recognizing the existence of certain inalienable human rights for everyone regardless of your race, your color, your sex, your religion, your political opinion, or the type of government that you're living under. I was glad to be asked to participate, and I'm proud to join Sting and Peter Gabriel, Youssou N'Dour, and Tracy Chapman in a tour that's gonna begin in early September and is gonna run for about six weeks. I'd like to dedicate this next song to the people of Amnesty International and their idea. So when we come to your town, come on out, support the tour, support human rights for everyone now, and let freedom ring." The band went into a gorgeous rendition of Bob Dylan's "Chimes of Freedom."

Jack Healey, leader of Amnesty in the United States, had the idea of celebrating the Universal Declaration of Human Rights, passed by the United Nations in 1948 and subsequently ratified by most nations, though enforced in its entirety by none. Its provisions include, besides the basic declarations of equal political rights that Bruce mentioned, equal rights in marriage, economics, the workplace, and, according to Article 24, "the right to rest and leisure, including reasonable limitation of working hours and periodic holidays with pay." Before long, the road crew, exhausted and jet-lagged from a schedule that jumped from Barcelona to Costa Rica to Canada, from Tokyo to New Delhi to Athens to Harare, had Article 24 emblazoned on a T-shirt.

The shows almost justified the weariness. Sting and Gabriel were at the height of their powers then, N'Dour a superstar of Afropop, Tracy Chapman the best singer-songwriter in many years. Bruce played the only rock and roll show and closed the night with an abbreviated hour's performance in which the hits just kept on coming as they hadn't since the MUSE concerts in 1980.

Each night began and ended with the musicians—including whatever local musicians were on the night's bill—singing Peter Tosh's anthemic "Get Up, Stand Up" and round-robin choruses of "Chimes of Freedom." Bruce dueted with Sting on "Every Breath You Take." Sting not only sang "The River" with Bruce but occasionally wandered into his set to take the piss, one night appearing with a vacuum cleaner. He was the best foil Bruce ever had, the first who stood next to him as an equal in celebrity and creativity. They referred to each other as long-lost friends, claimed to be spiritual and career advisers to one another, and there's no reason to think they were only kidding. On the last night, Sting and Gabriel appeared onstage as Bruce clones circa *Born in the U.S.A.*, right down to the black jeans and red bandanas.

The best moment perhaps was the next to last show, played in the Andes at Mendoza, Argentina, right on the border of Chile, still ruled by the fascist General Augusto Pinochet, installed by a U.S.–instigated coup in 1973. Among the "local acts" that night were some of the mothers of *los desaparecidos*, the "disappeared," murdered by the regime. These mothers regularly danced in protest, all by themselves, under risk of political persecution, and Sting had written a song, "They Dance Alone," telling their story. That night, they danced before the world, with a worldwide broadcast on the radio and, later, coverage on TV, too.

The next night, in Buenos Aires, Bruce paused before "My Hometown" to say, speaking slowly in an effort to make himself understood, "As a child, music filled me with many dreams—*de vida*, *de amore*, *de potencial humano*, *de sexo*—but most of all, *de libertad*. We are here tonight in the hopes of creating a world

A poster for the Amnesty tour featuring (*from left*) Sting, Tracy Chapman, Bruce, Youssou N'Dour, Peter Gabriel

without torture, without disappearances, without Pinochet, without leaders who govern with the blood of their people on their hands. Traveling around the world on this tour, I understood that though we lead different lives, at night when we go home to our families we dream the same dreams. As one American to another, let us dream and act together towards a world without oppression, where the human spirit sings as the voice of Argentina sings tonight. *Gracias*."

Confronted by the sight of his rock star friends dressed as himself, Bruce still got in the last word: "I wanna see your hands now. I wanna see you shake your hands now. We've been all around the world, we've been to places, we've played for people we ain't even seen before, yeah. . . . We went to England, we went to France, we went to Italy, we went to Spain, we went to India, we went to Africa, we went to South America. We went to *Philadelphia*. Now, I want you to know . . . yeah, I want you to know now . . . that there's one last thing we got to say before we go home. . . . *Uno! Dos! Tres! Quatro!* Well, shake it up, baby . . . twist and shout. . . ."

The boy had become a man, but not even the man could silence the boy.

Chapter Nine

No Miracles Here

"As fragile as each and every breath"

N LATE 1989, BRUCE announced that he was moving on to work with other musicians. This startled everybody, starting with the band members. All the more so when a November press release made the split public.

Apparently, Bruce hoped to accomplish things working with other musicians that he could not have done with the E Streeters. Whether he did remains debatable.

Given the number of stylists in the group, it would be hard to imagine the E Street Band changing musical direction. That was its glory and its limitation. Maybe Bruce decided that it need not be his limitation. Maybe he bought the loner artist myth and sought more individual glory. Maybe he wasn't sure what he wanted. The split was both amicable and, in the long run, ambiguous.

One night not long after the breakup, Bruce and Roy, both living in Los Angeles, went out to dinner. Afterwards Bittan played Springsteen a few tracks he'd been working on. A couple of the melodies caught Bruce's ear, and they wrote several songs together.

Roy became involved in the sessions for Bruce's next album, otherwise manned by Hollywood session pros, particularly drummer Jeff Porcaro and bassist Randy Jackson. The record they made—and made and made and made, for the better part of three years—sounded like the E Street Band with more polish and some soul touches, most provided by singers Sam Moore, of Sam and Dave, and Bobby King, another session veteran. It sounded like what linked every E Street Band recording was Bruce Springsteen more than the E Street Band.

By August 1990, that album seemed close to completion. Then Patti Scialfa, with whom Bruce lived since his first marriage broke up, gave birth to their first child. Bruce responded to the baby the way he'd responded to Elvis and the Beatles. He wrote "Living Proof" about the experience of watching his child being born. That set him off on a second set of songs, a whole different album project. Bruce worked almost alone on the second album—drummer Gary Mallaber was the only other musician who performed on all the tracks. Springsteen's heavier songs sounded very E Street; the rest sounded folk-rock with female vocal accompaniment.

The two albums didn't jibe lyrically any more than they did musically. The first group, which became *Human Touch*, represented love as a struggle without which life cannot be complete. The second group, which became *Lucky Town*, presented love as glory, something not without its difficulties but definitely offering more reward than risk.

By early 1992, he and Landau had convinced Columbia Records to release the two records separately but simultaneously. They arrived in the stores in April. It had been five years since *Tunnel of Love*.

BRUCE CERTAINLY WASN'T GOING to tour with the *Human Touch* players. Touring wasn't what those guys did. He toyed for a time with the idea of using Mallaber, but Mallaber's playing didn't work with the bulk of his material.

"I had some of the best drummers in Los Angeles come in," Bruce said during our 2005 interview. "It was fascinating, because I found a lot of guys at the time that could play a groove incredibly. They couldn't fill and then play a groove. I found guys that could move around the drums, like a Keith Moon, but couldn't keep solid time. So Zach Alford came in . . . Zach was a young black kid that had grown up with both funk and rock music. So he knew how to do both of those things. And I realized, after Max, 'cause Max had come up through all our music, and honed all of those different chops, that that was an uncommon ability."

Roy Bittan remained Bruce's keyboardist. His playing was a signature of the E Street sound, which guaranteed the new Springsteen tour wouldn't drift too far from the past.

Bassist Tommy Sims arrived with credentials even more diverse than Alford's—he was a young black kid who grew up with gospel, soul, and funk but professionally played country and contemporary Christian music.

Jimmy Iovine recommended Shane Fontayne as guitarist. Since age eighteen, Shane had toured with a variety of groups including Lone Justice. Bruce auditioned no one else.

Crystal Taliaferro was a touring pro who'd been in the bands of Billy Joel and John Mellencamp. She played guitar, saxophone, keyboards, all kinds of percussion, and she sang.

Aug. 11, 1989 – Garden State Arts Center, Holmdel, NJ
Bruce joins Ringo Starr and his All-Star Band onstage for "Get Back," "Long Tall Sally" (which he introduces by saying, "I never thought I'd play this song with Ringo Starr on the drums"), "Photograph," and "With a Little Help From My Friends."

Sept. 22, 1989 – Stone Pony, Asbury Park, NJ
At a Jimmy Cliff show, Bruce comes onstage to sing "Trapped," which was written and first performed by Cliff.

Sept. 23, 1989 – McLoone's Rum Runner, Sea Bright, NJ
The E Street Band, along with Little Steven, join Bruce for an impromptu forthieth birthday show.

Nov. 16, 17, 1990 – Christic Institute Benefit Shows / Shrine Auditorium, Los Angeles, CA
Bruce plays two full solo acoustic shows, which at this time is unprecedented. Songs premiered over the two nights include "Red Headed Woman," "57 Channels (And Nothin' On)," "The Wish," "Soul Driver," and "Real World." Jackson Browne and Bonnie Raitt join him for two encores each night.

June 8, 1991 – Los Angeles, CA
Bruce marries Patti Scialfa.

Sept. 26, 1991 – Stone Pony, Asbury Park, NJ
Southside Johnny and the Asbury Jukes play a show that is filmed for a sixty-minute VHS/laserdisc release to promote their new album, *Better Days* (produced by Little Steven). Bruce joins Southside and Little Steven onstage for the final numbers.

Mar. 26, 1992
The "Human Touch"/"Better Days" single is released.

Mar. 30, 1992
Human Touch and *Lucky Town* are released simultaneously by Columbia Records.

With Carol Dennis *(left)* and Bobby King *(center)*

Crystal became Bruce's new second banana, not as great a foil as Clarence Clemons—for one thing, the sexual charge changed—but with commanding stage presence and unstoppable energy.

Bruce hired five singers. Bobby King, who'd toured with Ry Cooder, provided a deep voice. The four female singers included Gia Ciambotti, who'd worked with rock singers like Patty Smyth, Belinda Carlisle, and Lucinda Williams; Angel Rogers, whose background was jazz and R&B; Cleo Kennedy, a veteran of gospel including a stint in the Gospel Harmonettes; and Carol Dennis, a gospel vocalist who'd toured with Bob Dylan in his Christian period.

Bittan and Ciambotti were white. Fontayne was English but with an Asian mother. Everybody else was African American.

Bruce had developed a very specific kind of audience. At its core, a kind of cult existed, a group of fans who had seen dozens or hundreds of shows and studied Bruce's songs and records with zealous attention to detail foreign to most contemporary music critics. The cult expressed itself in Internet discussion groups, fanzines, and parking lots before shows.

The cult's response couldn't be ignored. Its role in Bruce's career became crucial as soon as many such fans wanted to see multiple shows—repeat customers were and are the key to his reputation for selling out an extremely large number of shows in key cities.

Bruce's cult divided sharply in its response to the two new albums and especially to what came to be called in those circles the Other Band. Whether race had anything to do with that division and with the rupture that occurred between Bruce and his audience on the *Human Touch/Lucky Town* tour remains a divisive issue among these fans.

I'm sure race had everything to do with why so many of the Big Bruce Fans disliked the Other Band. It also had a great deal to do with why so many of them preferred the folk-rock based *Lucky Town* to the soul-inspired *Human Touch*. After years of arguing about it—I am, after all, a member of the cult—I'd say the ratio of hardcore Bruce cultists who prefer the former album to the latter is about three to one, and that the ratio of those who prefer *Lucky Town* to those who hated the Other Band is pretty much one to one.

Skin color means nothing here. I doubt if one in a million Springsteen fans hates black skin. Not one in ten million ever considered burning a cross. But it's also true that eyeballing the crowd at any E Street gig conveys the impression that about one in every ten thousand Bruce fans is something other than Caucasian. Based on all those discussions, it's probable that about the same percentage of Bruce fans harbors much awareness of funk, hip-hop, or contemporary R&B.

Hip-hop revolutionized popular music like nothing since rock and roll. By the early nineties, it had seized the

May 6, 1992 – Bottom Line, New York, NY
For the first time since the 1975 *Born to Run* shows, Bruce plays a show at the Bottom Line. The audience is made up of Columbia Records executives and staff. This is the first live concert Bruce plays with the new band he plans to tour with.

May 21, 1992
"57 Channels (And Nothin' On)"/"Part Man, Part Monkey" is released.

June 15, 1992 – Globe, Stockholm, Sweden
Opening night of the 1992–93 world tour.

Dec. 14, 1992 – Boston Garden, Boston, MA
Peter Wolf joins Bruce onstage for the final encore, "In the Midnight Hour."

top of the charts and most of contemporary music's spirit of invention. Bruce played the role of revanchist, holding the line against hip-hop's emphasis on polyrhythm, flagrant vulgarity, the importance of lyrical flow over narrative sense, electronics over virtuosity. With his four-square rhythms, caution and dignity, emphasis on narrative and craft, reliance on sounds played by hands and not triggered by synthesizer patches, Bruce Springsteen became an icon of reassurance. Rock and roll had come to signify whiteness and stability, a complete reversal of what it meant in the fifties and sixties, which was blackness and anarchy.

It's interesting to examine how Bruce was selected to play this part. He didn't volunteer—the volunteer was country singer Garth Brooks, explicitly marketed as not-rap. Yet Bruce's iconography remained a potent symbol of pop music's old regime. Bruce and Clarence, a little white guy and a big black guy out on the stage like Huck and Jim on their raft, had symbolized a kind of integrationist freedom at the beginning. By the nineties, the bond between Scooter and the Big Man signified other things. Among them was resistance to hip-hop's militant insistence that African American artists would speak in their own voices and use their own language. Just as important, it reinforced the notion that nothing really had to change in the music, in the iconography, or in the lives of those who lived and loved it.

Bruce sometimes tried to work against the resistance—

for instance, by having producer Arthur Baker remix his *Born in the U.S.A.* singles using hip-hop elements. That was a novelty that the cult could endure. But when Bruce went on tour with a band dominated by nonwhite people, he scrambled reassurance all to hell.

For the *Human Touch/Lucky Town* tour, Bruce had tape-cutting genius Peter Bochan work the sounds of the 1992 Los Angeles riots into a very hip-hop audio montage that introduced "57 Channels." Before that, Bruce introduced the song by saying things like, "Nineteen ninety-two. You see American cities in flames again. You reap what you sow." Bochan's aural montage worked to a hip-hop beat, linking Bruce's cultural critique with those by the likes of Public Enemy and N.W.A.

Bruce's cult didn't like that kind of music. Not the look—the sound.

If you pressed them, the main musician those cultists disliked was Zach Alford. They even convinced themselves that Bruce didn't like him much. In the midst of some songs, Bruce turned back to the drum kit and shook his head furiously as he shouted to Zach. Their exchange only ever happened during the stormiest songs, I always thought this was a way of exhorting and endorsing the sheer power of Alford's playing, which owed equal debts to both heavy metal and R&B.

Cultists felt it meant exactly the opposite, that Bruce was instructing Zach that he was playing "wrong."

Jan. 12, 1993 – Century Plaza Hotel, Los Angeles, CA
Bruce inducts Creedence Clearwater Revival into the Rock and Roll Hall of Fame and joins John Fogerty onstage for "Who'll Stop the Rain," "Green River," and "Born on the Bayou."

Mar. 23, 1993 – Count Basie Theater, Red Bank, NJ
Rehearsal show for the next leg of the tour. A twenty-three-song set includes "Viva Las Vegas" and "Achy Breaky Heart."

June 24, 1993 – Meadowlands Arena, East Rutherford, NJ
Billed as "The Concert to Fight Hunger," with special guests Joe Ely, Southside Johnny, Little Steven, Clarence Clemons, and the Miami Horns

But as far as I could tell, as a frequent visitor, not a hint of tension over Zach's playing existed backstage. And I've been around enough backstages to know this: If the front man is quarreling musically with the drummer, the problem never stays in the star's dressing room.

Bruce would also, early in the tour, tell Zach to count off a song, something he'd never done with Max. This was also "evidence" of Bruce's dissatisfaction with Zach. The idea seemed to be that anything Bruce did with the Other Band that he hadn't done with the E Street Band indicated error. It's not any harder to see the logic than it is to fault its premises. But listen to Zach on, say, "Badlands," against any live recording with Max that you please—it's not right and wrong, it's two different approaches to the same music.

In America, where rhythm's at issue, there lurks race.

The taste of Springsteen's Big Fans tends toward folk-rock and singer-songwriters. If they listen to Motown, the focus is on the harmonies and the songs, both of which are admittedly amazing. Motown's use of multiple rhythms, like its use of multiple melodies, in the same record is very subtle, nothing to antagonize white Americans, who, as James Baldwin once wrote in despair, "seem to feel that happy songs are *happy* and sad songs are *sad*, and that, God help us, is exactly the way most Americans sing them. . . ."

The irony is that Baldwin published those words in 1963, just as the Beatles arrived to finish the job Elvis started and show Americans the glory of making sad songs incorporate happiness and happy songs deal with sadness.

Hip-hop's much harder task is to move Americans—white Americans included—to hear beats as central rather than subordinate, which meant waging war against several centuries of European musical cultural supposition.

If I imagine looking through eyes wary of hip-hop's usurpation of the "natural" musical order, it's not hard to imagine being driven crazy by stuff like the "No justice, no peace" chant that followed the "57 Channels" audio montage. The backing voices, Crystal's percussion, the bass, and the drums charged at one another from oblique angles. The bass and drums continued to cut up the beat even after Bruce's vocal began.

That wasn't typical of the Other Band. It played Bruce Springsteen music, and you had to be a pretty big fan, I imagine, just to hear the difference between one group and the other. But it was possible for a listener to focus on beat—and more important, harder for a listener to ignore beat—with this group.

Between the two of them, Zach and Tommy made the bottom of Bruce's music new.

The rhythm no longer concerned itself only with drive and dramatic accent, but with more subtle things. In particular, Zach played way at the back of the beat. He had it exactly right for this band, with its many vocalists, because that style creates an exceptionally deep pocket in which to sing.

The idea of a beat as something that can be played correctly at various points in its duration flummoxes the musically naïve. It seems many Americans think of a beat as a Thing, indivisible as an atom (oops!). But beats function more like verbs than nouns—they express change, units of time that can be divided almost infinitely. So that a drummer, for instance, may push the beat by playing at the beginning of it, or hit it on the nose by landing smack dab in the middle of it, or lay back until the last millisecond before it fades into the next beat and becomes "wrong." It's not nearly as simple as counting to four.

What Zach Alford did that sounded "wrong" to the Big Bruce Fans was play deep in the back of the beat.

When he was younger, Max Weinberg tended to rush the beat, which amounted to speeding up the band. After some serious studying—nobody worked harder on becoming better than Max—he became a fantastic on-the-beat rock drummer who would lay back a bit when it seemed appropriate. But Max had other priorities, too—he followed and punctuated dramatic and comedic action better than anyone else I've ever seen. But compared to Zach, his time was quite rigid—Zach went for feel, something like Vini

Lopez but with more finesse and a steadier hand.

Not "wrong" but different—and if you expected Bruce to maintain consistency with his E Street sound, I suppose it wasn't hard to confuse the two. Not only with Zach but with pretty much the whole group.

Tommy Sims's bass lines rumbled with such intricacy that sometimes I went and stood beneath the stage, right under his spot, as a way of isolating his playing. It was like listening to a corkscrew cosmos inside the basic Bruce music, where the bass playing had always been defined by Garry Tallent's heartbeat rock and soul throb.

THEN THERE WERE THE SINGERS, on whose behalf, in a sense, all this went on. You're welcome to imagine whatever you'd like to the contrary, but about 90 percent of rock music—not to mention the music it takes its cues from—uses the band as a platform for the singers, and Bruce Springsteen's is far from an exception.

This time, he loaded the band with people who harbored fine voices and knew what to do with them.

Bobby King sings in blustering soul-man mode, a quintessential backup singer, unlike Sam Moore, for whom every duet becomes a duel. The female singers shone on new material and old. My favorite was Cleopatra Kennedy, who, though I didn't know it then, had been a gospel star as a teenager. Cleo had been through serious battles; she

June 25, 1993 – NBC Studios, New York, NY
Bruce appears on the final NBC broadcast of *Late Night With David Letterman* to sing "Glory Days."

June 26, 1993 – Madison Square Garden, New York, NY
The last night of the *Human Touch/Lucky Town* tour is a benefit for the Kristin Ann Carr Fund. Joe Ely and Terence Trent D'Arby are special guests.

Jan. 20, 1994 – Waldorf Astoria Hotel, New York, NY
At the Rock and Roll Hall of Fame induction ceremony, Bruce and Axl Rose perform "Come Together" as a duet without any rehearsal. The song is originally planned for Elton John and Rod Stewart, but Stewart is still in Los Angeles due to the recent earthquake.

March 1, 1994

"Streets of Philadelphia"/"Atlantic City" is released.

6 6th ANNUAL ACADEMY AWARDS
Monday, March 21, 1994
PRODUCTION
GEORGE TRAVIS

Mar. 21, 1994 – Dorothy Chandler Pavilion, Los Angeles, CA

Bruce performs "Streets of Philadelphia" live at the Sixty-sixth Annual Academy Awards ceremony. The song is nominated for (and wins) Best Original Song.

May 29, 1994 – Hollywood Palladium, Los Angeles, CA

Bruce joins the Rock Bottom Remainders, who include Dave Marsh, for "Gloria."

Shane Fontayne with Bruce during a taping for "MTV Plugged," September 22, 1992

101
TICKET NUMBER
ADMIT ONE THIS DATE

*** MTV PRESENTS ***
MTV'S UNPLUGGED TAPING
SEATING NOT GUARANTEED AFTER 7:45PM
SEP **22** TUE. 8:00PM
1992 WARNER HOLLYWOOD STUDIOS
1041 N. FORMOSA AVE
W. HOLLYWD
NO REFUND OR EXCHANGES
101
101
SEP 22
8:00PM
SEP 22

June 18, 1994 – McCabe's Guitar Shop, Santa Monica, CA

John Wesley Harding is joined onstage by Bruce for a version of "Wreck on the Highway."

July 16, 1994 – Stone Pony (outside tent), Asbury Park, NJ

Bruce, Patti, Max, and Jon Bon Jovi join Southside Johnny for seven songs.

Aug. 20, 1994 – Marz American Style, Long Branch, NJ

Joe Grushecky and the Iron City Houserockers are joined onstage by Bruce, who performs an entire fourteen-song set.

Zach Alford at the Globe Arena, Stockholm, Sweden, June 17, 1992

"Hungry Heart" or a variety of soul songs that made sense on their own terms, not just his, the way they always had before. On the final night of the tour, he found a way to take Woody Guthrie's "Lonesome Valley" to this church.

That night, with King and the women supplemented by Terence Trent D'Arby, a contemporary soul singer-songwriter who'd been practically brought up in his father's pulpit and whom Bruce had befriended, and Joe Ely, a West Texas boy whose roots encompassed the same kind of gospel, they turned the song from one of mourning to one that accepted the hardest things in life and still found transcendence: the gospel according to Bruce.

The gospel, period. For what Bruce brought to the morality of his show was not terribly different from what Baldwin recalled taking away from the Pentecostal churches where he worshipped and preached as a boy:

"There is no music like that music, no drama like the drama of the saints rejoicing, the sinners moaning, the tambourines racing, and all those voices coming together and crying holy unto the Lord," Baldwin wrote. "There is still, for me, no pathos quite like the pathos of those multicolored, worn, somehow triumphant and transfigured faces, speaking from the depths of a visible, tangible, continuing despair of the goodness of the Lord. I have never seen anything to equal the fire and excitement that sometimes, without warning, fill a church, causing the church, as Leadbelly and so many others have testified, to 'rock.'

told me once that she survived the bombing of her home church, Birmingham's Sixteenth Street Baptist, even though she was best friends with the girls who died, because, as the soloist, she hadn't finished choir practice yet. She and Carol Dennis (Dylan's second wife, it turned out) gave Bruce weapons not in his arsenal since Delores Holmes in the Bruce Springsteen Band. Gia and Angel filled in for Patti—Angel even flirted—except for the occasions when Patti came on for a duet.

You got a sense of what these ensemble vocals had to offer when Bruce turned them loose on songs like

Oct. 20, 1994 – Roseland Ballroom, New York, NY
Neil Young and Bruce join Bob Dylan for "Rainy Day Women #12 & 35" and "Highway 61 Revisited."

Oct. 21, 1994 – The Playpen, Sayreville, NJ
At a John Eddie gig, Greg Kihn, Elliott Murphy, Marshall Crenshaw, and Bruce come onstage for four songs.

Feb. 21, 1995 – Tramps, New York, NY
The show is filmed for the "Murder Incorporated" music video, to promote the new *Greatest Hits* album. It is the first E Street Band performance since 1988 and the first time Little Steven, Nils Lofgren, and Patti Scialfa perform together in the band.

. . . Their pain and their joy were mine, and mine were theirs—they surrendered their pain and joy to me, I surrendered mine to them—and their cries of 'Amen!' and 'Hallelujah!' and 'Yes, Lord!' and 'Praise His name!' and 'Preach it, brother!' sustained and whipped on my solos until we all became equal, wringing wet, singing and dancing, in anguish and rejoicing, at the foot of the altar."

The differences were many—there was ample warning, for one thing, the cries were different, the looks of wear meant something very different indeed. But in essence what sustained and whipped James Baldwin onward sustained and whipped Bruce Springsteen onward. To grow closer to that essence—to cause the church of his musical morality to rock—he went to its root.

Bruce preached his heart out on that tour. It was his old message of true love and rock and roll, the same exhortation to make that leap of faith he'd always encouraged, the same parody of the jackleg preachers who ran the televised part of his midnight world, the same fervor to reach out and touch . . . just . . . one . . . other . . . soul, in order that his own might be saved. He carried it into "Light of Day," he carried it through "Glory Days," he carried the ghost of it into his most forlorn numbers, always sung alone or with just the whisper of that backup he needed so badly. When he rocked, he meant to take the church with him, but he'd settle for just that one other soul. Never was this clearer.

Never was it clearer that there were lots of fans—people convinced that they understood him to his core—who just didn't get this part, didn't quite wish he'd shut up and sing but didn't see the point of all the witnessing, testifying, and taking it seriously, even when he took it seriously with a smile on his face and immediately undercut it with a joke at his own expense.

That last night, it took a seriously tangible form. He brought out D'Arby to duet on "My Hometown." That went well. Later, right after storming through "Who'll Stop the Rain," he brought Terence back to sing D'Arby's own "I Have Faith in These Desolate Times." This one, a long, slow recitation, almost an altar call, got booed. There weren't a lot of boos, there weren't any brickbats tossed to make the catcalls complete. But the booing happened; it was loud enough to be obnoxious. And what got booed was the very thing that made Bruce's show with the Other Band new.

I didn't register it as too much of a big deal at the time; there were plenty of other emotions flowing that night, and anyway, idiots abound in all crowds. But Bruce took it personally. Just before "Light of Day," he introduced D'Arby once more and added, "Need I remind some of you rude motherfuckers that everybody onstage is my guest?"

Feb. 28, 1995
Greatest Hits is released by Columbia Records, with four new bonus tracks recorded for the package: "Murder Incorporated," "Secret Garden," "This Hard Land," and "Blood Brothers."

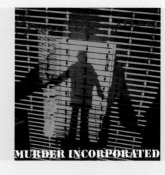

MURDER INCORPORATED

Mar. 1, 1995 – Shrine Auditorium, Los Angeles, CA
Bruce performs "Streets of Philadelphia," which is nominated for (and wins) Song of the Year at the Grammy Awards.

"Top o' the world, Mom!" called Bruce Springsteen at the 37th Annual Grammy Awards Wednesday night, accepting the song of the year award for writing *Streets of Philadelphia*. His mother sat next to his

HUMAN TOUCH AND *LUCKY TOWN*, the Other Band and the tour, even Bruce's split with Juli ("If Bruce couldn't make love work, where did that leave the rest of us?" as one fan said to me) combined to crack the illusion of a solid bond between the artist and his audience. You could add to those seismic pressures a host of other factors: Bruce's mass success, which disturbed the cult so much that fifteen years after *Born in the U.S.A.*, they'd be squabbling over whether a fan who didn't latch on 'til 1984 or 1985 was an authentic tramp like them, and plenty more. He'd been living in Los Angeles. He'd gotten divorced after being caught cheating, and his first child had been born without benefit of marriage. He was rich and lived in a big house—actually a couple of them, one in California, one in New Jersey. He continued to express allegiance to equality for the working class as many of his fans turned toward elitism in both Republican and Democratic forms. (So far as one could tell, none of this was an issue for his European fans.)

Bruce's pact with his fans turned on an idea of mutual support. He gave them a version of the greatest show on Earth. They gave him the freedom—or at least the space—in which to do work of depth and power, to explore topics other popular musicians never touched, to try to figure out how the pieces of this world fit together. Part of the pact was that he wouldn't travel the one-way street most stars found themselves on, ignoring his listeners.

It turned out to be a one-way street running in the other direction. When the star changed, a good part of his audience wasn't having it.

I think Bruce also maybe expressed a little aloofness toward the Other Band—he could flirt with Angel, and Crystal made a good foil, but there wasn't ten or twenty years of his life story standing next to him up there. The hallmark of that band was difference, and I can imagine that that was part of why he picked it, and it's part of why I loved it. But I can also see why for those who had their doubts, that lack of close bonding reinforced them.

Anyway, there's no helping it. When you become a superstar, one thing they should tell you is that the slope of the decline may be gentle but that the onset never is.

By the time he played the Meadowlands in July 1992, ten weeks after the records were released, he joked about the albums as flops: "Last time we were in the States we did that radio broadcast, right? Didn't I predict that, like, my records were gonna go zooming back to the top of the charts [*cheers*]? That's right. We've been away for a while, let's see how my prediction went. Has anybody got a *Billboard* magazine out there? Thank you, sir. All right, let me check out that Top Ten. All right—here's the Top Ten. There's, uh . . . Garth Brooks is still up there, I see . . . and Def Leppard, they're hanging in there, they're hanging in there. Oh shit . . . I must be in the Top Twenty, they must. . . . There's Elton John, he's older

Bruce and Steven Van Zandt join in on a Southside Johnny *(center)* video shoot, Asbury Park, 1992.

With Crystal Taliefero *(left)* and Shane Fontayne *(right)*, Globe Arena, Stockholm, Sweden, June 17, 1992

**"But anyway, we're here for bigger reasons than those damn record sales. We're here for bigger reasons than just to chase those big bucks all around. Can anybody tell me what those big reasons are? *Weeellll, aaah . . . LET'S ROCK!"*

—BS**

than me. . . . Where's Weird Al Yankovic, where's he? Shit, he's at fifty-seven. Where am I ?

"Jesus Christ, where am I? I must be on the other goddamn page. All right, wait. What? Gee . . . seventy-three! Wait a minute, *Lucky Town* at a hundred and fucking five [*laughter*]! I'm not in the Top 100?

"But anyway, we're here for bigger reasons than those damn record sales [*cheers*]. We're here for bigger reasons than just to chase those big bucks all around. Can anybody tell me what those big reasons are? *Weeellll, aaah . . . let's rock!"*

They did, for eleven sold-out Jersey shows. And Europe in '92 was damn near as glorious as Europe in '81. But it wasn't just the albums. Back home, Bruce suddenly couldn't sell out Cleveland, where the Brucemania used to be Jersey-like, and there were plenty of other places where they didn't sell out for the first time in about twenty years.

You could list all sorts of reasons: It was age, it was five years between albums, it was the lack of hit singles, it was the inevitable shrinkage of an audience inflated by the *Born in the U.S.A.* phenomenon. But mainly, it was a drag and an embarrassment because those shows were as good as any long run of shows I've seen Bruce do, which makes them as good as the shows I've seen anybody do.

The cultists saw them, too, I guess, and came to the opposite conclusion. Some of them, unaccountable as it seems to me, must have gone home disappointed and disaffected because . . . well, because it wasn't the same. Bruce's personal conservatism—his lack of rock and roll flamboyance, arrogance, misanthropy—attracted a cult that loved stability. His striving to please them made that cult think they ought to control him. Or something like that. Anyway, it didn't help, and the cultists were the ones who articulated the problems—most people who had trouble with what Springsteen was up to did the normal thing and stayed home.

They missed great shows. I saw enough of 'em to be sure of that.

THE OTHER BAND TOUR lasted almost exactly a year, from June 15, 1992, in Stockholm to June 26, 1993, at Madison Square Garden in New York. The final leg took Bruce back to Europe in April and May, wrapping up there on June 1. That was supposed to be the end of it but Bruce decided in late May that he'd play two final nights as benefits back home. The first would be a benefit for the Community Food Bank of New Jersey; the Food and Hunger Hot Line, which served the New York and New Jersey metropolitan area; and World Hunger Year, the food and hunger policy group founded by Harry Chapin and a priest-turned-disc-jockey-turned-activist named Bill Ayres.

The second night was a benefit for a new cancer-research charity, the Kristen Ann Carr Fund. Kristen Carr was the daughter of Barbara Carr and myself. Kristen was twenty-one when the sarcoma she'd been fighting for a little more than two years killed her. She'd worked on the tour, helping with merchandise sales in Europe during the summer of 1992. Bruce and she had known each other since she was a little girl, and he'd been a devoted visitor to her hospital room all through the final part of her illness. He spoke at her funeral, where he and Patti sang "If I Should Fall Behind," which they'd promised to sing at her wedding.

Kristen did more than figure out how many T-shirts to put on how many tables that summer. A lot of the Other Band was younger than Bruce—Zach, Tommy, and Gia weren't thirty yet, I don't think, and Crystal and Angel couldn't have been much older—and most of them had never been to Europe, or if they had, not on Bruce's fairly relaxed schedule. So Kristen and her fiancé, Michael Solomon, became the group's de facto entertainment directors. Kristen wanted to do her mother's work eventually, and that summer, she did a little bit of it—she helped keep a group that might have factionalized in good spirits. There were some real bonds there, and not only with the kids. I won't ever lose the image of Cleo and Carol freezing and in tears when they came to console us outside the funeral.

If you want to know what the end of Kristen's life was like, there are two good summaries. One is a line from *Tunnel of Love*'s "When You're Alone": "There are things that'll knock you down you don't even see comin' / And send you crawlin' like a baby back home." The other is a song Bruce wrote two years later, one that he has acknowledged contains Kristen's spirit. That is "Streets of Philadelphia." Every time I have ever heard it, she comes alive to me in the mournful way he sings a single line, "And my clothes don't fit me no more." That is not just how it was—that is how it *felt*.

We all wanted to create a lasting memorial; Kristen's doctor, Murray Brennan, chief of surgery at Memorial Sloan-Kettering, said he needed a permanently endowed surgical fellowship. That cost a little more than a million dollars.

Bruce said he'd play a show. He let us do stuff he'd never ordinarily do: The best seats cost $2,500, and those tickets came with a reception before the show (and he went to it), and there was a souvenir box set of every record he'd made up to that time. He gave us all the money—I mean all the money. We wound up with more than $1.5 million, enough to endow the fellowship in full, only six months after Kristen died.

Bruce asked me to come into his dressing room before the show. I think he had only done that once before, the first night he played Wembley Arena, a building he knew I'd been in a lot with other groups. We talked about how playing cities like New York and Los Angeles and London was different than playing anywhere else. They counted more, somehow.

This time, though, Bruce had a question for me, the strangest question he could have asked. He

wanted to know if there was anything special he could do that night. I was speechless. He was already doing everything—changing the lives of hundreds, maybe thousands of people with sarcoma, the rarest kind of cancer, that night, whether he knew it or not. Finally, I sort of stammered, "I just want a great Bruce Springsteen show." Which was, looking back on it, demanding something damned big. All I meant was, You've never let me down, I know you won't tonight.

When the house went dark, there were two spots on the stage. One was aimed at Bruce. The other was on a vase of Kristen's favorite flowers, pink "Anna" roses that Jon and Barbara Landau regularly brought to her hospital room. It was, I guess, Bruce or George Travis or somebody's idea of showing us that her spirit was there, even if she couldn't be.

The band filed onstage. A fiddle started up. The melody was achingly familiar. Bruce stepped up. "You gotta walk that lonesome valley," he sang. "You gotta walk it by yourself / Ain't nobody gonna walk it for you / You got to walk that lonesome valley by yourself."

Then Bobby King. Then Cleo Kennedy. Then Joe Ely. Then everybody.

They were telling Kristen's story, and the story of all those kids—and grownups too—who fight that battle.

Three songs in, Bruce stopped to explain the purpose of the show. He mentioned Kristen, as his friend, and he mentioned the need for money and for research. Then he got to the real point: "We're here not to mourn her loss but to celebrate her memory."

A few seconds later, he rocked back into the one that ends "Well if you can't make it, stay hard, stay hungry, stay alive if you can / And meet me in a dream of this hard land." I had my great Bruce Springsteen show. And Kristen had hers.

I remember the ending, too—lights up, me slumped in a chair, face wet, listening to Bruce sing about his own desolation when Steven left the band in "Bobby Jean," and winding up with "Follow That Dream," that story about everybody having a chance to give what they have to give, sung on behalf of somebody who did not get that chance. Turning something awful into something beautiful.

Ain't no miracle here. Just a further word on behalf of the tour sponsor. Bruce declared every night, in his introduction to "Leap of Faith," that he'd finally broken down and agreed to have one.

"I'm not out here tonight to try and sell you no beer," he would say, "and I'm not gonna try and sell you no sneakers, and I'm not gonna try and sell you no soda pop. Because our sponsor tonight is . . . love! That's right, that's right, our sponsor tonight is *love!*"

Maybe a little miracle after all. Or at least a very beautiful reward for someone who had earned it by walking that lonesome valley way too soon.

Chapter Ten

Pilgrim in the Temple

"Where it's headed everybody knows."

THE *GHOST OF TOM JOAD* tour began with a pair of rehearsal shows in little theaters in New Brunswick and Red Bank, New Jersey. It was just Bruce and twelve of his acoustic guitars on the stage for a couple of hours—unless you counted guitar tech Kevin Buell adding a keyboard lick or five from the wings, which I suppose we ought to.

Immediately after the second warm-up show at the Count Basie Theater in Red Bank, my first, I headed backstage, eager to see if what I thought I'd just seen Bruce pull off up there still made sense in the light.

Near the door, I bumped into Bruce, who'd stopped behind the curtains to talk to a couple of the techs.

"That was great," I said and clapped him on the shoulder. Then I took a step away and eyed him closely. "You're not wet." Bruce laughed and said, "Gee, I guess I'm not."

"You're always soaked after a show," I mused. Sometimes, in the outdoor shows during dog days, he'd even pour a bucket of water over his head. "So you don't need a shower, right?"

"Not right now, no."

"Well, I'm pretty sure we could get a drink in the office back here."

"Let's go," he said.

HE DIDN'T STAY DRY THROUGH lack of exertion. Bruce never worked harder than on the *Joad* tour. Never needed to. Never had to build a show around a set of songs whose challenges

212

At a rehearsal, Asbury Park, July 1999

involved singing the term *hydriatic acid* and making real a group of characters that include a vengefully homicidal hobo, a homeless Mexican boy turning tricks and huffing glue, a recently released convict looking for just one reason not to go about his criminal business, and a guy so fucked in the head over his relationship to a stripper—or is she a hooker?—that he can't figure out whether the dry lightning is out on the horizon or in his head. I was going to say it was a group of songs without a single moment of humor, but then I remembered the last song on the record, "My Best Was Never Good Enough," which used a series of clichés inspired by another homicidal maniac, the sheriff in Jim Thompson's hard-boiled novel *The Killer Inside Me*, to both mask and vent Springsteen's anger at the breakdown of his supposed relationship with his audience during the *Human Touch/Lucky Town* tour (or at least that is what the song is about in my opinion, the alternative explanation being that it is just a meaningless exercise, something I do not believe exists in any artist's public repertoire, let alone Bruce Springsteen's).

He stayed dry because it wasn't the kind of show where he jumped around a lot, or for that matter, even a little. *Joad*'s obvious antecedent is *Nebraska*, but it isn't a true solo album. Six of the twelve tracks include band accompaniment, and of the other six, Bruce augments his guitar and voice with keyboards on five. (The true solo number is

"The New Timer," the one about the homicidal hobo.)

So he could easily have justified taking some kind of band on the road, an ensemble that would feature some of the musicians on the record—E Streeters Danny Federici and Garry Tallent, *Lucky Town*'s Gary Mallaber, Patti Scialfa and her singing cohorts, Soozie Tyrell and Lisa Lowell, among them. But he chose to go it alone, stripping it down after the muddled messages sent by and to him on the Other Band tour, the way he'd stripped it down back in Asbury when Steel Mill and the Bruce Springsteen Band didn't work out.

Bruce spoke as if he'd done a lot of solo work over the years. He hadn't. If he did many one-man shows back in the Jersey days, it didn't show up in the papers or in people's memories the way his band work did. He'd done some, for a while, late in that period. As he was prepared by Appel and Columbia for the "new-Dylan" chopping block, he'd done a few more. During the *Joad* tour, he reminisced on stage about, for instance, working as Dave Van Ronk's opening act at Max's Kansas City.

He did a song or two solo in all his shows after *Nebraska*, sometimes doing two or three spots a night by himself or in a small ensemble setting, but never more than a couple of songs at a time, because he clearly lost too much of the attention of those arena and stadium crowds. You could tell from the bustle to the concessions and rest-

Apr. 5, 1995 – Ed Sullivan Theater, New York, NY
Live on the *Late Show With David Letterman,* Bruce and the E Street Band play "Money," "Murder Incorporated," "Tenth Avenue Freeze-Out," and "Secret Garden."

Apr. 5, 1995 – Sony Studios, New York, NY
The show is filmed as a promotional vehicle for the *Greatest Hits* album.

Apr. 11, 1995
"Secret Garden"/"Thunder Road" is released as a single.

rooms and a general loss of attentiveness (though that was far more the case in America than in Europe).

In October 1986, Bruce played the first of Neil Young's Bridge Benefits, shows that funded a school for special-needs kids, which Young's sons attended. Danny Federici and Nils Lofgren played on a number or two each, but mostly it was just Bruce up there. I need exaggerate nothing to tell you that it was, by a considerable distance, the most awkward show I ever saw him do, Bruce's invariably sure stage instincts abandoning him on matters of pace, even song selection—after singing Young's "Helpless" as a duet with Neil, he opened with "You Can Look (But You Better Not Touch)." It wasn't a brilliant reconception of the song, either. The entire show struck me as a shambles; its pieces just wouldn't fall into place.

I think it had something to do with not having worked in that format much, or in a long time, and I think some of the rest had to do with not being on the road at that point—it took place a year after *Born in the U.S.A.* ended, and eighteen months before *Tunnel of Love* would begin. A long layoff hadn't hurt him at all when he played MUSE, but then he'd been working in the studio with the band for the previous year.

Some of it, I wrote off to too much eagerness and too little rehearsal, and some of it may have had to do with the presence of Neil Young, always the member of the rock aristocracy to whom Bruce showed the greatest deference.

But anyway, it didn't give me great confidence in the *Joad* solo idea, not with that batch of songs.

Then again, I hadn't seen the shows that made many Springsteen fans greet the solo tour announcement eagerly. On November 16 and 17, 1990, Bruce played solo to benefit the Christic Institute, a group that sued the United States government and the C.I.A. in federal court, alleging that they trafficked in drugs as part of a scheme to undermine the legitimate government of Nicaragua, the revolutionary Sandinistas.

Across those two shows, Bruce debuted six songs: "Real World," "Soul Driver," and "57 Channels," which would appear on *Human Touch;* "Red Headed Woman," his recurrent live tribute to his sex life with Patti; and "The Wish" and "When the Lights Go Out," the former being performed infrequently over the rest of his career to date, and the latter vanishing altogether except for its inclusion on *Tracks,* his outtakes box set.

Bruce played mostly guitar, a little piano, at these shows. He introduced them volubly, and what he said prefigured some of what he'd do on the *Joad* tour (and later, on *Devils & Dust*). He asked for quiet at the beginning, and he made sport of his own personal foibles, speculated on his own sexual peccadilloes, and spoke of how becoming a parent had changed him.

Those shows energized fans, who raved about them for years. One story had it that Landau and Springsteen found

---

Apr. 12, 1995 – Carnegie Hall, New York, NY

The Rainforest Foundation Benefit Concert, at which artists perform songs by Elvis Presley. Bruce performs eight songs, five of them Elvis covers ("Viva Las Vegas," "Burning Love," "It's Now or Never," "Jailhouse Rock," and "Mystery Train").

July 9, 1995 – Café Eckstein, Berlin, Germany

A live video for "Hungry Heart" is filmed at this small bar. Bruce is backed by Wolfgang Niedecken and his Leopardefellband. One of the numerous "Hungry Heart" takes recorded during this performance is later officially released on the "Hungry Heart" CD EP (as "Hungry Heart [Berlin '95]") later, although it features Bruce's live vocals from the show laid over the original 1980 E Street Band instrumental tracks.

Sept. 2, 1995 – Cleveland Stadium, Cleveland, OH

Rock and Roll Hall of Fame concert to commemorate the opening of the museum. Bruce and the E Street Band perform an abbreviated eight-song set at this multiartist show. They also back up Jerry Lee Lewis and Chuck Berry.

the performances so compelling that they considered releasing a live album from them.

THE *JOAD* SHOWS OPENED on a virtually bare stage, Bruce alone before the microphone, holding an (amplified) acoustic guitar and wearing a harmonica in its holder around his neck. "Men walkin' 'long the railroad tracks / Goin' someplace there's no goin' back," he sang, investing the opening lines of "The Ghost of Tom Joad" with their full foreboding.

"Ghost," the title ballad from the album, updates the *Grapes of Wrath* character as if his speech, in Henry Fonda's voice, at the end of John Ford's film version, had come true: "I'll be all around you in the dark . . . I'll be everywhere . . . when you hear the guys yelling 'cause they're mad, I'll be there, when kids are laughing 'cause they're coming in at night to have their dinner, Ma, I'll be there, too."

Every song on Bruce's *Joad* proceeded on the premise that America had become such a hard, dark land that this spirit had been . . . lost? Shackled? Obliterated?

"Ghost" itself had several drawbacks. It was as wordy and almost as long as Woody Guthrie's "Tom Joad," a chapter-by-chapter synopsis of John Steinbeck's novel. It lacked an interesting melody or rhythmic complexity. This was song as story, bare to its bones. It riveted audi-ences. Bruce's voice made each line urgent, but he used another tool, something he'd rarely exhibited so nakedly: his charisma.

You couldn't turn away from him singing this long, wordy song because it was Bruce Springsteen up there, and not the Bruce Springsteen you thought you knew. This wasn't the prisoner of rock and roll. This was somebody else.

The *Tunnel of Love* tour represented the point where he began the turn. The Other Band tour represented a first effort at expressing it. *The Ghost of Tom Joad* tour, though, brought this new—this adult, mature, sober—Bruce Springsteen into full view.

When "Ghost" finished, Bruce spoke to the audience. In those early shows, he hemmed and hawed a bit, but with-in a month, in Austin, he had it down pretty well: "This is where I give my little speech about, you know, trying to get the audience to be quiet. I don't think it's necessary, but just in case," he chuckled at his own nerve, "I just wanna say singing and clapping along tonight will be viewed as a psy-chotic event by the people sitting around you. And it is a community event, so if somebody around you's making too much noise, please feel free to band together and very politely and constructively ask them to shut the fuck up." And he was off into the next song, usually "Adam Raised a Cain," transformed from its electric-guitar rage to some-thing much more meditative as he sang those adolescent truths without a band at his back.

Oct. 17–24, 1995 – "October Assault" Tour
Bruce joins Joe Grushecky and the Houserockers for every date on their October 1995 tour and plays most of the show as a guitarist in the band, joining Joe for a few numbers at the mic.

Nov. 19, 1995 – Shrine Auditorium, Los Angeles, CA
At Frank Sinatra's Eightieth Birthday Tribute Concert, Bruce performs Sinatra's "Angel Eyes."

Count Basie Theater, Red Bank, New Jersey, 1995

An illustration by Paul Leibow from the *The Ghost of Tom Joad* tour book

Most nights, he sang the great majority of *Joad's* twelve songs intermingled with some of the most psychologically probing of his earlier material: "Darkness on the Edge of Town," "Spare Parts," and for uplift's sake, "Does This Bus Stop at 82nd Street" and "This Hard Land." There was plenty of room to add songs from all across his repertoire: "Murder Incorporated," left off *The River*, "If I Should Fall Behind," his recent hit "Streets of Philadelphia," an acoustic "Born in the U.S.A." that turned it from anthem into slide blues lament, "Reason to Believe," seeming even bleaker here than it had fifteen years before, "Brothers Under the Bridge," which concerned Vietnam veterans who were in the same homeless, desperate straits as the *Joad* characters. After a while, once he gained full confidence that the tenor of the new album

dominated, he even felt free to let in more light with songs like "No Surrender" and "Two Hearts."

He could have gotten more love, bigger applause, and probably higher ticket prices if he'd sung more old stuff, not just because it was old but also because it made fewer demands on the listener's conscience (and often, patience). But he never backed off the *Joad* material as he had with the previous two albums. At that show in Red Bank, he did eleven of *Joad's* twelve songs. The last night of the tour, in Paris eighteen months later, he did ten of them. (Most nights, he left out "The New Timer," perhaps because even he found its vengeful spirit unsettling; that last night, he didn't do "My Best Was Never Good Enough," either.)

He talked much more than he had on other recent tours, but this time he didn't spin improbable yarns or immerse the crowd in dramatization. He no longer played the perpetual good guy; in New Brunswick, when some

Nov. 21, 1995
The Ghost of Tom Joad is released.

Nov. 21, 1995 – State Theater, New Brunswick, NJ
Opening night of the *Ghost of Tom Joad* tour. The entire show is performed solo on the acoustic guitar.

For his debut, *Greetings From Asbury Park, N.J.*, Springsteen penned lyrics as poems, then attached melody and beat, a formula he subsequently abandoned.
"Music is important in formulating characters," he says. "You set a certain rhythm, and it's the rhythm of the man you're singing about."
Creating the vivid characters and despairing yarns on *The Ghost of Tom Joad* was "more like screen writing or short-story writing," he

Nov. 27, 1995 – NBC Studios, Burbank, CA
Bruce appears on *The Tonight Show* for the first time and plays "The Ghost of Tom Joad."

Mar. 25, 1996 — Dorothy Chandler Pavillion, Los Angeles, CA
Bruce performs "Dead Man Walkin,'" which is up for an Academy Award for Best Song but does not win.

Apr. 16, 1996 — Royal Albert Hall, London
The song "Pilgrim in the Temple of Love" is played for the first time.

Apr. 22, 1996 — Royal Albert Hall, London
First ever known performance of "The Angel" from *Greetings From Asbury Park, N.J.*

folks called out requests, he snapped back, "What do I look like—a jukebox?" And he kept up that attitude. More often, he was wryly reflective. Introducing "Dry Lightning," he remarked, "This is a song about one of those relationships where you can't seem to get it right. I had one for about, *mmm*, thirty-five years with different women. But it was the same one. It was really with myself. . . ." He termed "Born in the U.S.A." the most misunderstood song since "Louie Louie," but noted that "the singer gets the last word," before singing his blues version, with the notes of triumph all peeled away to leave just bruises and a broken heart showing. He went into some detail about conditions for the poor, especially the migrant poor, as he sat on a stool to sing the trilogy of *Joad* songs that featured stories about them and the people who chased them down: "Sinaloa Cowboys" (with the "hy-dree-at-tic acid"), "The Line," and "Balboa Park." Before "Youngstown," he often discussed the book that inspired it, *Journey to Nowhere*, by writer Dale Maharidge and photographer Michael Williamson, but he always ended by remembering "the men and the women who built this country, who built the buildings that we live in and the bridges that we cross, who gave their sons and their daughters to the wars that we fought, and who were later deemed expendable."

The details of these raps varied from night to night, but mostly, it was the same monologue—but clear and for the most part, concise. You can't take Freehold out of the boy, he said, in one way or another. He lived in that bourgeois house in the Hollywood Hills—actually now that the kids were in school, Bruce and Patti were living in a bourgeois house in the New Jersey suburbs—but his heart and, more important, his allegiance, still belonged to the people and places he'd grown up with. He proved this decisively on the *Joad* tour, doing shows in Asbury Park to benefit local charities and even one at Freehold's St. Rose of Lima Church, where he'd been educated and brutalized by the nuns.

The connection to the early part of his career was also clear. The theme remained "growin' up." In that sense the most beautiful and telling of the raps was the one that preceded "Spare Parts," a *Tunnel of Love* song about an unwed mother who fails to drown her baby.

"I think when you're young," he'd say, "you always feel like you can change the world in some fashion. I remember when I first picked up the guitar and got in a band, I said, 'Man, if I could just write the right song or if I could hit the right chord, you know. . . .' And then the world bit by bit hits you in the face, and then you get to a place, I think, where in some ways, you've got that uphill battle against cynicism.

"This is a song about somebody who does change the world. I guess it's sort of like somebody that takes part in a real-life miracle, where on a given moment on a given day there's a decision made not to add to the violence or

Sept. 19, 1996 – Performing Arts Center, Providence, RI

A new song, "There Will Never Be Any Other for Me but You," is played for the first time.

Sept. 24, 1996 – Miller Auditorium, Kalamazoo, MI

Bruce writes a song called "In Michigan" specifically for the show and performs it live.

Sept. 29, 1996 – Woody Guthrie Benefit / Severance Hall, Cleveland, OH

Bruce performs with Joe Ely, Arlo Guthrie, and Pete Seeger at this benefit performance for the Woody Guthrie Foundation and Archives. Material from this show is released in 2000 on *Til We Outnumber 'Em: The Songs of Woody Guthrie* (Righteous Babe Records).

brutality that exists in the world. And in doing so, how someone can change themselves and, and maybe in that way, maybe that's the only way you can change the world. . . . Well, this is about a woman that takes that step."

The *Joad* tour was a singular rock star's way of trying to make just such a maneuver, to make sure his music still mattered and that his self remained an honest version of the one he'd set out to create. In that respect, he could have sung "Born to Run" and made it fit. But he never did. This tour did not concern itself much with innocence. The last song, every night on the first leg, the initial set of dates in America, was always the one that ended "For you, my best was never good enough."

CHANGES CAME. BRUCE STILL insisted on quiet, he could still be abrupt, sometimes even a little rude with those who shouted out requests and cries of devotion between songs—his most withering riposte to "I love you" being, "But you don't really *know* me," keeping his distance in a way he rejected before this.

The music couldn't change that much, given not only the unwieldy songs of *Joad* but also the limited instrumental palette he allowed himself: just the voice, the guitars (a line of black Takamines displayed at the back of the stage in their many tunings), the harmonicas (in their many keys),

and the occasional keyboard accents contributed by Buell from offstage. He scrambled the set order—around the time he played the Woody Guthrie tribute concert at the Rock and Roll Hall of Fame in Cleveland, he opened with Woody's "Tom Joad" for a spell; later he tried out "The River" in that spot. He added some songs, including less likely ones as he gained confidence, so that by the time he played the Asbury shows in November 1996, he could do "Spirit in the Night," "Racing in the Street," and "Rosalita" and have them (sort of) fit.

In "The Promised Land," among his hoariest rock anthems, Bruce found a superb vehicle for extending the musicality of the one-man acoustic show. Not only did he innovate the yodel at the end, but he also began toying with how to play the song on guitar. By the end, he turned the Takamine into a tuned drum, slapping and pounding its hollow body much more than he picked or strummed its strings. This left his reedy but always passionate voice close to unaccompanied, which drained the songs of their bravado and lent them the spirit of true courage.

He could drop "My Best Was Never Good Enough" from the end now. Not only had he made his point, however obliquely, he also had discovered a dramatic ending that required no comment—this version of "The Promised Land" broke through into a new kind of freedom, solitary because it had been won that way, but not disconnected.

Oct. 27, 1996 – Anti-Proposition 209 Rally, Los Angeles, CA
Bruce performs "The Promised Land" and "No Surrender" at this televised rally to defeat Proposition 209, an anti–affirmative action bill. The bill passes.

Nov. 8, 1996 – St. Rose of Lima School, Freehold, NJ
Bruce plays the auditorium of his childhood alma mater and debuts a song he writes for the occasion, "Freehold."

BRUCE SPRINGSTEEN
SOLO ACOUSTIC TOU
PARAMOUNT THEATRE
ASBURY PARK,NJ
SUN NOV 24, 1996 8:0

BUT WHILE BRUCE SPRINGSTEEN could make the morality of the show look that easy, he could never stand to keep it that simple.

So he also introduced a few new songs into the mix. At the tour's official opening show, at the Wiltern Theater in Los Angeles, he hauled out "It's the Little Things That Count," a song of seduction (and one of the several since then where the protagonist is a goner as soon as his lover's tongue slips into his mouth). But that was the only one he came up with that felt at all in keeping with his newfound maturity.

On the other hand, several of the others were quite adult, the exception being "In Michigan," which he came up with in Detroit one night to deal with the fact that every time he sang "Highway Patrolman," a very sad song, Michigan chauvinists would cheer at the line that names a road after the state.

"So," he said, "because I'm sitting backstage with nothing to do before I come out here, these are the thoughts that are running over in my mind: Jesus, a kid wanted to hear 'Highway Patrolman,' but when I sing 'Highway Patrolman,' the word 'Michigan' is gonna come up, and when the word 'Michigan' comes up, *somebody*, I don't know who, is gonna shout, either filled with local pride or just because, for some reason, that's the strange thing that people do when they hear the name of their home state. But the thing is, you don't do it at home, you don't sit in front of the TV and every time you hear the word 'Michigan,' jump out of the couch and go 'Woo!' I don't do it when I hear the words 'The great state of New Jersey.'

"But then I got to thinking, as I must, because I'm sitting back there with nothing to do for two hours before I come out, I'm thinking, wait a minute, instead of being worried that 'Michigan' is gonna inspire applause, what I should be doing is I should be thinking that's where the money is, the money is in writing songs with people's hometowns in 'em. Now, it really doesn't matter what you say in the song at all as long as their hometown comes up regularly.

"And so, because I'm sitting back there for two hours with nothing to do before I come out here, in about the last ten minutes before I hit the stage, I said, 'I'm gonna write one of these suckers right now.' And I do have to tell you it's one of the greatest songs I've ever written—gonna make 'em forget all about that 'Born in the U.S.A.' bullshit, this is the one." He did point out, when he finished singing the silly thing—which begins, "Well, my mother rolled over and died in Michigan / My dog got hit by a truck and I cried in Michigan / I got drunk and puked my guts in Michigan"—that "the last word to this song will be 'Ohio' tomorrow night."

Nov. 13, 1996 – Landmark Theater, Syracuse, NY
"The Hitter" is played for the first time.

Dec. 2, 1996 – Sunrise Auditorium, Miami, FL
Dion guests on "If I Should Fall Behind."

Feb. 26, 1997 – Grammy Awards Broadcast / Madison Square Garden, New York, NY
Bruce performs "The Ghost of Tom Joad." The album wins the award for Best Contemporary Folk Album.

Those idle hours backstage must have dragged heavy on many a night, because a series of these songs emerged—well, a couple more, anyway. There was "Sell It and They Will Come," a memorable social commentary on the phenomenon of late-night telemarketing programs, featuring the "abacycle," the Evel Knievel stimulator that "removes all pain from your life," haircuts performed with vacuum cleaners, Dionne Warwick and her psychic friends, Tony Little, "America's personal trainer," and Bruce's own T-shirts for sale outside in the lobby. Once he even sang "Sell It" in Germany, to some effect, since, apparently, German television was also infested with such gimcrack nonsense.

There was "There Will Never Be Any Other for Me But You," which featured Prince Charles's desire to become his beloved's tampon, the latest of the many loves of Elizabeth Taylor, Elvis and Priscilla, Jim Bakker and Tammy Faye, the Trumps, all described as "a love that's hard / Like a pitbull on your ass, in a very small backyard."

This was what maturity had wrought? Well, at least it was an adult response to boredom. Mature content.

For "Pilgrim in the Temple of Love," almost certainly the most outrageous song Bruce Springsteen will ever write and beyond any shred of doubt the most ludicrous he has written and performed before an audience for money, I harbor within my vast resources of rationalizations not a single excuse.

It's a classic shaggy-dog story. On Christmas Eve, in a strip joint parking lot, Bruce espies in the car parked next to his a man in a Santa suit receiving a blow job. Inside the bar, he's chatting with a stripper—about her kid and the lames she dances for—when Santa stumbles in. The bartender knows him well enough to take the vodka off the shelf without a word; Santa knows the bar well enough to ask if his wife has called.

Bruce asks Santa how the kids are this year. Santa offers in return "a merry fuck you." The owner greets Bruce saying he's never had "a real superstar in this place." The superstar leaves not long after, Santa not far behind.

Mister Claus pukes on the hood of a car, Springsteen hands him a handkerchief and pulls out onto the highway (classic Springsteen imagery!). As Bruce rolls toward home, where there are toys to assemble, he sees . . . well, you've heard ten thousand variations of this, you know what he sees, and you pretty much know what he hears.

Backstage, it might have been boring. Out front—from time to time—it could get to be a laugh riot. Or as someone should have leaned over to me and said, "Toto, I don't think we're in 'Jungleland' anymore."

IT'S ALL ABOUT BALANCE, this maturity thing. Without "Pilgrim in the Temple of Love" or something like it (say,

Mar. 8, 1997 – Tradewinds, Sea Bright, NJ
Bruce plays five songs with Jakob Dylan's band the Wallflowers.

May 5, 1997 – Polar Music Prize Ceremonies, Stockholm, Sweden
Bruce is awarded the prestigious Polar Music Prize from the Royal Swedish Academy of Music. His Majesty King Carl XVI Gustaf of Sweden presents the award at a gala ceremony that is televised live in Sweden. Bruce performs "The Ghost of Tom Joad" and "Thunder Road."

May 26, 1997 – Palais des Congrés, Paris, France
Final show of the *Ghost of Tom Joad* tour.

Count Basie Theater, Red Bank, New Jersey, 1995

the introduction to "Red Headed Woman," a testimonial to the virtues and maritally restorative powers of cunnilingus), the *Joad* show wasn't a drag—but it wasn't complete, either. Bruce had never been afraid of the sentimental, now he wasn't even afraid of being vulgar. That is by my measure a liberation in itself.

But for the most part, the *Joad* show was a very serious enterprise, as well it should have been. Lou Cohan, a long-time Springsteen fan, editor of an early fanzine, and a veteran high school teacher in South Gate, a Chicano part of Los Angeles, gave the album a listen and told me, "That's [Governor] Pete Wilson's California he's singing about." I told this to Bruce, who responded, "Of course. I lived there."

After he played a benefit for the Steinbeck Library in San Jose, he went to Los Angeles on his day off and played at a rally urging the defeat of the anti-immigrant Proposition 209. The proposition, a model of racist xenophobia and a harbinger of worse to come after 9/11, passed, but that's beside the point.

Bruce joked often between songs on the *Joad* tour about his wealth and his do-gooder image. But he also took his role in society seriously, the more so now that the lives of his own children were at stake—as the lives of all children are, so long as some children are treated as without value. "We've decided, I guess, that some Americans are expendable and that their lives and their dreams are simply the price of doing business," Bruce would say, introducing "Murder Incorporated."

The Ghost of Tom Joad was Springsteen's statement—quiet but firm—that fame and wealth had changed him. In some ways, the process had transformed him. The romantic innocence of "Incident on 57th Street" seemed so far away now.

In other ways, and *Joad* was also about this, fame and money didn't touch him.

Some would say that his very wealth made his allegiances incongruous or even invalid. But a 1040 form isn't a loyalty oath. He knew exactly what the stakes were and he knew how thin the margin was. He said so often in another way he had of introducing "Youngstown."

"I think you spend your life and learn a craft, it's hard to do . . . and somebody decides you're obsolete and . . . you know, people who built the infrastructure of the country itself, the highways, the buildings, the bridges that we cross, steel that was shipped out here for Oakland Bridge, you got over here. What would you do, what would I . . . ," he said, and he wasn't just musing, he was offering up the product of his seeking. "I just sat there and said, 'What would I do if I couldn't . . . if I came home and I couldn't take care of my kids and, and . . . and I couldn't make sure that they would be healthy and that they would be safe. . . .'"

So Bruce Springsteen's pilgrimage through adulthood—from the strip mines to the strip joints—continued.

Anaheim, California, 2000

Chapter Eleven

Rebirth and Renewal

" 'Cross this river to the other side"

INVENTED A WHOLE BUNCH of reasons for avoiding the first few concerts on 1999's Bruce Springsteen and the E Street Band reunion tour. They opened in Europe, for one thing. I had work to do, and covering Bruce Springsteen wasn't really my work anymore. There were probably a couple more.

Really, the idea of the tour made me as nervous as a spurned lover about to meet his darling once again. What if they weren't as great as I remembered? What if this turned out to be another run-of-the-mill rock-band reunion, guys going through the motions to cash in or try to recapture a little of the old glory. They only had one new song—unless you counted the four CDs of vault material that made up the box set *Tracks*, issued in November 1998.

Irrational worries and I knew it. They'd come together in 1995 to make some new tracks for *Greatest Hits*, and even played a full set while making a video for one of its "new" tracks, "Murder Incorporated" (actually from the *River* sessions). That show was splendid, and although "Murder" was the only new song they did, they played a wonderful array of their standard repertoire while the cameras set up, from "Spirit in the Night" to "Ramrod" to "This Hard Land."

More recently, I'd seen the band play at Bruce's Rock and Roll Hall of Fame induction in March and, in that four-song set, they sounded fantastic. But I didn't go to either of the rehearsal shows they played in Asbury Park later that month, nor any during the opening week of the tour, although it started in Barcelona, where I loved the Springsteen fans. *Tracks* included a bunch of songs that ranked with my Springsteen favorites—if they played "Loose Ends," a dream would be realized. (They did and it was, though not often enough—how greedy is *that?*) There were also some stray songs— "Streets of Philadelphia," the tracks from *Greatest Hits* and the *Blood Brothers* video that went with it. But to carry a whole tour on the strength of even Bruce's 150 or so oldies and one new song, no matter how great "Land of Hope and Dreams" was? From those materials, could even Bruce Springsteen make an exciting and creative show?

So, I waited 'til ten days into the tour and flew to meet my wife and the rest of Bruce's posse in Milan.

The next afternoon I walked into the end of sound check in Milan's Forum and heard "Lion's Den" and "Don't Look Back," a pair of *River*-era rockers from *Tracks*, and a "Nebraska" that picked up where the band had left off.

Then Roy Bittan started to play something familiar. At first I thought "Thunder Road," then "Racing in the Streets." Then I realized it was the old monster itself, "Jungleland." (Roy told me later that the introductions to a few of the songs from that period are so similar that he sometimes wonders if he's playing the right one.)

The music washed not so much over me as into me, and tears welled in my eyes. I remembered being tired of "Jungleland" when Bruce played it in every show, that I was glad when he more-or-less dropped it from his set. And I wondered how jaded my heart had become, to feel that way about this glorious noise.

What could I have been thinking to wait so long?

Then the sound check ended with "Trouble River," a song from *Tracks* where the singer wakes from a dream in which "all I seen was smiling faces staring back at me," and the problem didn't strike me as quite so individual anymore.

FOR THE ACTUAL SHOW, I sat with two Sony executives at the opposite end from the stage. There was no seating on the floor, and the fans down there crowded to the stage, leaving a large empty space between us and them.

Maybe that was why it felt as if the show took a few songs to kick in, but the impression was pretty subjective—I was looking for what was different about this show, how things had changed or stayed the same. Bruce opened with a *River*-period song from *Tracks*, "My Love Will Not Let You Down," which struck me as a curiosity, then "The Promised Land," "Two Hearts," and "Prove It All Night." It might have been 1980.

Then they hit "Darkness on the Edge of Town," and I got it. The band did exactly what it had always

"I'm so glad to be in your lovely city of Milano tonight. But we're not here on a vacation tonight, we're here with a message."
—BS

done—better. Although the details weren't immediately evident in that first instant, the picture came into focus: The E Street Band had grown. Everybody played better, including Steven Van Zandt, who'd ended his prodigal's sabbatical. Bruce had grown as a singer, too, so that he could invest a twenty-year-old song like "Darkness" with new shades of emotion, find nuances in its story that had lain untapped. It took a while to hear it, *especially* if you were looking for differences, because the difference was not in the arrangements or the style, the difference was in the substance. They did the same things. Pretty much exactly the same things. They did them better. That was the story of the reunion tour.

By the time they were halfway through "The River," I got up and headed down into the crowd—the Sony executives came with me. (They might have stayed in their seats those last couple of songs—one of which was the off-your-ass "Rendezvous"—so as not to offend a foreigner too dumb to relocate.) Just as I arrived at the pack before the stage, the band erupted into the first full-band "Youngstown" I'd ever heard—all the implications of the album arrangement turned into a hard-rock explosion, its edge almost metallic. They rocked relentlessly for the next hour, through "Youngstown," "Murder Incorporated," "Badlands"—with the invariably sweet harmonies of thousands of Italians on the wordless bridge— "Darlington County," "Tenth Avenue Freeze-Out" (incorporating the Curtis Mayfield gospel-soul number, "It's All Right"), with Bruce slowing the pace for the most extended, funny, and potent preacher parody I'd ever heard him do, a sermon that witnessed the morality of the show in the most explicit, hilarious, and, no doubt to the Italians, barely comprehensible terms. Then, not letting up, "Where the Bands Are," another of those lost *River*-era rockers, and "Working on the Highway," before finally slowing for "The Ghost of Tom Joad." And then, before the encores, "Born in the U.S.A.," "Jungleland," a warhorse that still had its legs, and as a finale, "Light of Day," with preaching that made what Bruce did in "Tenth Avenue" sound tame.

"I'm so glad to be here in your lovely city of Milano tonight," he declaimed in a hoarse, rasping half-shout. He spoke without a break, as if in one long sentence, with pauses for gulps of air that might have been greeted, in an actual service, by "amen" but here were just occasions for whoops and stamping. "But we're not here on a vacation tonight, we're here with a purpose, we've come a long, long journey and we're here with a message. That's right! And I've come a long, long way to impart this message." Here, he went through the towns he'd been to, the miles he'd traveled, as if for the very first time.

He slowed the tempo, lowered his volume just a trifle for what came next, then accelerated bit by bit as he reached his main point.

"I know that you're feeling downhearted . . . and I know, I *know* that you've been dispossessed, I know that you're feeling dispirited . . . I know you've been analyzed, downsized, stigmatized, retro-

A crowd gathers outside a rehearsal for the reunion tour at Convention Hall, 1999

Sept. 4, 1997 – MTV Video Music Awards / Radio City Music Hall, New York, NY

Bruce performs "One Headlight" with the Wallflowers, who are nominated for Best Group Video.

Dec. 7, 1997 – Kennedy Center Awards / John F. Kennedy Center for the Performing Arts, Washington, D.C.

Bruce performs "The Times They Are A-Changin'" at the Kennedy Center Awards, where Bob Dylan is being honored.

Jan. 30, 1998 – Sgt. Patrick King Benefit / Count Basie Theater, Red Bank, NJ

At this concert to raise money for the family of slain Long Branch police officer Sgt. Patrick King, Bruce performs along with Jon Bon Jovi, Southside Johnny, Little Steven, Max Weinberg, and Patti Scialfa.

Apr. 4, 1998 – Bay Street Theater, Sag Harbor, NY

Bruce performs "Oh What a Beautiful Morning" and "The Ghost of Tom Joad" at this performance to dedicate the Elaine Steinbeck Stage at the Bay Street Theater.

May 21, 1998 – *Where It's At: The State of the Union*

Bruce and Danny perform "The Ghost of Tom Joad" and "Across the Border" on this TV special produced by *Rolling Stone.*

Nov. 6, 1998

Tracks, a four-CD box set, is released.

psychedelicized." Max punctuated each of these. Now Bruce was back to his full head of steam. "And I wanna tell you that I'm here tonight, I'm here tonight, I'm here tonight to resuscitate you, to reeducate you, to regenerate you, to reconfiscate you, to reindoctrinate you, to rededicate you, to *reliberate* you with the power! With the promise! The majesty! The mystery!" He took a deep breath and uttered the rest in a roar. "THE MINISTRY OF ROCK AND ROLL!"

And, he slowed it again. "Now I want to tell you that I cannot, I *can*not, I *cannot* promise you life everlasting. . . . But I can promise you life . . ."—a split second's pause that seemed like an eon, then he bellowed, as loud as I've ever heard him bellow anything—"RIGHT NOW!!!"

It was a tour de force of what the band could do. They'd been up there, by then, way over ninety minutes— sixteen songs, about a dozen of them torridly paced. No intermission, just straight through from one to the next to the next. Except during "Tenth Avenue," Bruce didn't say much—talking would have disrupted the groove and anyway, this music spoke for itself if any rock and roll ever did. They rocked without respite, they showed neither themselves nor the crowd any mercy. Not only that, they fit together better than ever.

THE ENCORES KICKED OFF with "Streets of Philadelphia," which played it like it had been intended for them. Then more warhorses: "Hungry Heart," "Born to Run," "Thunder Road" complete with Bruce's climactic slide across the stage on his knees while playing the guitar. Then "If I Should Fall Behind," another that fit the E Streeters like they'd been waiting for it.

As Bruce stepped to the microphone for the next song, Susan Duncan-Smith, our close friend who runs Sony Music's Rome office, found me in the crowd and said, "We're leaving straight after the show, so Barbara wants you to come to the van now." It was either that or spend the next hour or two waiting for a lift, so I went.

But I dragged my heels, because Bruce was speaking. I went over toward the right side of the stage past security, then stopped.

"We thank you for the twenty-five years of support of our music," he said. "So these are sort of a special series of concerts, they're sort of a rebirth and a rededication of our band and our commitment to serve you. This is . . . 'Land of Hope and Dreams.'"

The music started—the drums and then a guitar lick that called a rock and roll believer to the altar. Danny's organ went into the mix, and then the rest of the band. "*Let's go!*" Bruce shouted.

Dec. 10, 1998 – Paris Concert for Amnesty International / Omni Palace, Bercy, Paris, France
Bruce appears with Peter Gabriel, Radiohead, Tracy Chapman, Youssou N'Dour, and others at this Amnesty International concert in Paris. He performs "Get Up, Stand Up" with Gabriel, Chapman, and N'Dour, followed by four more songs, two of which are included on the DVD of this show released in 1999.

Feb. 26, 1999 – *Late Night With Conan O'Brien*, NBC Television Studios, New York, NY
Bruce appears with the Max Weinberg 7 on Max's last appearance on the show before tour rehearsals for the reunion tour, due to begin in March. They perform "Working on the Highway."

Mar. 16, 1999 – Rock and Roll Hall of Fame Inductions / Waldorf Astoria, New York, NY
Bruce is inducted into the Rock and Roll Hall of Fame. The E Street Band join him onstage for four songs. Later in the evening, there is an all-star jam session with Bruce, Bono, Billy Joel, and Paul McCartney, among others.

The van was waiting. I turned to go. Jon Landau and Barbara stopped me. "You need to hear this," my friends said and let me linger.

I listened, first with thanks, then with awe.

I grew up listening to soul music right alongside rock and roll, and the truest description of what was going on then came from the mouth of my brother Rob Tyner of the MC5. "We all really wanted to sing like soul singers." Which meant, it turned out, bringing church into the mix, too. To bring all that music together, for me, that was the rock and roll grail. It was the revolution and it was the healing, too.

Here was my dream, then. A song patently based on "This Train Is Bound for Glory," though more likely Sister Rosetta Tharpe's version than Woody Guthrie's rendition. You could hear in it Curtis Mayfield, Sam Cooke, but also the Rolling Stones, Bob Dylan, and everybody else who'd tried to shoulder some of that burden.

Steven Van Zandt's guitar rang out like a mandolin, Bruce and Nils answered him with rock and roll chords, Max rifled off snare shots, Patti's harmonies swelled above the rest, Garry's bass throbbed beneath. Danny and Roy carried the weight down in the mix. The Big Man stepped up for his solo and blasted it out—he'd been to church, all right.

I need your passports!!

Please bring them to the venue tomorrow, Friday.

I need your passports!!

You have not read this far without knowing that song, or its lyrics, its promise not just of faithfulness to an ideal—to a morality—but to reach out to everybody and to make it, make it through whatever comes, as long as everybody sticks together and keeps it honest, keeps it as real as we know how. Then "dreams will not be thwarted . . . faith will be rewarded." And, the song asked (asked me, even if it doesn't ask you), if not, what are we here for?

Rock and roll is the language of individualism, but it is also the language of the human bond, the story of each struggle and the realization that all those struggles are one. At moments like those, it is both sides of that equation at once. When the music gets to that place, we have come to the land of hope and dreams, where all of us—saint and sinner, whore and gambler, lost souls—come together. It is just as James Baldwin wrote in "Sonny's Blues": "For, while the tale of how we suffer, and how we are delighted, and how we may triumph is never new, it always must be heard. There isn't any other tale to tell, it's the only light we've got in all this darkness."

One new song. The oldest of them all.

Apr. 9, 1999 – Palau Sant Jordi, Barcelona, Spain
The reunion tour starts in Barcelona.

Apr. 24, 1999 – Stadthalle, Vienna, Austria
This show features the one-time performance of "Dollhouse."

May 21, 1999 – Earls Court, London, England
Bruce performs "Meeting Across the River" during this show for the first time since the end of the *River* tour on Jan. 1, 1979.

Convention Hall, Asbury Park, New Jersey, September 1999

IT ALL SHOULD HAVE been like that—not necessarily my little epiphanies beside the stage, nobody gets those every time out—but so smooth, so much love, so much camaraderie, so much great music.

For the most part it was. They'd started the tour in Europe because, quite simply, Bruce had been for the last several tours a bigger act overseas than at home. His surest sellouts were in Spain, Italy, and Scandinavia—and New Jersey, of course.

There was another thing, and it made the difference in Milan. The audiences in Europe—especially in the places where Bruce was most popular—knew how to give him rapt attention, dead silence when it was required, and the most fervent call and response when the moment was ripe for that.

Convention Hall, Asbury Park, New Jersey,
September 1999

It was different in the States, especially in New Jersey, New York, and Philadelphia. Demand in New Jersey remained great enough to sell out fifteen nights at the Meadowlands (the equivalent of four shows at Giants Stadium next door). With days off and arena scheduling conflicts, it took literally a month to get through those shows. They did another six nights in Philly.

I tried not to catch myself comparing the American shows to the ones in Europe, but really, it couldn't be helped. When Bruce sang quieter songs in the States, the crowd's restlessness was audible and visible—those fans simply didn't have much patience for that kind of listening. You could feel the strain when he did unfamiliar songs, too. Although in Philly, Bruce ad-libbed "I wanna be where the fans are" at the end of "Where the Bands Are" (another of the lost gems from *Tracks*), it wasn't always so clear that the crowds were willing to be where he was. To me, it always seemed like most of his listeners in American arenas wanted to hear just the warhorses—you couldn't say hits, they'd have been as satisfied with an album track like "Racing in the Streets" as with a hit like "Brilliant Disguise," much more satisfied with "Racing" than, say, "Cover Me," with its disco tang. You could feel them tugging Bruce toward their version of him, not quite willing to give up the romantic innocent or the kid dis-

Bruce and Jon, 1999

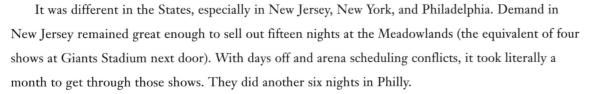

**June 2, 1999 – Bercy,
Paris, France**
Elliot Murphy joins Bruce for "Hungry
Heart."

**July 15, 1999 – Continental Airlines Arena,
East Rutherford, NJ**
"Freehold" is performed at the first of a record fifteen sold-out
shows at the Meadowlands.

Bruce
Springsteen
& the E Street
Band
01

covering his adulthood for the grown-up guy who wanted —needed—to throw some songs about the pleasures of domesticity into the mix.

So that took the edge off it a little bit. But just a little.

And in Boston, where Bruce did five nights in '99, there was an added edge—it was the one place in America where some parts of the show were better than even the best European Springsteen concerts, because the crowd and the artist spoke the same cultural language, the evangelical parodies shot home. But mainly, Boston became the best place in the United States to see Bruce Springsteen because the audience there was the most enthusiastic, reveling in whatever he gave them, and deafeningly, riotously happy when what he gave was what they'd hoped for.

EVERY TOUR, IT SEEMED, one song crystallized the band's playing—"Kitty's Back" served that function for the early E Street lineups, "Prove It All Night" held the place for a while, at one point "She's the One" made an unlikely move to center stage. On this tour, "Youngstown" filled that role. It wasn't the song that set the theme; it was the thermostat that reported how well and how intensely the band played.

Even on the *Joad* album, "Youngstown" smoldered with electric guitar energy—it was the one track there that cried for a band. Now, it kicked off with a suggestion of Celtic bagpipes in the intro, the grainiest vocal in the show, and climaxed with a guitar extravaganza after the song's protagonist prays to be sent to hell—riffs breaking like waves and ending in sheer feedback thunderation, a thick stew of sound.

Steven Van Zandt's return had a lot to do with it. He brought with him his very Anglophile, extremely sixties, slightly psychedelic sensibility, which helped create a sound more massive in every way. Steven's guitar might have added clutter, but his tone was different than either Bruce or Nils, a little less open and determined—a stubborn sound that knew its own mind and didn't bend much at the knees. He loved the Stones, but he always sounded more like Pete Townshend to me.

With three nasty guitars, two keyboards, Max playing as mightily as he ever had, Garry Tallent anchoring the

Aug. 1, 1999 – Continental Airlines Arena, East Rutherford, NJ
"Backstreets" opens the show for the first time ever.

Aug. 7, 1999 – Continental Airlines Arena, East Rutherford, NJ
"Don't Look Back" is included in tonight's set, last played in Boston in 1977.

Bruce Springsteen & the E Street Band

08

Aug. 9, 1999 – Continental Airlines Arena, East Rutherford, NJ
"Frankie" is played during this show for the first time since April 1976.

enterprise, five voices, the E Street ensemble could roll like a tank division when it wanted to. On "Youngstown" and to a lesser extent "Murder Incorporated," "Darkness," "Prove It All Night," and "Atlantic City," it wanted to send a message of the danger in power, and it succeeded.

None of those songs came from *Tracks*, and surprisingly little of that album's music made the regular setlists—on the *Live in New York City* album, released from the shows at the very end of the tour, only the night's opening song, "My Love Will Not Let You Down," and one bonus track, "Don't Look Back," came from the box set. Only "Land of Hope and Dreams" and "Murder Incorporated" joined the core group of songs accurately reflected by that album's lineup. The eleven main songs there included three from *The River*, two each from *Darkness* and *Nebraska*, one each from *Joad* and *Born to Run*, and nothing at all from *Tunnel of Love*, *Human Touch*, *Lucky Town*, or the two pre–*Born to Run* albums.

That's not quite fair to the sets, which more often included two dozen songs (and would have extended the *New York City* set to three or four discs). But a comparison of the album to the last two shows (of ten, a house record) at Madison Square Garden, from June 29 and July 1, 2000, doesn't change the ratios much. On the 29th, Bruce played four songs from *Born to Run*, three each from *Darkness* and *The River*, two of the previously unreleased tracks from *Greatest Hits* and *Tracks*. On the last night, one of the most

expansive shows he ever played, the distribution was the same except that there was also a second *Nebraska* number, and he played a song from *Greetings*. The distribution accurately characterizes the tour—it was a standard repertoire tour, and given the tendency of rock bands to beat such material to death, that makes the vitality of the music all the more impressive.

Band rehearsal, Asbury Park, New Jersey, 1999

The catch is that "Land of Hope and Dreams" wasn't any longer the only new song in the set. On the last night, he played four unrecorded songs: "Code of Silence," which he cowrote with his friend Joe Grushecky, opened the show, which also included "Further on Up the Road," which he'd debuted the week before the Garden series began, in Atlanta, and "Land of Hope and Dreams," which had ended every show on the tour.

THE FOURTH NEW SONG was "American Skin (41 Shots)." The lyric was based on the shooting by New York City police of an unarmed African man, Amadou Diallo. Diallo was gunned down in his Bronx apartment building vestibule by four members of the Street Crime Unit, a confrontational plainclothes squad. The officers claimed to have mistaken the wallet Diallo held for a gun.

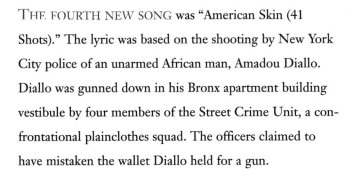

Aug. 11, 1999 – Continental Airlines Arena, East Rutherford, NJ
Tonight the set includes "New York City Serenade," which has not been played since August 1975 at the Allen Theater in Cleveland.

Aug. 27, 1999 – Fleet Center, Boston, MA
Peter Wolf joins the band onstage for "Raise Your Hand" during the encores.

Sept. 3, 1999 – MCI Center, Washington, DC
Bonnie Raitt, Bruce Hornsby, Mary Chapin Carpenter, and Shawn Colvin join the band onstage for "Hungry Heart" and "Red Headed Woman."

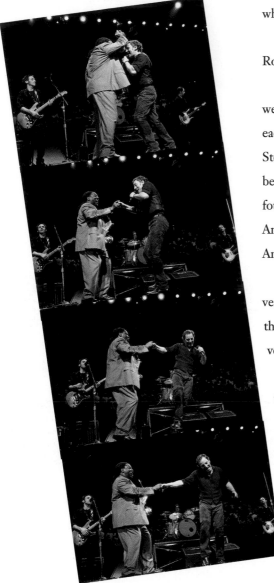

Diallo was hit by nineteen of the forty-one bullets the police fired. A public frenzy ensued and was never adequately resolved, especially when the trial was moved from the majority black Bronx to majority white upstate Albany and the officers were acquitted of all charges.

Bruce premiered "American Skin" in the same Atlanta show in which he did "Further on Up the Road." He didn't say a word of introduction.

He didn't need to. He never presented a song more dramatically than "American Skin." The stage went black. A pinpoint spot hit the mic at center stage. Against a brooding synth riff and brushed drums, each of the singing members of the E Street Band stepped forward and sang "forty-one shots." Patti, Nils, Steven with his voice cracking, Clarence sounding totally outside his usual bravado, somewhere between bewildered and frightened, then Bruce leaning in amongst them as they sang it as a chorus, over and over, four more times. Then Bruce asked for quiet, and he began to tell his version of what had become an American legend: "It ain't no secret, no secret my friend / You can get killed just for living in your American skin."

In light of the response from people who *had never heard the song*, it's worth pointing out that the first verse told the story from the cop's point of view—and very sympathetically, with the cop leaning down to the shattered man, praying he'd live. (Diallo, hit so many times, must have been dead when he hit the vestibule floor.)

It's a haunting song, especially the second verse, where a black mother makes her son promise never to challenge the police. The song tackled the reality of race, the truth that all of us fear one another and that it gets some of us killed, and that it's people with the "wrong" skin who do almost all of the dying.

Bruce Springsteen took the cops at their word: The Diallo shooting had been a horrible mistake. He had his eye on other questions, the kind that didn't get asked in the media furor over the case, with reporting polarized on the issue of the cops' honesty. His lyrics implied that the more important matter was why the cops were there, armed with an attitude.

A transcription of the lyrics immediately hit the Internet. The transcription popped up in the *New York Post*, the flagship of Rupert Murdoch's reactionary media empire (which had just spawned Fox News).

Oct. 15, 1999 – America West Arena, Phoenix, AZ
Phoenix resident Sam Moore (of Sam and Dave) joins Bruce for "Soul Man."

Feb. 28, 2000 – Bryce Jordan Center, Penn State University, PA
First show after a three-month hiatus. The opening song is "Lion's Den" in honor of the Penn State Nittany Lions.

Anaheim, California, 2000

The city's law 'n' order mayor, Rudolph Giuliani, and the police unions fired at Bruce without listening. They declared that, since the cops who shot Diallo had been acquitted, further public comment was out of order. This didn't reflect even an honest reading of the lyrics, which made clear Springsteen's empathy for the police as well as their victim.

A police union spokesman capped the whole controversy by calling Bruce "a floating fag" (a term that remains undefined, despite diligent research). The nonsense comment showed up the controversy for what it was: an attempt to cut off any dialogue about what had happened since Giuliani had turned the city's dark streets over to cops on "stop and search" missions.

Bruce had those ten shows at the Garden coming up, and the last thing either the cops or Giuliani wanted was such a discussion to take place. (Giuliani's administration later paid the Diallo family $3 million to settle a wrongful death lawsuit. But guilt wasn't the real issue—hiding from racism and its consequences was the issue.)

Everyone knew Bruce would sing "American Skin" at the first New York City show on June 12. That night, with Diallo's parents seated just to stage left, the Garden felt close to the edge of real violence. I was scared as hell. I don't know how Bruce or the band felt, but when your opponents are armed and angry, just singing the song takes some guts.

Bruce not only didn't back down, he opened with "Code of Silence," whose lyrics—portraying a love relationship that died because communication had suffered a total breakdown—metaphorically addressed the cops' objections. After four more songs, "American Skin" rang out. The band sang as if in mourning. Springsteen has walked the edges of despair in a lot of his songs. Here, it was impossible to see how he maintained his equilibrium, for what he skirted was the American abyss.

Confronted this time not with mere expropriation but overt official hostility, he argued back with just his voice and his band, and this gave him an indomitable dignity. He sang "American Skin" at every show he did at the Garden, and the mayor and the cops just shut up after that first night. Bruce still didn't need to say a word of introduction. Once more, the music spoke for itself. Once more, the morality of the show won out.

IF THAT HAD BEEN the climax of the reunion tour, it would have been a defeat. But it was nowhere near its climax. By July 1, "American Skin," which just about everybody called "41 Shots," had become an engrossing part of the whole show but not the main event.

The last night, the band pulled out everything it had, as it always did for a tour's conclusion—it's just that this time they had more to pull out, and maybe more to cele-

Mar. 14, 2000 – Altel Arena, Little Rock, AR
The set includes "Mary, Queen of Arkansas," which is played for the first time since March 1974.

114 A 7 COMP
LOWER SECTION 0.00
HARTFORD CIVIC CENTER
BRUCE SPRINGSTEEN
&
THE E STREET BAND
NO CAM/REC/LASER POINTERS
SUN MAY 7, 2000 7:30PM

June 4, 2000 – Philips Arena, Atlanta, GA
Live debut of "American Skin (41 Shots)."

brate, too. Not many bands come back together after a decade and make better music than they had the first time, but almost everyone who saw the show, virtually every reviewer even, thought that was exactly what Bruce Springsteen and the E Street Band had done.

Bruce pulled out some rare treats for that last night. They did "The E Street Shuffle," and made its "move on down to the scene" even more graceful than ever. Without fanfare, he did a Vietnam commentary, playing "Lost in the Flood" and "Born in the U.S.A." back to back.

After the usual brief break to cool off—he was soaked with sweat that night, all right—Bruce came back out and sat at Roy's piano. He played the opening chords of "The Promise" to cheers, and when the crowd settled, did it with an air of exhaustion that made the tragedy of self-betrayal seem even more powerful.

When he finished and walked toward his usual position in the center, he found the whole band gathered, applauding. That one, I don't think they'd rehearsed.

He played the encores that night, as on so many final nights, to exhaust himself, to get it all out 'til the next time, which was who knows when: "Ramrod," "Bobby Jean," "Born to Run," "Further on Up the Road," a full-bore "Thunder Road" 'til the sweat streamed down him. The band kept up; I don't see how, the pace was enough to weary anyone.

Then "If I Should Fall Behind," in that beautiful doo-wop arrangement. This night, you could take it less as a commitment between lovers than as a commitment between friends—bandmates, an artist and his audience, a man and the world he struggled to understand and change at least a little bit for the better.

Then he spoke. "The first night we played, I came out and we did this song, and before we started, I said I was hoping that our tour would be the rebirth and the renewal of our band and our commitment to serve you. I hope we've done that well this year, and we'll continue to try and do so."

They played it, and to my ears it sounded as glorious as ever, and it seemed like they were done. Then arose a keyboard drone. It went on for half a minute, and then the other keyboard joined in and Max tapped his cymbals on the beats. Bruce started to sing "Blood Brothers," the song he'd written to describe what happened to men who give up their comrades to cope with the rest of life, an emotionally inside-out sequel to "Tenth Avenue Freeze-Out."

When he got to the end of the second line of the last verse, he stopped singing and signaled to the band.

He began a new version of that last verse, which originally declared that he did not know how he felt at that moment. The new one said exactly the opposite. He sang every line of it with the rededication, the renewal of

June 12, 2000 – Madison Square Garden, NY
Bruce performs "American Skin (41 Shots)" on the opening night of a seven-night stand at the Garden, the last shows of the tour. The New York State Chapter of the Fraternal Order of Police denounces both Bruce and the song.

July 1, 2000 – Madison Square Garden, New York, NY
The final show of the reunion tour is filmed and will largely comprise the soon-to-be-released *Live in New York City* DVD and CD. "Lost in the Flood" is played for the first time since 1978. The show ends with an emotional rendition of "Blood Brothers."

Nov. 3, 2000 – Stone Pony, Asbury Park, NJ

Bruce joins Joe Grushecky and the Houserockers onstage after their first two songs and plays for nearly two hours.

Dec. 17, 18, 2000 – Convention Hall, Asbury Park, NJ

Bruce, Patti, Little Steven, Garry, Nils, violinist Soozie Tyrell, Southside Johnny, Bobby Bandiera, and the Max Weinberg 7 play two rollicking Christmas concerts to end a spectacular year.

Apr. 3, 2001

Live In New York City is released.

turned himself into a preacher, promising to spread "the ministry of rock 'n' roll."

He dropped to his knees, spread out his arms and worked the crowd like a gospel singer. The house lights stayed on through much of the show; Mr. Springsteen wanted the audience to join in, and wouldn't rest until it did (although he met no resistance). He was also bonded with the band, sharing a microphone with all the musicians whose instrumentals were portable, even trading vocals on a love song, "If I Should Fall Behind."

promise he'd found in this reunion. There were tears in his eyes—you could see them on the video screens at the sides of the stage.

> Now I'm out here on this road, alone on this road tonight
> Close my eyes and feel so many friends around me
> In the early evening light
> And the miles we have come, and the battles won and lost
> Are just so many roads traveled, so many rivers crossed
> And I ask God for the strength, and the faith in one another
> 'Cause it's a good night for a ride, 'cross this river to the other side
> My blood brothers

Having honored the band's devotion, and his own, he released them, freed us all to bask in the exuberance of the song's coda, let its spirit wash over us. Like a lot of Bruce Springsteen music, it was sentimental as hell. And undeniable as a baby's cry.

When it was done, he declared, "We'll be seein' ya!" and strode out of sight again for a while.

From left: Jon Landau, Garry Tallent, Roy Bittan, Steven Van Zandt, Clarence Clemons, Max Weinberg, Bruce Springsteen, Nils Lofgren, Patti Scialfa, Barbara Carr

May 27, 2001 – Stone Pony, Asbury Park, NJ

Bruce joins Southside Johnny and the Asbury Jukes onstage for a full hour at their Labor Day Concert at the Pony.

Aug. 18, 2001 – Clearwater Music Festival, Asbury Park, NJ

Bruce plays a short acoustic set at this outdoor festival.

Aug. 18, 2001 – Stone Pony, Asbury Park, NJ

Later the same day at the Clearwater Festival, Bruce joins Nils Lofgren onstage for four songs, and also plays a song with John Eddie at the same venue.

Sept. 1, 2001 – Stone Pony, Asbury Park, NJ

Clarence Clemons and his band are joined by Bruce for a four-song set.

Chapter Twelve

No Fairy-Tale Ending

"Dust on my shoes, nothing but teardrops"

N SEPTEMBER 2001, JUST AFTER two airplanes crashed into New York's World Trade Center buildings and killed three thousand people, many of them from central New Jersey, Bruce Springsteen pulled out of a parking lot at the beach in Sea Bright, near his home. A man driving by rolled down his window and shouted to him: "We need you—*now!*"

Suppose that guy had driven past thirty seconds later, after Bruce had pulled out of the lot. Suppose he'd shouted but Bruce hadn't heard him. Suppose whatever you'd like. The next time Springsteen took the stage, he'd still have been very involved in what happened on September 11, 2001, to his hometown, his native region, and his country.

It's not so much that Bruce created an image of himself as an artist who struggled mightily with the most consequential human issues. It's not that he also played the local hero, the guy who never turned his back on the people he grew up with, the rock and roll star who never forgot the way life might look from the most distant seat in the house.

The thing is, Bruce Springsteen took those roles seriously. They were—and are—his moral imperatives. He understood rock and roll as a way of describing the way the world looked. He took it to be a method of dancing in the face of disaster, a way of releasing woe, believed you could rock your bones 'til the troubles fell away, at least for an instant (which was considerably more relief than seemed possible before the backbeat began). Onstage, he bopped 'til he dropped and encouraged—nay, commanded—you to do the same, not just this time but every time.

Backstage at the Bell Center, Montreal, Canada, April 19, 2003

The day had long passed when anybody could be everybody's rock and roll hero. But for a certain group, Bruce Springsteen remained a compass and a comfort. Many were people who lived near him in Monmouth County. The 9/11 attacks devastated Monmouth, especially Rumson, the wealthy town where he lived and his kids went to school.

It wasn't that he was expected to respond to the plight of these neighbors. It was that he expected himself to respond.

ON SEPTEMBER 21, 2001, Bruce debuted a new song on a national telethon, *America: A Tribute to Heroes*. He'd played "My City of Ruins" the previous December, at his Christmas shows at Asbury Park's Convention Hall. Those shows featured Bruce accompanied by the Max Weinberg 7, the band his drummer led on Conan O'Brien's late night show; Nils Lofgren; Southside Johnny; Steven Van Zandt (now Little Steven); Patti Scialfa; Soozie Tyrell; and local guitarist and bandleader Bobby Bandiera.

The Christmas shows partly represented Bruce's love of the holiday season. He had made two famous Christmas records, both chestnuts, both recorded live: "Santa Claus Is Coming to Town," and "Merry Christmas Baby," a remodeling of Otis Redding's update of Charles Brown's original, recorded on the *River* tour.

They also represented a continuation of the concept that his success ought to give something back to the communities that supported him. The Christmas shows were a chance to make the spirit of "My Hometown" real.

But which hometown? Freehold had been gentrified into a modern and moderately prosperous little town. Asbury Park had suffered through a series of redevelopment failures that left it ever poorer, and not incidentally, ever blacker. Freehold had, outside its Hullabaloo club, pretty much rejected him. Asbury had offered the shelter and inspiration of the Upstage.

Not to mention, Freehold didn't have any concert halls. Asbury had Convention Hall—drafty, frigid, frightful with echoes, in sore need of rehabilitation and yet still standing proudly right on the shore.

Freehold had St. Rose of Lima Roman Catholic Church, where he had been christened, confirmed, failed as an altar boy, and educated up through junior high. Asbury was the hometown of his soul.

Bruce had become involved with some of Asbury's business owners and one or two government officials. He supported the local NAACP, and through them, developed an association with a black choir on the West Side, the city's black and poor neighborhood. "My City of Ruins" was a gospel song in sound and structure, and at the Christmas show, he sang it with his band accompanied by members of the choir.

Sept. 21, 2001 – *America: A Tribute to Heroes*, New York, NY

This live, nationally televised program to commemorate those who saved lives on September 11, 2001, opens with "My City of Ruins." The song is played by Bruce on acoustic guitar and harmonica, accompanied by backing vocalists Patti, Steven, Clarence, Delores Holmes (former vocalist with the Bruce Springsteen Band), and her daughter Layonne. The show is released soon after on a two-CD set and DVD.

Oct. 18, 19, 2001 – Count Basie Theater, Red Bank, NJ

These concerts are arranged as a benefit for the Alliance of Neighbors to raise money for Monmouth County families who were impacted by the events of September 11. Jon Bon Jovi, Joe Ely, Joan Jett, Sonny Burgess, and Phoebe Snow are on the bill also. Bruce joins Sonny Burgess for "Tiger Rose," which he had written for Burgess's record; Joe Ely for "All Just to Get to You"; Joan Jett for "Light of Day" (a Springsteen song she had recorded); and he also plays his own five-song set.

In Asbury Park, "My City of Ruins" spoke to its immediate surroundings in the devastated city. "Young men on the corner / Like scattered leaves / The boarded up windows / The empty streets" described what one saw driving into Asbury on the West Side. Springsteen performed it as a prayer for the restoration of the city and the lives in it—that's the meaning of its final choruses of "Rise up!"

Opening the *Tribute to Heroes* telethon, "My City of Ruins" described something much more metaphoric—the city represented New York City and its metropolitan surroundings, and also the nation under attack; the "young men" symbolized all citizens. You might even have understood those "young men . . . like scattered leaves" to include those who in their fury and desperation steered the planes, although it's unlikely that very many viewers took it that far. The telethon represented the end of national mourning. Two weeks later, America bombed Afghanistan.

BACK IN MONMOUTH COUNTY, dozens of families had lost their main means of support in the World Trade Center massacre. On October 18 and 19, Bruce and such friends as Joe Ely, Joan Jett, various E Streeters, most notably Garry Tallent, and rockabilly Sonny Burgess came together at the Count Basie Theater in Red Bank in a benefit for the Alliance of Neighbors, a group that counseled, funded, and offered other support for those families.

Introducing "My City of Ruins" at those benefits, Springsteen said, "This was a song that I wrote for Asbury Park. Songs go out into the world and hopefully they end up where people need 'em. So, I guess, this is a gift from Asbury Park to New York City in its time of need."

Now it came back home—all the way home, to the neighborhood in which he wrote it. Many Rumson residents worked for the investment firm Cantor Fitzgerald, perhaps the single company most devastated by the Trade Center attacks. However different the lives of rock stars and investment bankers may be, a lot of those people took Bruce as an inspiration.

After 9/11, Bruce did more than play the telethon and benefit shows. Responding to calls from the grieving, he spent hours listening to 9/11 widows and children. He heard their cries more often and probably more intensely than he heard the guy shouting at him on the street.

Dec. 3, 4, 6, 7, 8, 2001 – Convention Hall, Asbury Park, NJ
The Max Weinberg 7 are the house band for this year's Christmas shows. Nils, Patti, Southside Johnny, Bobby Bandiera, Soozie Tyrell, Elvis Costello, Bruce Hornsby, and Garland Jeffreys join Bruce for these concerts. Inspired by George Harrison's recent passing, the first night's show opens with "Something" and "My Sweet Lord."

Dec. 15, 2001 – Continental Airlines Arena, East Rutherford, NJ
Tim McLoone's Holiday Express Band is joined onstage by Bruce for the final two encores, "Merry Christmas Baby" and "Santa Claus Is Coming to Town."

Jan. 11, 2002 – Foxwoods Resort and Casino, Mashantucket, CT
At Clarence's birthday show in the B. B. King's Night Club at Foxwoods, Bruce plays four songs onstage with the band. For the final song, "Glory Days," they are joined onstage by B. B. King.

At the Bell Center, Montreal, Canada, April 19, 2003

But he kept his work with 9/11 victims invisible. The next Bruce Springsteen appearances came at his four Christmas shows at the Convention Center. He played those shows with the same accompanists as last year, adding his early seventies New York City singer-songwriter comrade, Garland Jeffreys. The shows were more intense than the previous year's, and he dredged up a lot of old songs, the material from the first two albums most influenced by his life at the Shore. Still, those songs themselves often had the air of a lark. His mission may have become more complex, but his purpose remained exactly what he said it was at the end of the reunion tour: a "commitment to serve you."

Introducing "My City of Ruins" that night, he talked about Asbury, how "there's just a lot happening in town." He mentioned the local charities funded by proceeds from the shows, summer events like the Clearwater Festival, the new city government (as crooked as the rest but no one knew that yet), beachfront redevelopment (as crooked as the last such effort but again, who knew?), and a host of local businesses, from delis to art galleries. He had immersed himself in his hometown, had come to know its pride and its shame, and he brought the morality of his shows to it.

WHEN HE PLAYED THE Christmas shows, Bruce already had begun writing his most important new songs in years. Of them, only "My City of Ruins" had anything to do with Asbury Park. Almost all of the others related to the aftermath of the 9/11 attacks. Not the attacks themselves but their consequences. And not their geopolitical consequences so much as their emotional and psychological consequences.

Early in 2002, he began work with producer Brendan O'Brien in Atlanta. By early summer, the record, titled *The Rising*, was complete, and the group had reassembled for rehearsals at the Shore.

This was the E Street Band at its most expanded: Soozie Tyrell was added on violin and backing vocals. That made the group a ten-piece, the same size as the Bruce Springsteen Band that had crashed in 1970 and the *Tunnel of Love* band with its horn section.

But the E Streeters remained mainly a rock band. Clarence played the only horn; Patti Scialfa and Soozie Tyrell's harmonies displayed traces of girl group pop, rock and roll, and country, as well as soul and R&B. There were soul-tinged tunes among the songs on *The Rising*, but especially since O'Brien's production emphasized guitars, most of it sounded like what it was, Bruce's first unmitigated rock album since *Born in the U.S.A.*

The Rising was received as the first major artistic statement about 9/11. Not the first major rock work; the first important work of any kind.

July 26, 2002 – Convention Hall, Asbury Park, NJ
Warm-up show for the *Rising* tour, for contest winners and guests. Violinist Soozie Tyrell has been added to the band.

July 30, 2002
The Rising is released.

July 30, 2002 – Convention Hall, Asbury Park, NJ
The Today Show broadcasts live from Convention Hall; four songs are played. Later on the same day a rehearsal show is played to a live audience.

Still, the album received relatively little radio airplay—although it sold about three million copies in the United States, it produced no hit single, the title track peaking at number fifty-two, which happened to be Bruce's age at the time.

Very few popular musicians get the kind or amount of print and TV coverage that Bruce received. Established magazines, not just *Rolling Stone* and its ilk, reviewed it, diving for pearls amongst its verbiage and virtually ignoring the noises that accompanied the words. Bruce himself had cachet once more: *The Today Show* broadcast an entire two-hour edition featuring rehearsal performances by Bruce and the band, and *Nightline* devoted an entire hour to an interview with Springsteen by Ted Koppel. The E Street Band appeared on David Letterman's show on consecutive nights.

If anything, Bruce acted like respectability took the pressure off. He even allowed strangers to attend late July rehearsals at Convention Hall and the Meadowlands. Bruce displayed an unprecedented lack of secretiveness or even caution.

Anyone expecting that his lyrical subject matter predicated a dour Bruce Springsteen and the E Street Band should have been immediately dissuaded by the opening show on August 5 at the Meadowlands.

Bruce came out with a stern look on his face and kept it as he stepped up to sing "The Rising," with its invocation of the fiery stairwell, the priest (Father Judge, in real life)

"wearing the cross of my calling," the full panoply of heroism that leads to the very ambiguous "rising" of the title—a call for the resurrection of the dead (a call from the dead themselves, it may be), perhaps also a call for the resurrection of the spirits of the living, and of the way we value life itself. But with the second number, "Lonesome Day," which hid its sadness in a joyful noise, he took off into cool-rockin'-daddy mode, not only aware of the world's woes, but celebrating in their face.

They played eleven of *The Rising's* fifteen songs that night, and those songs fit easily into a selection of Springsteen's standards: "Prove It All Night," "Darkness on the Edge of Town," "Promised Land," "Two Hearts," "Badlands," the inevitable "Born to Run." The older songs highlighted the brightness of some of the new material (Bruce left out the most difficult songs on the album, including a landmark of despair called "Nothing Man"). The set wasn't lighthearted—"41 Shots" was there—but it ended in rising spirits, with "My City of Ruins," "Born in the U.S.A.," and "Land of Hope and Dreams."

For the first two weeks, the set list varied not at all, as stable as on the *Tunnel of Love* tour, when he'd also put together a uniquely coherent group of original songs. When he finally began changing it as the group swung west, one of the first things to go was "41 Shots." Months into the tour, he still did eleven or more songs from the new album every show.

Aug. 1, 2002 – Ed Sullivan Theater, New York, NY
Bruce plays "The Rising" and "Lonesome Day" on *The David Letterman Show.* The second song is broadcast on the show the next night, and Bruce is also interviewed, his first talk-show interview appearance.

GA   GA4 84   ADULT
GEN ADM STANDING   20.00
CONVENTION HALL
BRUCE SPRINGSTEEN
ticketmaster
& THE
E STREET BAND
✱✱ REHEARSAL SHOW ✱✱
FRI AUG 2, 2002 2:00PM

Aug. 7, 2002 – Continental Airlines Arena, East Rutherford, NJ
Opening night of *The Rising* tour

Aug. 29, 2002 – MTV Video Music Awards / Museum of Natural History Planetarium, New York, NY
This TV broadcast includes "The Rising." The rest of the nine-song set is played for a live audience outside in pouring rain.

Bruce also kept mute on his political stance, even though some of the songs—especially "Lonesome Day," with its line "A little revenge and this too shall pass," and "Empty Sky," whose revenge-driven protagonist declares "I want an eye for an eye"—invited misinterpretation by the revenge-minded.

That changed in the West, too. Late in the encores in Tacoma on August 21, Bruce said, "Once again, just a couple of public service announcements: For Food Lifeline out there in the lobby on your way out, please stop by and give 'em a hand and check out the good work that they're doing here in town. Those are the folks that are on the frontline in the fight against hunger and poverty here in Washington [state]. Also, we're in the midst of a rollback of civil rights. I think it's a good time to sort of keep your eyes open. Civil rights are a reaffirmation of our strength as a nation of laws, due process. Usually, you don't think about it 'til it's a little too late. So keep your eyes open. I think that vigilance and responsibility comes with the turf when you're born in the U.S.A."

That statement broke Springsteen's own rules—he always separated his charity comments (on this tour, made in the prelude to "My City of Ruins") and his political commentary (on this tour, right before "Born in the U.S.A."). But what he said in Tacoma, and throughout the rest of the American dates that year, interwove his work with the food banks and other community groups with an

expressly political stand, and it came very close to telling his audience not only what he thought was right and wrong, but that he believed they ought to think it, too. Bruce believed in the "big tent" much more avidly than any of the politicians who played games with the term, so moving that far represented a major shift.

Springsteen couched his disagreement with government policy carefully in moderate civil libertarian terms, even with the tissue-thin lies that sent America to war in Iraq flying furiously. But then, Bruce wasn't particularly political. The songs on *The Rising* managed to speak about one of the central political events of his lifetime without taking a stand on anything crucial to what happened there—the nature of the U.S. role in the Middle East, for instance, or the role played by monotheistic fundamentalists. He took care to avoid racism against Arabs, in the exotica of "Worlds Apart" (which strikes me as the story of the righteous love between an American soldier and a Muslim woman) and the graceful and eloquent "Paradise," which attacks vengeful and suicidal beliefs, secular and religious, as being equally opposed to real spirituality. As he always had, Bruce eschewed comments on policy and ideology.

But the lyrics aren't all there are to those songs. Bruce's sound cried out where his words were silent, a shouted warning against the madness of the jihadist bombers and the insanity of American imperialism. It did its best not to

---

side with evil, to endorse no nation or religion, and to seek justice, not an eye for an eye or a tooth for a tooth. *The Rising* came from Graham Greene territory—if you can imagine Graham Greene writing in the voice of a New Jersey altar boy who attended the Upstage instead of Oxford. It wasn't political, it was moral. The question was, Could you stay in that moral territory and not take some kind of side?

By the time he got back East, to Boston in early October, he'd taken another step. He made his venerable encore announcement about the charitable organizations in the house, made his nonusual comments about eroding civil rights, then added: "There's also a lot of war talk in the air. However you feel about it, it's never served our nation well to go rushing into a war. We should demand a full debate." Once again, he reminded the crowd, "that vigilance and responsibility come with the turf when you're born in the U.S.A."

A week later, they went to Europe for just two weeks. They played in France, Spain, Italy, Germany, Holland, Sweden, and England—countries outside "the coalition of the willing," or inside by virtue of the government flouting popular opinion. Each night, Bruce would introduce "Born in the U.S.A." by thanking the audience for its long-time support, and say, in the native tongue, "I originally wrote this song about the Vietnam War. I want to play it tonight as a prayer for peace." Given what happened to the Dixie Chicks less than six months later for saying that they were embarrassed by George Bush, it's worth wondering what would have happened if he'd gone further.

But Bruce didn't.

As he adjusted the show for the remainder of the American tour, the major change was a deeper dip into his back catalog. Songs that he hadn't played for twenty years suddenly began appearing in the sets: "Streets of Fire," unheard onstage since New Year's Day 1979, the very last date of the *Darkness* tour, cropped up in Lexington, Kentucky. Songs from the first two albums like "Incident on 57th Street," "Does This Bus Stop at 82nd Street," and "It's Hard to Be a Saint in the City" became regular features of Bruce's solo piano spot. He dusted off other orphans: "Human Touch," "Darlington County," "The Promise," "So Young and In Love," "Where the Bands Are." A

BRUCE SPRINGSTEEN & THE E STREET BAND

DATE			PAGE
Tue -Feb 25	TRAVEL DAY		
Wed -Feb 26	LOAD IN	DULUTH, GA	1
Thu -Feb 27	LOAD IN/ REHEARSALS	DULUTH, GA	2
Fri -Feb 28	ARENA AT GWINNETT CENTER	DULUTH, GA	3
Sat -Mar 1	TRAVEL DAY/ DAY OFF	DULUTH, GA	4
Sun -Mar 2	FRANK ERWIN CENTER	AUSTIN, TX	5
Mon -Mar 3	DAY OFF	AUSTIN, TX	6
Tue -Mar 4	JACKSONVILLE COLISEUM	JACKSONVILLE, FL	7
Wed -Mar 5	DAY OFF	JACKSONVILLE, FL	8
Thu -Mar 6	RICHMOND COLISEUM	JACKSONVILLE/ RICHMOND	9
Fri -Mar 7	BOARDWALK HALL	RICHMOND, VA	10
Sat -Mar 8	DAY OFF	ATLANTIC CITY, NJ	11
Sun -Mar 9	DAY OFF/	NY/ WEEHAWKEN, NJ	12
Mon -Mar 10	DUNKIN' DONUTS CENTER	NY/ WEEHAWKEN, NJ	13
Tue -Mar 11	BLUE CROSS ARENA	PROVIDENCE, RI	14
Wed -Mar 12	ALL FLY HOME	ROCHESTER, NY	15
Sat -Mar 15	TRAVEL DAY		16
Sun -Mar 16	TRAVEL DAY		17
Mon -Mar 17	TRAVEL DAY		18
Tue -Mar 18	TRAVEL DAY/ LOAD IN	MELBOURNE, AUS	19
Wed -Mar 19	REHEARSALS	MELBOURNE, AUS	20
Thu -Mar 20	TELSTRA DOME	MELBOURNE, AUS	21
Fri -Mar 21	TRAVEL DAY	MELBOURNE, AUS	22
Sat -Mar 22	SYDNEY CRICKET GROUNDS	SYDNEY, AUS	23
Sun -Mar 23	DAY OFF	SYDNEY, AUS	24
Mon -Mar 24	TRAVEL DAY	BRISBANE, AUS	25
Tue -Mar 25	BRISBANE ENTERTAINMENT	BRISBANE, AUS	26
Wed -Mar 26	BRISBANE ENTERTAINMENT	BRISBANE, AUS	27
Thu -Mar 27	TRAVEL DAY	BRISBANE, AUS	28
Fri -Mar 28	WESTERN SPRINGS STADIUM	AUCKLAND, NZ	29
Sat -Mar 29	ALL FLY HOME	AUCKLAND, NZ	30
Sun -Mar 30	CROSSLOAD TEAM FLY HOME		31
Tue -Apr 8	TRAVEL DAY		32
Wed -Apr 9	ARCO ARENA	SACRAMENTO, CA	33
Thu -Apr 10	DAY OFF	SACRAMENTO, CA	34
Fri -Apr 11	PACIFIC COLISEUM	VANCOUVER, BC	35
Sat -Apr 12	DAY OFF	VANCOUVER, BC	36
Sun -Apr 13	PENGROWTH SADDLEDOME	CALGARY, AL	37
Mon -Apr 14	SKYREACH CENTRE	CALGARY, AL	38
Tue -Apr 15	DAY OFF	EDMONTON, AL	39
Wed -Apr 16	DAY OFF	NEW YORK/ MONTREAL, QC	40
		NEW YORK/ MONTREAL, QC	41

Oct. 16, 2002 — Palau Sant Jordi, Barcelona, Spain
Part of this show is broadcast live on VH1 in Europe, and the entire show is later made available on a DVD titled *Live in Barcelona*.

Nov. 2, 2002 — Tradewinds, Sea Bright, NJ
At the Third Annual Light of Day Benefit for the Parkinson's Disease Foundation, Bruce joins Joe Grushecky, Garland Jeffreys, and Gary Bonds onstage.

Nov. 19, 2002 — BJCC, Birmingham, AL
Emmylou Harris sings "My Hometown" with Bruce, accompanied also by Patti and Soozie.

At the Bell Center, Montreal, Canada, April 19, 2003

stronger hint of the standards set he'd developed on the reunion tour, but every show still featured almost all of *The Rising*, in part taking the measure of how well those songs fit in with the new ones.

The Rising tour was the longest Bruce had done in ten years, continuing into the new year, after a substantial break from mid-December to the end of February.

On February 19 and 20, 2003, Bruce played shows at the Somerville Theater, a tiny movie theater just outside Cambridge, Massachusetts. Sporting ticket prices up to $500, they were intended to raise enough money to resuscitate *Double Take Magazine*, a project of his friend, Harvard psychologist and civil-rights veteran Robert Coles. The magazine never published again, but the shows remain among the most important Bruce has ever done. At this "Intimate Evening of Conversation and Music," he played solo, although the setup was a little more musically elaborate than the *Joad* tour, adding piano to guitar.

He organized the show into a peculiar "And then I wrote . . ." format. He would describe his state of mind, living conditions, hopes, and problems at the time he made an album and then play a song that demonstrated the sometimes improbable results. Is there any concrete description that could quite account for the lyrics of "Blinded by the Light"?

A more relevant question: Could anyone imagine a show where Bruce Springsteen took a paying audience—even a tiny paying audience—through "Does This Bus Stop at 82nd Street" line by line, explaining context ("I was on a bus going up to Eighty-second Street where a friend of mine had a crash pad . . ."), whim ("I just liked that"), and broad intention: "The *Daily News* asks her for the dope / She says, 'Man, the dope's that there's still hope.' That's the song.

"Without that, the song doesn't get on the album," Bruce concluded. "I don't have it. I got close to it but I didn't have it. But—somebody once said that a good rock song is only one good line, you only need one good line that gets you where you want to go, and the other stuff is kind of like getting there, and I think that's true, as long as you find that one good one that takes it and puts it on the record."

It was like hearing Springsteen interviewed by himself. And what he laid out, predictably enough if you'd followed him all these years, was pretty much that he knew what you wanted to know, and was willing to answer the parts he could ("Advertisers on the downtown train"? "Poor working stiff"?), and cop to the parts he couldn't ("'Queen of diamonds, ace of spaces, newly discovered lovers of the everglades.' Let me, uh, refer to my notes . . . nothing special.")

Juxtaposing the hope and promise of "Thunder Road"

Nov. 23, 2002 – American Airlines Arena, Miami, FL
Bruce is joined onstage by Bono and Dave Stewart for "Because the Night." Dion sings a duet with Bruce on "If I Should Fall Behind." The encores are introduced by *The Sopranos'* "Big Pussy," Vincent Pastore.

Dec. 4, 2002 – Mellon Arena, Pittsburgh, PA
Joe Grushecky joins Bruce to perform "Code of Silence," a song that they wrote but had not previously performed together.

Feb. 23, 2003 – Grammy Awards / Madison Square Garden, New York, NY
Bruce performs "London Calling" for a Clash/Joe Strummer tribute along with Little Steven, Elvis Costello, and Dave Grohl. Bruce and the E Street Band perform "The Rising." *The Rising* is nominated for Album of the Year.

"And we are in concert.
band is performing for y
that evening. And you h
to take this thing as hig
I come out at night, ther

with the nihilism of "Nebraska," "The River," and "Sherry Darling," he proved an adept critic of his own music and the music from which he had borrowed and stolen over the years.

On this truly revealing night, he told the story of going to Washington for the Kennedy Center Honors, the year he played "The Times They Are A-Changin'" by special request of Bob Dylan. And of taking Patti by the Vietnam Memorial, where they sought out, among the names of the dead, Bart Haynes, the first drummer in the Castiles, and Walter Cichon, lead singer of the Motifs, then seeing Robert McNamara, the war's architect and advocate, at the ceremony that evening.

Back to the beginning, and then into the future, with a song inspired by that trip, and by a clipping Joe Grushecky sent him about a week later—he credited Grushecky with cowriting the song "in some fashion," although he didn't spell out the process—called "The Wall." It wasn't about his bandmate Bart. It was about Walter, an older guy, someone he knew much less well but in whom, once upon a time, Bruce had seen a version of his dreams and whose dreams had bled out somewhere in the jungle.

It's not necessarily a great song, at least from what you can tell so far—Bruce has only performed it a couple of times other than at the two *Double Take* shows, and never with the band. It reads like a letter to a lost companion or maybe just a diary entry. But it's a revealing song, and what it exposes is that by the beginning of 2003, his thinking about war and government had taken a turn:

> You and your boots and black T-shirt
> Ah Billy you looked so bad
> Yeah you and your rock and roll band
> Was the best thing this shit town ever had
> Now the man who put you here
> He feeds his family in rich dining halls
> And apology and forgiveness have no place here at all
> At the wall

In those lines, he finds the place Graham Greene used to locate, the place where politics and morality come so close together—always, a place of immorality—that distinguishing between them, while possible, really isn't worth the trouble. It's a song about Walter Cichon, a song about Robert McNamara, a song about Bruce Springsteen, young and old. It's another side of "My City of Ruins," except in "Ruins," Bruce sounds sad and weary. Here, he's pissed off and irreconcilable.

"The Wall" is a song about war, and not just any war. It's about Vietnam and the shadow it still casts, from that monument in D.C. to the streets of Baghdad and beyond. It's also about all the things around the war, the issues of power, control, greed, and contempt surrounding the men who instigated the war—the very kind who'd turned their back on Bobby Muller and his comrades when they came

Mar. 4, 2003 – Jacksonville Coliseum, Jacksonville, FL
Hank Ballard's "Let's Go, Let's Go, Let's Go" is performed for the first time in honor of Ballard's recent passing.

Mar. 6, 2003 – Richmond Coliseum, Richmond, VA
Bruce is joined onstage by former Steel Mill vocalist Robbin Thompson as well as Bruce Hornsby.

Mar. 22, 2003 – Cricket Ground, Sydney, Australia
Because of a loss of power during four songs, the show ends up being "only" three and a half hours long, and "Rosalita" is played as a treat for the audience.

home shattered. By singing "The Wall" on stage—no matter how small a stage—Bruce Springsteen demonstrated that he had made a decision. It wasn't about which side he was on—he made that choice when he first linked up with Muller and the veterans. It was a decision about what his success was worth.

The *Double Take* shows closed with a unique question-and-answer dialogue about the songs with the audience. On the first night, this elicited some revealing material, which Bruce basked in; on the second night, the crowd went after nonsense and trivia, and Bruce grew exasperated. But the event itself ranks as one of his most successful stage efforts, and a prelude to part of his future.

RESUMING THE BAND'S TOUR with a handful of Southern dates, rescheduled from the fall when the group lost Clarence for a couple of weeks to emergency surgery for a detached retina, there wasn't much change. "Born in the U.S.A." remained "a prayer for peace."

Bruce always felt more comfortable back home, and when the tour got back East, for a March 7 show at Atlantic City's Boardwalk Hall, the change came. The setlist was even more fun than usual, incorporating "Roll of the Dice," "Jersey Girl," and a one-off pass at the Beatles' "Tell Me Why." After he sang "Empty Sky," though, Bruce decided to clarify its lyrics once and for all.

"That was the last song I wrote, I think, for *The Rising*. I was looking for a cover, and a fella that was coming up with some ideas sent me over a . . . just a picture of an empty sky. I thought it was an important metaphor but there's one thing that always bothers me a little bit: Occasionally when I play that song, I hear some applause for the line 'I want an eye for an eye.' As a songwriter, you always write to be understood, and I wrote that phrase as an expression of the character's anger and confusion and grief. It was never written to be a call for blind revenge or bloodlust." He got cheered for that, no big surprise—there was never a lot of applause for the "eye for an eye" line, after all.

"So, I just thought, given the times we live in, you can't be too clear about these kinds of things these days, and I realize that it could've been a well-meaning few or perhaps borderline psychotics out there who may have misunderstood. But . . . living in a time when there's real lives on the line and there's enough destructive posing going on out there as it is, I wanted to make sure that that line was clearly understood."

As Bruce described it to *Backstreets*, his politically articulate American fanzine, "I have no compunction about stopping and telling someone what I mean. There's a moment to do that. And so, hey, I had the stage at the moment [*laughs*], and generally if I feel any sort of recurring misunderstanding that's occurred more than a few

Apr. 29, 2003 – Count Basie Theater, Red Bank, NJ

Billed as "The Hope Concert," the show is staged to raise money for the health care of Bobby Bandiera's son. Bruce joins the Bobby Bandiera Band, Gary Bonds, Jon Bon Jovi, Southside Johnny, and the Max Weinberg 7.

May 2, 2003 – Stone Pony, Asbury Park, NJ

Soozie Tyrell does a show to mark the release of her first solo album, *White Lines,* and is joined onstage by Bruce and Patti for two songs.

nights running, I'll say, 'Okay, there's a few people. . . .' Maybe there's a hundred, maybe there's ten. Maybe there's two. Maybe I'm just hearing the guy who's making the noise at that moment. But in the end, I am speaking to you. I'm speaking to you individually. And so I don't have a problem stopping at a particular moment and making clear my intentions. And now with the fabulous help of the Internet [*laughs*], those intentions are instantaneously around the world, and it helps clear things up even faster." That's about as far from letting the music speak for itself as you can get.

A week later, in Providence, he moved another step. "I wrote this song in the early eighties about the Vietnam War," he declared. "I wouldn't want to have to write another one like it. I'll send this out tonight as a prayer for peace, a prayer for the safety of our sons and daughters, the safety of innocent Iraqi civilians, and to add our voices to no war in Iraq."

So "Born in the U.S.A." went out into the twenty-first century.

BRUCE HAD JUST LANDED in Melbourne for a quick (five shows, eight days) tour of Australia and New Zealand when the war came on March 19. "What will follow will not be a repeat of any other conflict. It will be of a force and a scope and a scale that has been beyond what we have seen before," declared Donald Rumsfeld, who had McNamara's old post as secretary of defense. Every day of the tour, the Americans battered the Iraqis, meeting little effective resistance. (If this was a repeat of any other conflict, it wasn't Vietnam but the Nazi blitzkrieg of Poland in 1939.) Maybe because he was among strangers, perhaps because like everyone else who opposed the war, he was a little taken aback that it had begun with such flimsy pretexts and against so much good evidence that those pretexts were lies, Bruce said little—just more prayers for peace. Nor did he expound during a few West Coast and Canadian shows, or on the road in Europe, where the band spent May and most of June.

He did take to letting the music speak for itself in a slightly different way for the next five weeks of the tour, not opening with "The Rising," as he had done on virtually every show on the tour, but with a solo acoustic number, often "Born in the U.S.A.," that shouted the antiwar theme most unambiguously. The tour ended in a spectacular deluge at San Siro Stadium, in Milan, one of Europe's most legendary soccer stadiums.

Stadiums were the next tour tactic back in the States, too. The announcement that Springsteen would play Boston's Fenway Park, the oldest baseball stadium standing and one of American sport's citadels, made headlines in both the entertainment and sports sections. The tour would hit baseball parks in Pittsburgh, Philadelphia, Chicago, San

July 21, 2003 – Giants Stadium, East Rutherford, NJ
Vini Lopez plays drums on "Spirit in the Night."

Sept. 6, 7, 2003 – Fenway Park, Boston, MA
Two shows are performed at legendary Fenway Park. Both shows start with "Take Me Out to the Ballgame" and end with "Dirty Water"; Peter Wolf appears as a special guest. Fans line the streets cheering as the band's van enters and leaves the stadium.

Sept. 10, 2003 – Skydome, Toronto, Canada
The show starts with a cover of "My Ride's Here" in honor of Warren Zevon, who had recently died. This performance was later included on *Enjoy Every Sandwich: The Songs Of Warren Zevon*.

Francisco, Los Angeles, Toronto, Detroit, Denver, Milwaukee, and end with three nights at Shea Stadium, home of the New York Mets, the first weekend in October.

A batch of football stadiums also appeared on the itinerary, highlighted by seven shows (spread out over six weeks in July and August) at Giants Stadium back home in New Jersey. The final leg of the *Rising* tour began there on July 15. Bruce came out ready to escalate his political stance.

"Once again I wanna thank everybody for coming out to the show tonight," he said at the very end. "What I like about it, I know people with all different kinds of political beliefs come out and see us, and I, I like that, you know. We welcome all. There's been a lot of questions raised recently about the forthrightness of our government and this playing with the truth has been part of both Democratic and Republican administrations in the past, and it's always wrong—never more so than when there's real lives at stake. The question of whether we were misled into war with Iraq isn't a liberal or a conservative question, or a Republican or a Democratic question, it's an American question. Protecting the democracy that we ask our sons and daughters to die for is our responsibility and it's our trust. Demanding accountability is our job as citizens. That's the American way. So may the truth will out. That's

A rehearsal at Shea Stadium, New York, New York, October 2003

our public service announcement for tonight. This is 'Land of Hope and Dreams.'"

That one felt scripted. By July 24, still at Giants Stadium, he'd found a more natural voice for it: "This is where I kind of make my little public-service announcement," he began much less nervously. "We got people of all different political beliefs and they come to the show and we like that and we welcome everybody. . . .

"There's been a lot of questions in papers lately about the forthrightness of our government. I think that you can see that playing with the truth during wartime has been a

At Fenway Park, Boston, Massachusetts, September 2003

part of both Democratic and Republican administrations in the past, and it's always wrong—never more so when there's real, real, real lives at stake. I think the question of whether we were misled into the war in Iraq isn't a liberal or a conservative question, but it is an American one, and protecting our democracy that we ask our sons and daughters to die for is our sacred trust as citizens—and demanding accountability from our leaders is our job, that's the American way. I'll do this tonight hoping that the truth may will out and as a prayer for our troops in Iraq and the peace of the Iraqi people. This is 'Land of Hope and Dreams.'"

A very different, much less ambiguous prayer. A partisan prayer. It struck home, though not always as Springsteen intended. Walking through the Fenway crowd as Bruce made his antiwar spiel there, I heard a woman moan from her very good seat, "Oh, just shut up!" The tone didn't imply that she was a warmonger or a Republican. It implied that she'd come to dance and couldn't be bothered by the rest of the world.

Well, that was the true battleground, the people who just didn't want to know. The ones who booed vigorously, and there were always some, had already made up their minds. Bruce Springsteen made his journey into the fire seeking out the bored or at least the uncommitted.

He still spent less time talking politics than rummaging through his old songs and picking one or two every night to sing, even virtually unknown stuff like "County Fair" (one of the more obscure tunes from *Tracks*). "I tended to keep my comments down to approximately two minutes at the end of the night, which I felt was a pretty good balance to the three hours that we'd spent playing, you know?" Bruce told *Backstreets*.

Left and right: At Fenway Park, Boston, Massachusetts, September 2003

But one of the songs he revived after a year's layoff, starting in mid-September at a show in Chapel Hill, North Carolina, and then a few nights later in Hartford, Connecticut, was "American Skin (41 Shots)." He hadn't done it all year, not since the previous December, when he played it in Atlanta, where he'd debuted the song on the reunion tour, and in Cincinnati, which was in the midst of a similar crisis over police brutality.

On October 1, beginning the final weekend of the tour at Shea, he stuck "41 Shots" into the middle of the set. It was a night for awareness of open wounds—he opened with "Souls of the Departed," his *Lucky Town* song about the first Iraq war, and included the Vietnam vets' anthem, "Who'll Stop the Rain." Or, it was a look back to the last time he'd ended a tour with a big engagement in New York City. Or, it was a night when he just felt like hearing those harmonies.

The New York City Police Department's Shea Stadium security detail took it as an attack. They didn't do anything that night. Two nights later, though, the tension between the cops and Springsteen's crew became overt. When the band left the stage, after a show in which "Into the Fire" was played for a New York City fireman who'd recently been killed on the job, the expected police escort wasn't there to shepherd them away from the traffic jam. The cops explained—to George Travis and other crew members, to the promoter, and to the press—that the escort was a courtesy and that Springsteen had insulted them at the first show by singing "41 Shots" and they therefore owed him no courtesy. Naturally, then, the final night of the tour opened with "Code of Silence," a song Bruce hadn't played since Joe Grushecky joined him onstage in Pittsburgh (Joe's hometown) the previous December. Bruce said nothing conciliatory during the show. An escort appeared after the show.

By then, the last thing on anybody's mind was the cops, or maybe even politics. For the opening encore, they played Moon Mullican's "Seven Nights to Rock," as they had been doing for several months. "My City of Ruins" should have come next, but instead, Bruce went to the microphone. "Yeah!" he shouted. "We have my great friend and inspiration Bob Dylan with us tonight."

Dylan, dressed in his usual jeans and ratty hooded sweatshirt, came out with an electric guitar, and the band ripped into a song. After a few seconds, someone shouted in my ear, "What are they playing?"

Antics at Giants Stadium, East Rutherford, New Jersey, July 2003

"For the first two lines, it was 'Highway 61 Revisited,' but now I'm not sure *what* it is," I answered. It may not have been the most elegant performance of a Dylan song Springsteen and the E Streeters had ever done, but it was by far the most passionate.

After they finished and Dylan departed, Bruce stepped up again.

"It was Bob's work that when I was first trying to write songs . . ." he began, then started over. "At a particular time in our country's history, he was one of those fellas who came along and has been willing to stand in the fire. I remember when I was growing up in my little town, he just made me think big thoughts, you know. His music really empowered me and got me thinking about the world outside of my own little town. I don't know if great men make history or if history makes great men, but for me, Bob's one of the greatest—now and forever. So I'm gonna dedicate this one to him tonight. I wanna thank him for gracing my stage and for being such an inspiration.

"When I wrote this one, I was trying my best to follow along in his footsteps. It's a time right now in our country when there's a lot of questions in the air about the forthrightness of our government. Playing with the truth during wartime has been a part of both Democratic and Republican administrations in the past. And once again the lives of our sons and our daughters are on the line. So it's a good time to be good vigilant citizens. Protecting the democracy we ask our sons and our daughters to die for is our sacred trust. Demanding accountability from our leaders and taking our time to search out the truth, that's the American way . . . and I learned that from Bob Dylan.

"This is 'Land of Hope and Dreams.'"

The show didn't end there. This night it had to end on another peak, one that let him, his band, and his listeners let go of one another for a while. So while he brought out more and more old friends—Garland Jeffreys and Willie Nile, his record company president Donnie Ienner and Jon Landau—they romped through "Rosalita," "Dancing in the Dark," and then "Quarter to Three" with Gary U.S. Bonds, "Twist and Shout," and finally, "Blood

Dec. 5, 7, 8, 2003 – Convention Hall, Asbury Park, NJ

Three Christmas shows end the year. The Max Weinberg 7 are the house band. Jesse Malin, Garland Jeffreys, Southside Johnny, Nils, Steven, Soozie, and Sam Moore also appear with Bruce. "I Thank You" is performed as a duet with Bruce and Sam Moore.

Mar. 16, 2004 – Beacon Theater, New York, NY

Bruce joins Jackson Browne onstage for his final encore, "Take It Easy." The previous night Bruce had inducted Jackson into the Rock and Roll Hall of Fame.

Sept. 15, 2004 – Paramount Theater, Asbury Park, NJ

Bruce joins Patti during her show for "As Long As I Can Be With You" and "Love (Stand Up)." This is Patti's first tour as a solo artist. He will also appear with her in New York at the Bowery Ballroom and the Roxy in Los Angeles.

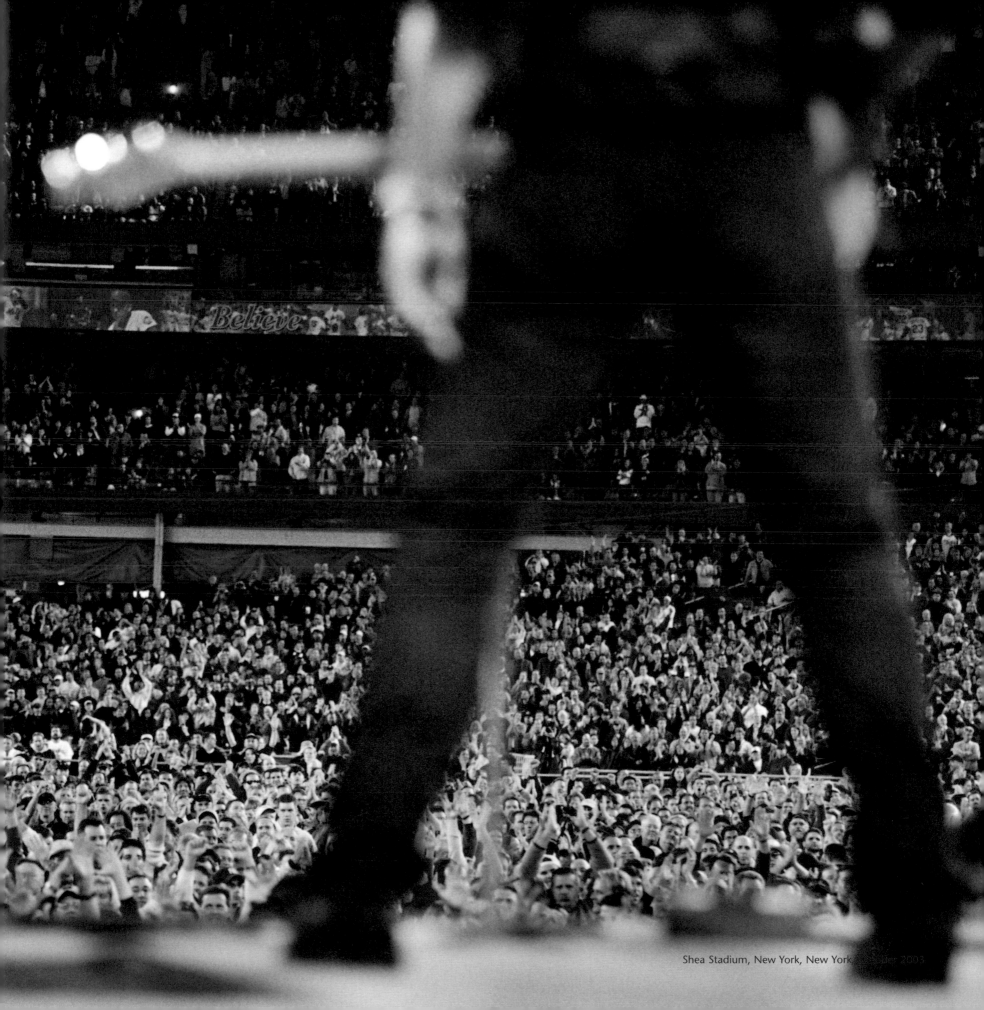

Shea Stadium, New York, New York, October 2003

At Shea Stadium, October 2003

Brothers." Onstage and out in the cold, damp stadium, old friends embraced, not knowing just when they'd see one another again.

ALMOST EVERYBODY CAME home for four Christmas shows the first week in December. This time, soul man Sam Moore owned the event. Although suffering badly from the flu, Sam took the whole place to school with three of his old Sam and Dave hits and a star duet performance on "My City of Ruins" that not only showed Moore's gospel roots but also made a case for him as still the greatest live soul singer.

What was on his mind besides Christmas, charity, music-making, his kids, and the future of Asbury Park came across in the next-to-last song each night which was not a holiday song by any means. "(What's So Funny 'Bout) Peace, Love, and Understanding," written by British anti-hippie Nick Lowe in 1974 and made famous by Elvis Costello's 1979 rendition, speaks in furious power-pop terms about the ideals of the age and why abandoning them is a mistake.

Lowe, a confessed cynic, observed these things with a jaundiced eye—the over-the-top tone is established by the song's first lines: "As I walk through this wicked world / Searching for light in the darkness of insanity."

But Costello and most of those who sang it after him, certainly including Springsteen, took the song as an anthem of their commitment to the ideals of the 1960s. Steeped in soul-gospel rhetoric, they took the chorus—"'Cause each time I feel it slippin' away, just makes me wanna cry"—at its face value. Which of course was not quite the values of the sixties, anyway, since to express the passions of the movements, the line would have needed to end "just makes me wanna fight." But still, the song served. It brought together dreams and realities in a kind of post-Woodstock Apostles' Creed.

The shows ended, of course, not with "Peace, Love, and Understanding" but with a less contentious fantasy, "Santa Claus Is Coming to Town." It was a family affair, with Bruce's kids and a couple dozen others all sporting red Santa hats with white pom-poms, singing along with the band and its musical guests.

When they finished singing it on the fourth night, this beloved musical community dispersed, to be gathered together again, who knew when.

Senator John Kerry and Bruce Springsteen at the Gund Arena in Cleveland, Ohio,
October 2, 2004

Chapter Thirteen

Public Service Announcements

"The country we carry in our our hearts is waiting."

BRUCE SPRINGSTEEN WAS OUT OF sight for the first eight months of 2004 and expected to stay there. Patti Scialfa had at last released *23rd Street Lullaby*, her second solo album. (She'd put out her first, *Rumble Doll*, eleven years before.) She had a tour planned for mid-September. With no desire to upstage her, Bruce was playing the role of rock and roll house-husband, his most public plan to play guitar on a couple of numbers at her nearby shows.

Rumors did abound that Springsteen would lead a troupe of artists in support of the Democratic Party's presidential ticket, Senators John Kerry and John Edwards. Most of those rumors emanated from the rich fantasyland of the right-wing press, particularly the *New York Post*, vehicle for the tempest around "41 Shots." (Bruce put it best in his interview with *Backstreets:* "I do run into people who thoroughly believed the *New York Post*'s interpretation of that piece of music! But I've also run into a lot of people who completely understood what I was trying to say.")

The rumors were true. A July 25 *Los Angeles Times* story got almost all the details right, and probably nailed the motivation, too: "Insiders disagree on the unifying rhythm of the celebrity coalition. Some say it is the promise of the John F. Kerry candidacy, but at least one emphasizes the fear of President Bush's reelection. 'There is a range of feeling about Kerry,' the source said, 'but a uniform belief that Bush must go.'"

Backstreets, either prescient or very well informed, offered: "If you're worried about all those acts taking up precious Boss Time, fear not: Rather than all the artists being on the same bill,

"That's why I'm here today, to stand alongside Senator Kerry and to tell you that the country we carry in our hearts is waiting. And together we can move America together toward her deepest ideals. And besides, we had a sax player in the White House . . . we need a guitar player in the White House!"

—BS

sources tell *Backstreets* that numerous concerts will likely take place throughout each state on a given night, with different artists in various venues/cities. How about Bruce and R.E.M. for starters?"

That's almost exactly the lineup of the Vote for Change tour announced on August 4, although John Fogerty and Bright Eyes were also added to the Springsteen part of the package. Other artists involved included Pearl Jam, the Dave Matthews Band, the Dixie Chicks, Jackson Browne, Babyface, James Taylor, John Mellencamp, Bonnie Raitt, Death Cab for Cutie, Ben Harper, Jurassic 5, Keb Mo, and My Morning Jacket. Not a wide representation of America's music culture, but broader, for instance, than the Amnesty International tour or most charity events.

The tour would last almost exactly a week, with thirty-four shows planned for twenty-eight cities. The idea was to storm each of the so-called swing states (those whose electoral votes for president were in doubt), with concerts in several different cities, all on the same night, in venues ranging from clubs to arenas, maximizing media exposure.

The artists issued a joint statement about why they were undertaking the tour: "We share a belief that this is the most important election of our lifetime. We are fighting for a government that is open, rational, just, and progressive. And we intend to be heard. We plan to do something never done before— to concentrate our energies in the states where the election is expected to be closest. We hope this commitment of time and effort by so many artists and our willingness to take our energy to so many parts of the country will help inspire our fellow citizens to take a hard look at what is at stake in this election, at the federal, state, and local level, and to get involved in trying to move our country in a truly compassionate and humane direction. . . . Most importantly, we wish to communicate our concerns to our fellow citizens and join with them in the effort to change the direction of our government toward one that will make our country as great as it can be."

The political sponsor of Vote for Change was moveon.org and its MoveOn PAC, an ultraliberal, antiwar-based group founded on the Internet by recent college graduate Eli Pariser and funded largely by billionaire investor George Soros. Soros and two wealthy Silicon Valley entrepreneurs also provided most of the funding for America Coming Together (ACT), which would be the recipient of all the money raised by the tour. ACT used the VFC money for voter registration and get-out-the-vote efforts.

Bruce, the biggest name in the pack, followed up the announcement with a small media blitz on August 4 and 5. He appeared on ABC-TV's *Nightline*, and did interviews with the Associated Press and several other print sources, including an extensive *Rolling Stone* interview with editor Jann Wenner.

"I always believed that it was good for the artist to remain distant from the seat of power, to retain your independent voice, and that was just the way I liked to conduct my work," Springsteen told *Backstreets* editor Chris Phillips. "But the stakes in this one are just too high. I felt like, given what I've written about, the things that I've wanted our band to stand for over the years, it's just too big a battle to lay out of."

He made his position even clearer with "Chords for Change," an op-ed essay in the August 5 *New York Times.* "I have been partisan about a set of ideals: economic justice, civil rights, a humane foreign policy, freedom, and a decent life for all of our citizens," he wrote, reiterating that "the stakes have risen too high" to stay uninvolved.

Springsteen didn't simply oppose Bush, saying he believed that "we need an administration that places a priority on fairness, curiosity, openness, humility, concern for all America's citizens, courage, and faith," and that he thought that Kerry and Edwards were "interested in . . . working their way toward honest solutions." The energy in his essay was its attack on Bush administration policies: "We dived headlong into an unnecessary war in Iraq, offering up the lives of our young men and women under circumstances that are now discredited. We ran record deficits, while simultaneously cutting and squeezing services like after-school programs. We granted tax cuts to the richest one percent (corporate bigwigs, well-to-do guitar players), increasing the division of wealth that threatens to destroy our social contract with one another and render mute the promise of 'one nation indivisible.'"

Even to me, a veteran member of America's great third party—the nonvoters who don't believe that either Republicans or Democrats can be trusted—he had a plausible case. Kerry had been a leader—albeit, the most conservative leader—of the Vietnam Veterans Against the War. He opposed the death penalty. He wasn't George Bush, and he wasn't surrounded by George Bush's cabal.

It's just that Kerry's speeches contradicted so much of it. Kerry supported continuing the war in Iraq, he had no fair taxation plan, he lacked a coherent health care policy. He also proved to be as empty of charisma as a floor lamp.

The last paragraph of Springsteen's essay offered a stranger perspective, casting the political in religious terms. He used a muted version of populist prophetic rhetoric, nearer the bombast of William Jennings Bryan than the subtlety of Graham Greene. "It is through the truthful exercising of the best of human qualities—respect for others, honesty about ourselves, faith in our ideals—that we come to life in God's eyes," Springsteen wrote. "It is how our soul, as a nation and as individuals, is revealed."

MCI Center, Washington, D.C., October 11, 2004

Exploiting spiritual belief in politics is dubious business no matter who does it. But the conclusion of "Chords for Change" was pure Bruce Springsteen: "It is time to move forward. The country we carry in our hearts is waiting."

KERRY PLAYED THE SPRINGSTEEN card every day, entering each rally with "No Surrender" as his theme song.

Bruce and John Kerry did know one another, at least a little bit, through Bobby Muller. Kerry, unquestionably, provided the easiest personal fit of any Democratic contender since Springsteen became an adult. But Vote for Change had more to do with the role of celebrity in politics, the loopholes in the campaign finance laws, and the desperation of folks who operated from the kind of politics of grassroots empowerment and universal dignity Springsteen had long implicitly advocated. It was Bush, not Kerry, who accounted for taking a stand in this election.

The E Street Band came together behind Bruce. You couldn't really know what any of the other guys thought, except that Bruce deserved their support. There was one exception: Steven Van Zandt's "I Am a Patriot" from his most famous solo record, *Voice of America*, declared, "I ain't no Democrat and I ain't no Republican / I only know one party and it's name is freedom."

Tickets initially went on sale for the shows with Bruce,

R.E.M., Fogerty, and Bright Eyes on August 21. The Philadelphia concert was an immediate sellout, but three days later, seats remained available in Detroit, Orlando, St. Paul, and Cleveland. (Arena-level concert tickets that don't sell right away are often never sold at all.) That same day a seventh show was announced. After weeks of dickering, a Miami date couldn't be arranged, so a D.C. show was added for October 13. Every artist on the VFC roster would appear in a four-hour show. In addition, celebrated documentary directors Albert Maysles and D. A. Pennebaker would film the event. After a long struggle complicated by the partisan politics, Robert Redford's Sundance cable channel agreed to air the concert live, along with the Maysles film, as a five-hour special called *National Anthem: Inside the Vote for Change Tour*.

What about the audience? It's hard to imagine that after all he'd done, Bruce Springsteen could still be construed by some of his ardent admirers as at base a political conservative—but there were those who took his endorsement of Kerry, let alone his active campaigning for the Democrats, as an affront. "Shut up and play!" became the cry of his right-wing fans. But then, since they managed to maintain that misimpression after the Reagan contretemps, twenty years of supporting the homeless and the hungry, about thirty years of stories about growing up poor, *No Nukes*, *The Ghost of Tom Joad*, and "41 Shots," those fans could not be accused of listening acutely.

Oct. 1, 2004 – Oct. 13, 2004 – Vote for Change Tour
Bruce and the E Street Band join R.E.M., John Fogerty, Tracy Chapman, Jackson Browne, Eddie Vedder, and Bright Eyes for the *Vote for Change* concerts staged by America Coming Together (ACT) on the eve of the 2004 Presidential Election. The Oct. 11 show at the MCI Center in Washington, D.C. is broadcast nationally on TV. The tour ends on Oct. 13 at Continental Airlines Arena in East Rutherford, NJ.

Oct. 28, 2004 – John Kerry Election Rally, Madison, WI
Bruce plays two acoustic songs at this rally for Democratic candidate John Kerry. He will also appear at Kerry rallies in Columbus, Miami, and Cleveland.

Cleveland, Ohio, October 2, 2004

Nov. 6, 2004 – Stone Pony, Asbury Park, NJ

At the Fifth Annual Light of Day Benefit, Bruce joins Joe Grushecky and his band onstage for several songs.

Dec. 2, 2004 – Heinz Hall, Pittsburgh, PA

At the "Concert for Flood Aid" for the victims of devastating recent floods in the area, Bruce joins Joe Grushecky, Jesse Malin, and Exit 105 during their sets and also performs three songs solo.

Dec. 19, 2004 – Harry's Roadhouse, Asbury Park, NJ

Two Christmas shows are played on the same day. Bruce is backed by Bobby Bandiera's band for the show, and is also joined by Patti, Max, Southside Johnny, and Willie Nile for various songs.

Mar. 14, 2005 – Waldorf Astoria, New York, NY

Bruce inducts U2 into the Rock and Roll Hall of Fame and joins them onstage for one song, "I Still Haven't Found What I'm Looking For."

Bruce joins fellow musicians Eddie Vedder *(left)* and Jackson Browne *(right)* backstage on the Vote for Change tour.

Some Republican Springsteen fans said they'd go to the show anyway. Some said they'd never spend another nickel on his music in any form. It didn't make any difference for attendance at these concerts, because Vote for Change would play one show per city in places where there had always been enough demand for multiple arena shows for Bruce alone, as long as he toured with the E Street Band. It's likely that party registration was less of a deterrent to ticket sales than knowing that Bruce would be playing for "only" ninety minutes and that R.E.M. would co-headline. As with the Other Band and *Joad* tours, there were some people who wanted all three rings or no circus at all.

But that wasn't the main tension among Bossmaniacs that fall. The real question was whether Springsteen, who had committed so much energy to building a version of community in his audience, had spent his credibility wisely or foolishly, whether he would forge a closer bond with those who stayed within that community by stepping up for his beliefs or whether his adoption of a partisan position demolished that community.

If you were looking for a show with something at stake, Philadelphia's Wachovia Center on October 1, 2004, the opening night of Vote for Change, had it on offer.

BRUCE EMERGED AS THE evening's master of ceremonies. Just after 7:30 P.M., he and R.E.M.'s Michael Stipe introduced Bright Eyes—a young singer-songwriter named Conor Oberst who'd been making records for ten years, since he was fourteen, and was known, if to anyone in the house that night, mainly to what remained of R.E.M.'s indie rock audience. Bruce declared that Oberst's most recent record "floored me."

Springsteen set the tone of the evening in two ways. First, politically, by saying that all the musicians were there to "fight for a government that is open, forward looking, rational, and humane—and we plan to rock the joint while doing so." Then, artistically, saying in his most deadly humorous tone, "I will come out and slap you silly. We have too much great music tonight. No *BRUUUCING!*"

An hour later, he gave R.E.M. a rousing send-off—his affection for both players and music obvious even before he said they'd been an inspiration to him for twenty years—then joined them for "Man on the Moon," the set closer, adding some deliberately unsubtle Elvis moves.

A few minutes later, just after 10:00 P.M., he came back out with the E Streeters. He took center stage armed with a twelve-string guitar and a slide and ripped out a staggering country-blues arrangement of

"The Star Spangled Banner," the most memorable instrumental revamping of the song since Jimi Hendrix's electric-guitar extravaganza at Woodstock. (If you could imagine Jimi's version without any amplifier or any distortion except what you can achieve with a bottleneck, you'd have the sound.) Then he kicked into "Born in the U.S.A.," the mournful way. In one stroke, Springsteen established his patriotism and his passionate dreams of the better country he carried in his heart.

Then the band crashed into its frenzied little set, all anthems up front: "Badlands," "No Surrender," "Lonesome Day," "Lost in the Flood," "Johnny 99," and "Youngstown," Nils Lofgren burning up the night in a way that let you know whose side he was on, all right.

They stopped for a few seconds, brought out John Fogerty, fifty-nine years old and bouncing on the balls of his feet as they snapped into "Centerfield," "Déjà Vu (All Over Again)" (a new song about the parallel between Iraq and Vietnam), and the capper, the song Fogerty, an Army veteran, spit into the eye of the chicken hawks back in Creedence Clearwater Revival, "Fortunate Son," whose lines about being born with a silver spoon and inheriting star-spangled eyes never seemed more resonant than now. Bruce kept John, one of his major inspirations, out there and got him to sing a duet on "The Promised Land." Then "The Rising," reminding us what had happened.

Stipe came out to sing "Because the Night" like he'd been born for the task. He stuck around for "Mary's Place," and they added R.E.M. guitarist Peter Buck and bassist Mike Mills for "Born to Run" (which can never have too many guitars, after all). Fogerty came back for "Proud Mary"—they were in the encores now, but it happened so fast, it felt like about fifteen minutes had gone by, not an hour and a half.

"(What's So Funny 'Bout) Peace, Love, and Understanding" ripped through the room, on point because, for all the reasons that Bush had earned their enmity, the war in Iraq—based on lies and destructive of both that country and America—was the biggest. Then, a surprise, the finale: Patti Smith's "People Have the Power," Stipe warbling it, Bruce shouting it, Oberst trilling it, Fogerty preaching it, Max, Garry, Mills, and the boys pounding it home.

They spent two hours on the stage rather than Bruce's typical three or four. True, there was a little more politicking—maybe three minutes instead of two.

The "public service announcement" came as the introduction to "Born to Run."

"The money we raised tonight will go directly into mobilizing voters, voter education, getting people to the polls, and bringing out the progressive vote on November second," said Bruce, maybe a little more out of breath than usual at this point. "We remain a land of great promise, but it's time. We need to move

"We remain a land of great promise, but it's time . . . to move America toward the fulfillment of the promises that she's made to her citizens—economic justice, civil rights, protection of the environment."

—BS

"America is not always right—that's a fairy-tale that you tell your children at night before they go to sleep. But America is always true and it's in seeking these truths that we find a deeper patriotism—don't settle for anything less."

—BS

America toward the fulfillment of the promises that she's made to her citizens—economic justice, civil rights, protection of the environment, respect for others, and humility in exercising our power at home and around the world. These core issues of American identity are what's at stake on November second. I believe that Senator Kerry and Senator Edwards understand these important issues, and I think they could help our country move forward.

"America is not always right—that's a fairy tale that you tell your children at night before they go to sleep. But America is always true, and it's in seeking these truths that we find a deeper patriotism—don't settle for anything less.

"So, we've got some work to do between now and election day. If you share our concerns, find the best way to express yourself, roll up your sleeves, and get out there and do something. And remember, the country we carry in our hearts is waiting."

BY ALL ACCOUNTS IT WENT that way for all six shows. Not all the Vote for Change bills worked out so successfully, either in terms of tickets sold or aesthetically (the Sundance special was not unmitigated bliss), but the Springsteen/R.E.M./Fogerty sets had charm, charisma, intensity, great music by three of American rock's finest veterans, and standing room only. And they had the one thing missing from almost all shows, rock or otherwise: purpose. You didn't have to share that purpose—you didn't have to think that "America is always true" is anything but another fairy tale—to get excited in its presence.

The real last Vote for Change show—the encore, as it were—came two nights after the televised D.C. show, at the Meadowlands (where else?), Bruce and the E Streeters accompanied by Fogerty, Jackson Browne, Patti Scialfa (doing a full solo set), and surprise guest Eddie Vedder, of Pearl Jam.

The Jersey show came about because of a startling experience Bruce had while reading the newspaper. As he "explained" in the midst of "Mary's Place": "I'm so glad to be here in my home state tonight. I'm so glad to be home. . . . Are you having fun out there?" The cheers said they were.

"I'm glad, but of course you know we're here tonight with a purpose. We're here tonight on a mission. All the wonderful musicians and the mighty E Street Band have risen up to take you down to the river of change and to help you to cross over to the other side. That's right, I wanna be washed in the waters of democracy! That's right!

"I've been hearing an awful lot about these swing voters . . . swinging. It's *October eleventh*, what the hell are you doing? You mislead the nation into war, a man loses his job—it ain't rocket science. In the words of that other great pathological New Yorker, 'You're fired' when that happens.

On the Vote for Change tour. *From left:*
John Mellencamp, Clarence Clemons,
Bonnie Raitt, Dave Matthews, James Taylor.

"There I was, one nice, sunny morning. I'd come down after a wonderful night of sleeping, and I'm sitting at the breakfast table about to enjoy my eggs and my orange juice. I put on my reading glasses. And I glance over the front page of the morning paper, and it says, 'Election race tightens up in New Jersey.' It says, 'New Jersey—close.' 'New Jersey turning into a swing state.'

"So the first thought that came to my mind of course was . . . *Great God Almighty!* The second thought was *What the Bejesus!* [*chuckles*]. The third thought was *Get me to the Meadowlands now!* I can't have it, I can't have it.

"So all I wanna say out there is if you're swinging, if you're swanging, if you're sweeping, if you're swooping, if you're switching, if you just can't decide . . . if you wanna be even temporarily released from the burdens of Republicanism . . . you can be saved *right now*!

"Do I have a volunteer? Ladies and gentlemen, I need your help, I need a minute to close our eyes and say Hally-burton three times real fast. Let the healing begin. Go home and tell your neighbors, tell your neighbors that a change is coming. And all I wanna know is [*at the top of his lungs*] ARE YOU READY?"

(Perhaps they were, since Kerry won New Jersey.)

What made the night so outstanding was the music—especially the three songs mid-set with Vedder, a true inheritor of Springsteenian commitment, courage, and raw power. Vedder sang "No Surrender" with Bruce, then they put him out front for "Darkness on the Edge of Town," where he sounded amazingly like the young Bruce. Finally, to return the favor, as he said, the E Street Band played the hell out of Pearl Jam's "Betterman."

A song later, Fogerty came out and they crashed through the four-song miniset they'd been doing throughout the tour. Another song and then Jackson Browne sang "Racing in the Street" like it had been written for him. (Earlier, Bruce sang "The Pretender" in Browne's set, with the same effect.) The encores opened up with three Creedence hits, the usual "Proud Mary," plus "Bad Moon Rising" and that old E Street encore favorite, "Travelin' Band."

At the end of such an exhilarating evening, the election seemed to be going very well.

JOHN KERRY AND HIS HANDLERS thought it was going well, too, but they didn't want to take any chances. So they asked Bruce to accompany the candidate for what the Kerry camp called Fresh Start for America rallies on the last few days of the tour.

The first, on October 28 in Madison, Wisconsin, drew eighty thousand people, twenty thousand more than anticipated, to see Bruce and the band Foo Fighters as well as Kerry. Later that day, they went to Columbus, Ohio, for the same presentation to another stadium-size audience.

The Springsteen family with Senator John Glenn (center) and Senator John Kerry (right). Bruce and Patti are joined by daughter Jessica (left) and sons Evan and Sam.

In Madison, where the event was broadcast live on C-SPAN, Bruce, serving as Kerry's introductory presenter, played an acoustic "The Promised Land," then prefaced Kerry's appearance with a short speech. "As a songwriter, I've written about America for thirty years. I've tried to write about who we are, what we stand for, what we fight for. I believe that these essential ideals of American identity are what's at stake on November second. The human principles of economic justice . . . health care, feeding the hungry, housing the homeless, a living wage so folks don't have to break their backs and not make ends meet, the protection of our environment, a sane and responsible foreign policy, civil rights, and the protection and safeguarding of our precious democracy here at home.

"I believe that Senator Kerry honors these ideals. He has lived our history over the past fifty years, has an informed adult view of America and its people. He's had a life experience, and I think he understands that we as humans are not infallible. As Senator Edwards said during the Democratic convention, 'Struggle and heartbreak will always be with us,' and that's why we need each other. That's why 'United We Stand,' that's why 'One Nation Indivisible' aren't just slogans, but they need to remain guiding principles of our public policy.

"And he's shown us, starting as a young man, that by facing America's hard truths, both the good and the bad, that that's where we find a deeper patriotism, that's where we find a more complete view of who we are, that's where we find a more authentic experience as citizens, and that's where we find the power that is embedded only in truth to make our world a better and a safer place.

"Paul Wellstone, the great Minnesota senator, he said, 'The future is for the passionate and those that are willing to fight and work hard for it.' Well, the future is now, and it's time to let your passions loose. So let's roll up our sleeves. . . . That's why I'm here today, to stand alongside Senator Kerry and to tell you that the country we carry in our hearts is waiting. And together we can move America together towards her deepest ideals. And besides, we had a sax player in the White House . . . we need a guitar player in the White House!"

Bruce wasn't proposing himself as president; he was referring to Kerry, an amateur guitarist. But as Springsteen swung into the Kerry campaign's theme song, "No Surrender," you didn't have to be a cynic

Meadowlands Arena, East Rutherford, New
Jersey, October 13, 2004

to wonder whether, of the two guys on that stage, the wrong one was the candidate.

The Kerry campaign found the turnout and the media attention so successful that they quickly added a rally with Springsteen for Miami the next day. Kerry aides said it was Bruce's idea, that he'd told the Senator that "he didn't want to wake up Wednesday [the morning after Election Day] and wish he'd done more."

On November 1, election eve, Springsteen appeared at the campaign finale, a late-night rally in Cleveland, also nationally televised. Bruce added a third song, "Thunder Road," dedicated to Kristen Breitweiser, a Kerry supporter, "who is actually a neighbor of mine, just a few minutes away from me in New Jersey.

"She was one of the 9/11 widows known as the Jersey Girls, who, when the administration was stonewalling the 9/11 Commission, held their feet to the fire and got the truth out. So I want to do this tonight for her," Springsteen said.

His introduction, given with Patti and all three of his kids standing just behind him, was the most expansive political speech he'd ever given.

"Now, nobody's got all of the answers to all of America's problems. And when John Kerry wins tomorrow [*cheering*], it's just the beginning of the work that we need to do ourselves to create a humane American society. I got involved in this election because I saw the opportunity to have somebody in the White House with a heart, that would honestly ask the hard questions, that would respect our most struggling citizens, and a spirit that would seek the solutions to bring us closer to fulfilling America's promise for everybody. I believe that Senator Kerry honors these ideals and that he'll work for them. He's lived our history over the past fifty years, he has an informed and adult view of America and her people. . . .

"I was speaking to Senator Glenn the other night, and he said that politics is supposed to be the personnel department of the Constitution. It is supposed to be shining service. And that's why we need good, wise, and trustworthy servants to put our ideals in action. Senator Kerry, since he was a young man, has shown us, by having the courage to face America's hard truths, both the good and the bad, that that's where we find a deeper patriotism, we find a more complete view of who we are, we find a more authentic experience as citizens, and that's where we find the power that is embedded only in truth to make our world a better and safer place for our kids to grow up in. These are the things that have brought me here tonight."

The roar of the crowd was among the many things that made Kerry supporters think they'd won Ohio—and whoever won Ohio was going to be president.

When Bruce Springsteen woke up the next morning, the lawn of his Rumson, New Jersey, home had been covered with "Bush for President" signs. George Bush won Ohio.

Chapter Fourteen

Finger on the Trigger

"No shadow, no darkness, no tolling bell, shall pierce our dreams."

M Y FIRST *DEVILS & DUST* CONCERT, in Los Angeles in May 2005, inspired more trepidation than I have ever had at a Springsteen show.

My doubts stemmed from the *Devils & Dust* album. It got great reviews for its lyrics, and deserved them, but the music struck me as dry bones in a valley of interior monologue. Most of the interest came from the touches added by producer Brendan O'Brien and percussionist Steve Jordan. Bruce's vocals were way too cautious and mannered, relatively bloodless readings. There are songs on the *Devils* album that I cherish—the title track, "Jesus Was an Only Son," "All I'm Thinkin' About," "The Hitter"—but even those are never as exciting as they could be.

Devils & Dust was put together out of a handful of new songs. Bruce built it, from what I can hear, on the foundation of the title track, which is about the war in Iraq and about living in the America that could have chosen the deceitful coward rather than the honest war hero to rule it. If America was always true, Election Day 2004 suggested that the truth was somewhere between pitiable and contemptible. In his terrorized tale of a blasted landscape enveloped in the smell of blood, one could hear Bruce coming to terms with this.

Devils also included a fair share of songs that had been hanging around for several years: "Long Time Comin'," one of its better songs, had first appeared on the *Tom Joad* tour in 1996, almost ten years earlier. "The Hitter" had also been around for a spell, and those weren't the only

Devils & Dust, 2005

ones. The album had a certain sound (the things I didn't like were central to it, maybe), and it had a certain point of view—as always in solo mode, Bruce was at his bleakest.

He wasn't in *true* solo mode on the album—besides O'Brien and Jordan, several others participated in the sessions—but he sounded isolated in the songs and in the way he sang them. It was no real surprise when Bruce decided, after a couple of rehearsals with other musicians (among them, Nils Lofgren), that he would tour solo.

The *Devils & Dust* tour opened in Detroit on April 25. It's not like I didn't want to see the show—I'm a Bruce Springsteen fan, and I have witnessed musical miracles when the lights went out. But solo renditions hardly seemed likely to enrich the *Devils* music.

The reviews of the first three shows got me more excited. Well, not the reviews so much as the setlists. Bruce included a fantastic harvest of old material: "Part Man, Part Monkey"? "Real World"? "Reason to Believe" sung through his harp mic?

Still, what could he do with that listless new batch?

Oh, me of little faith!

First, he could come out on a stage dressed for the occasion, curtained to catch and enrich every color in the lighting and with a Tiffany lamp on the grand piano, and a chandelier to add a note of funky chic.

He could play not just guitar, harmonica, and the piano, but a pump organ, dobro, electric guitar, electric *piano*. He could not just use that harp mic to make a virtue of his voice as distorted blur, but he could also use it to create a species of atmospheric blues. No guitar, just foot-stomping on "Reason to Believe," but when he came out for an encore "Johnny 99," he had his vocal run through the harp mic again and added the dobro for one of the weirdest musical effects he'd achieved.

Musically, he cracked open the new album, performing nine of its eleven songs, every one not only better but he cracked livelier than the record, the vocals with a clarity and assurance and the focus of the playing crystallized. He could speak about the songs, what they meant, why he wrote them, weaving an autobiographical tapestry. He could develop a setlist with some of the strongest juxtapositions of his career, "Incident on 57th Street" straight into "If I Should Fall Behind." He did that at the piano, and another thing this show could do was show how good a pianist he'd become. He could sing "The Promised Land" as starkly as he had ever sung it, slapping the guitar silly and never strumming the strings, measuring the cost of every line of the song's affirmations.

He could leave you a little embarrassed that you'd doubted. He could leave you lusting for more.

THE *DEVILS & DUST* tour had something to do with the album but more to do with Bruce not just rummaging but rampaging through his body of work. From April 25 to November 22, 2005, he played 72 shows—and 140 different songs. (His Sony Music Website, brucespringsteen.net, lists 243 songs. Of the 5 songs he played at all 71 shows, three were from the *Devils* album (the title track, "Jesus Was an Only Son," and "Reno"); the others were "The Promised Land" and "The Rising." ("Matamoras Banks" was dropped from just one show, the night he did a duet with Bruce Hornsby on its prequel, "Across the Border.") Over the course of the tour, he played every song from *Devils* and *Nebraska*, all but one song ("Balboa Park") from *The Ghost of Tom Joad*. No surprise—those are the solo albums.

He also played every song from *Tunnel of Love* at least once, which he hadn't done in the eighteen years since the album was released. He played seven of the nine songs from *Greetings from Asbury Park, N.J.*—he probably hadn't done that many since *The Wild, the Innocent, and the E Street Shuffle* (from which he played only two songs) came out, thirty-two years before. He played fifteen of the twenty songs from *The River*, which is a much higher percentage than any time except *The River* tour and all the more startling because those fifteen included "Drive All Night" and "Fade Away," fan favorites because they expressed a passionate romanticism that vanished with *Born in the U.S.A.* He played "Drive All Night" at eight shows—the same number at which he played "Born in the U.S.A." (He played "Born to Run" just once.)

It goes on like that: Thirty-seven times he hauled out "Part Man, Part Monkey" (three times he went to the well for "Backstreets"). Fifty-six times he played "Reason to Believe" (once he did "Prove It All Night"). He never played "Jungleland," but he did "State Trooper" twenty times. He did "Thunder Road"

Continental Airlines Arena, East Rutherford, New Jersey, May 19, 2005

With Nils Lofgren, 2005

one night; he did "Thundercrack" seven nights. He played "The Fever," but he never played "Badlands."

The most startling thing he did was go back to the very earliest days of his career, songs that until the release of *Tracks* had been known only from bootlegs, and which he'd never done on the reunion tour. "Thundercrack," which feels like the component parts for half of the *Born to Run* album, is one of those. But he also played "Santa Ana," "Iceman," and on the last night of the tour, the most storied lost song of them all, "Zero and Blind Terry," which as far as I can tell he hadn't played live since February 1974. There were only six known performances of it prior to that night. (As fan Matt Orel said, "He's finally become a Bruce Springsteen fan.")

He spoke in wonderment, punctured with his typical hoarse chuckles, of writing such songs, so verbose and yet full of the narrative dreamwork that sustained him through his first three albums. He said he didn't know where he came up with the stories or conjured the myriad fantastical names for the people and places. A surprise, since on this tour, he'd often told stories about where his songs came from—which is to say, often about where he came from and, more surprisingly, given how cautious and private he is, about how things were at home today, too.

He did much of this reminiscing at the piano. For instance, introducing various songs, often early ones ("For You," "Incident on 57th Street"), he explained why he didn't write many love songs early in his career. "Well, I got mixed signals at home, you know," he told the Cleveland audience. "My mother had on the Top Forty radio in the morning and I heard all the beautiful 1950s doo-wop love songs, 'In the Still of the Night' and 'Gloria.' That was an unusual moment because all the men on the radio at the time were attempting to sing like beautiful women and had these beautiful, angelic, high voices and there was some recognition that women were the repository of love as, uh, men were the repository of confusion [*chuckles*]. So you had all these men transforming themselves, you know, transforming themselves—[*sings in doo-wop falsetto*] Glor-ee-aaa. . . . I can't do it very well but it was a beautiful sound. So, my mother would have it on every morning, and she'd be like, 'What a lovely song, that's my favorite song.'

"And then my dad was kind of sitting there at the kitchen table, and he had a very simple approach, his approach was, 'Bruce, all love songs are a government conspiracy. They are there simply to get you married so you'll have to pay more taxes.' That was his approach, so, I mean, makes sense. I mean, it's no crazier than, 'Hey, we'll find a bunch of old trailers, and we'll convince everybody they're mobile weapons labs.'

Apr. 4, 2005 – Two Rivers Theater, Red Bank, NJ
Bruce performs a solo acoustic show to promote his new album, *Devils & Dust,* on VH1's *Storytellers* series. The concert is shown on April 23 and is later released on DVD.

Apr. 21, 22, 2005 – Paramount Theater, Asbury Park, NJ
Two public rehearsal shows are held prior to the start of the solo acoustic *Devils & Dust* tour.

Apr. 25, 2005 – Fox Theater, Detroit, MI
Opening night of the *Devils & Dust* tour

Apr. 26, 2005
Devils & Dust is released by Columbia Records.

"At any rate, so what I, I ended up doing was I ended up hiding my love songs, so I'm gonna pop a few of 'em on you here, let me see if I can." He played "Incident on 57th Street" and the not-so-early but definitely apt "Stolen Car."

Sliding the politics into the personal stuff wasn't all that unusual this time, either. In London, he pointed out that *Inherit the Wind,* the 1950s movie about the Scopes trial over teaching evolution, would be too controversial to make in present-day America—but so would the Flintstones because of "the whole neanderthal setting, not to mention the homosexual undercurrents between Barney and Fred." Bruce never sounded bitter about the Kerry loss, but he mocked Bush relentlessly (he hardly needed to be cautious any longer), with a particular focus on the war and the lies that generated it, and on the campaign against evolution— which is where those thirty-seven renditions of "Part Man, Part Monkey" came in, to give him a chance to say, as he did in Philadelphia, "Personally, I think that the president believes in evolution too, but he can't say he does because the monkey vote didn't put him in the office."

But most of the stories, whether they introduced very old songs or brand-new ones, concerned the theme of *Devils & Dust.* That's been mostly interpreted as mothers and sons, in contrast to Springsteen's earlier focus on fathers and sons. True, several songs in that set focus on mothers and their male offspring—"Black Cowboys," "Jesus Was an Only Son," "The Hitter," "Silver

Palomino"—but two of the most important songs, "Long Time Comin'" and "Matamoros Banks," concern fathers.

I thought the theme could be better stated as parents and children, until I realized that half of the album is about marriage or wanting to be married or failing at couplehood. What *Devils & Dust,* as a group of songs, is really about is love and commitment, with parenthood, especially mother-hood, as the epitome of that commitment, its deepest and most difficult aspect. Or as he said introducing "Reno," the one where he shocked his listeners by having a whore quote the narrator the price for anal intercourse ("two-fifty up the ass"), "A song about love, not being able to handle the real thing . . . and not being able to handle the wrong thing."

That might not snap into focus until you heard the new songs with the old ones, and that might be part—

Apr. 30, 2005 — Glendale Arena, Phoenix, AR
Nils joins Bruce for "This Hard Land."

May 3, 2005 — Pantages Theater, Los Angeles, CA
Nils joins Bruce on "Waiting on a Sunny Day."

May 17, 2005 — Tower Theater, Philadelphia, PA
Live debut of "Iceman"

ITER RIGHT +0.00 RESTO
NO CAMERAS/RECORDERS
BRUCE SPRINGSTEEN
A NEDERLANDER THEATRE
SOLO ACOUSTIC TOUR
PANTAGES THEATRE
6233 HOLLYWOOD BLVD
ON MAY 2, 2005 7:30PM

Paramount Theater, Asbury Park, New Jersey, April 2005

though it certainly wasn't all—of the motivation for that rampage through the catalog. In the show, Bruce's whole world came into play and he used the *Devils* tour to reestablish its meaning, on the ground of an adult life, with grown-up ambitions and a middle-aged man's wry, slightly impatient humor.

I can't think of a rock and roll parallel, or, for that matter, a close parallel in any form. (If I knew a little more about Jacques Brel, maybe I could, though there was no question this was a rock show, not any nation's cabaret.) I can tell you quite a lot about what the *Devils* show wasn't. It wasn't quite a confessional, and it certainly wasn't a Tin Pan Alley "And then I wrote . . ." or even what you get on VH1's songwriter's forum, *Storytellers* (although he took a lot from his own episode of that series). It wasn't theatrical—there weren't sets, or a fixed narrative of any kind, and given the way Bruce scrambled his setlists, even the emotional maneuvering couldn't quite be predicted from night to night. It wasn't a drama. It certainly wasn't a comedy, although he gave himself more laugh lines than he ever had before, and told the shaggiest of his numerous shaggy-dog stories. The tragedy involved wasn't particularly surprising—just the human dilemma and the political crisis and the ways in which they fit together (and didn't). It wasn't religious, although it was certainly interested in spiritual things. It was, of course, intimate but he played a lot of arenas, scaled-down but still sometimes to audiences of eight thousand to ten thousand.

It was enchanting. It was revealing. It was as personal as any night I've ever spent in a theater. You never quite knew which layer of skin Bruce might peel off next or how his most absurd premises might yield his deepest insights. It was entirely unpredictable.

Does that make this one-man show—in which, before the tour was over, the regularly featured instruments included a ukulele, a harmonium, and an autoharp—a rock and roll concert?

What *else* could you call it?

FOR ME, THE NIGHTLY APEX was "Jesus Was an Only Son." The way he did it brought to mind my favorite painting, Raphael's *The Fall of Jesus on the Road to Calvary*, which portrays the love of Jesus and his mother for one another in the last hours of his life. Raphael shows them both on their knees, reaching out, unable to touch except with their eyes.

Bruce set his song in Gethsemane and presents it as the story of why Jesus allowed himself to be crucified, but the idea's pretty much the same.

Bruce prefaced the song in various ways. The best I heard was in his Philadelphia show on November 9, just two weeks before the tour ended. He'd been given a map

June 23, 2005 – Scandinavium, Gothenburg, Sweden
"Fade Away" is played at this show for the first time since Mar. 5, 1981.

June 29, 2005 – Keflavik International Airport, Keflavik, Iceland
During a fuel stop for his private jet on the way home from the European leg of the tour, Bruce gets off the plane and plays a six-song set in the airport terminal for a small audience of airport workers.

July 23, 2004 – Philips Arena, Atlanta, GA
"Sad Eyes" and "Valentine's Day" are both played at this show for the first time ever.

BRUCE SPRINGSTEEN DEVILS & DUST
Welcome to Arena at Harbor Yard
Wednesday, July 20, 2005
In order to assure a great experience for all, please be sure to observe the following:

•Tonight's show is a solo/acoustic performance, set in a theatre style arrangement.

• The artist requests that you do not bring flowers/gifts. No gifts/flowers will be admitted into the building.

• All guests must be seated by the start of the first song. There will be **no seating until the end of the third song.**

of the neighborhood of his childhood, when "I probably had sixty relatives living within a hundred yards," and with St. Rose of Lima, the church, rectory, convent, and school right there, too. His use of this visual aid took about five hilarious minutes, and it was tricky to spot the moment when it shifted into something about which he was perfectly serious, although in retrospect it's pretty obvious—it's when he talks about how the dread instilled by the Catholic Church influenced his songwriting. He makes the statement into a laugh line, mostly through vocal tonality, but now he's not just riffing on his weird life, his oddball youth, or his strange relatives (all of which he did riff on). Now he's getting down to business.

"All of those things made a big impression on me," he said as the laughter died. He struck a seemingly tentative chord on the piano. "But as I was writing on the last record, I was writing about parents and children quite a bit, and my mind wandered to thinking of Jesus just as someone's son, and of the destiny that . . . that we are all locked into our children's destinies. So, this is 'Jesus Was an Only Son.'"

He struck the chord anew, made you recognize it this time—the melodic shape, Bruce's version of church music, quite close to "My City of Ruins"—and sang the first verse, which describes Jesus walking up Calvary Hill, his mother beside him, and as a boy in the hills of Nazareth, reading *Psalms* "at his mother's feet."

He kept playing, started talking. "As soon as you have your kids, you realize, this feeling appears in your gut, that there isn't anything to do to keep them safe, and that their destiny will be your destiny." He sang the next section of the song, in which a mother prays for her child's safety.

"If you figure our choices are given their meaning by the things that we sacrifice, I always figure that Jesus had to be thinking about the part of life he was gonna lose. And that it was really beautiful down in Galilee this time of year, and that there was this little bar across from the beach that needed a manager, and that Mary Magdalene could tend bar, and he could save the preaching for the weekend—the hell with it. And that they could have a bunch of kids, and get to see the sun fall on their faces, and watch their lungs—watch 'em breathing. And get to see the next day. And the day after that. And the day after that. And the day after that."

He just sang the rest of the song, which is beautiful, mystical, and reasonably coherent for something that talks about the "soul of the universe" and "a sea whose distance cannot be breached."

For me, that little story he tells is better than the poetic language, though, and closer to the meaning of Bruce's music all along.

In the Philadelphia show, two songs after "Jesus Was an Only Son," Bruce picked up his autoharp and sang one

July 31, 2005 – Schottenstein Center, Columbus, OH
"Lift Me Up," a song written by Bruce for the soundtrack of John Sayles's 1999 film *Limbo,* is performed live for the first time.

Oct. 3, 2005 – WBJB-FM Studios, Lincroft, NJ
Bruce performs "All the Way Home" and "If I Should Fall Behind" and does an interview for the Fall Membership Drive in his first live radio performance in decades.

Oct. 17, 2005 – Wachovia Center, Philadelphia, PA
Bruce and Patti join U2 onstage for a version of Curtis Mayfield's "People Get Ready."

Nov. 1, 2005

E Street Radio goes on the air as part of Sirius Satellite Radio to coincide with the release of *Born to Run's* thirtieth-anniversary package. The channel will be on the air until January 31, 2006. In addition to rarities such as recordings of Bruce dating from early 1973, *E Street Radio* features track-by-track album discussions, behind-the-scenes insights, and conversations with E Street Band members and others associated with Springsteen throughout his career.

Nov. 8, 2005 – Wachovia Center, Philadelphia, PA

"Drive All Night" is performed by Bruce on the piano. The song had not been performed onstage since Sept. 11, 1981.

Nov. 9, 2005 – Wachovia Center, Philadelphia, PA

"Santa Ana" and "Thundercrack" are played, both for the first time since 1973.

Nov. 15, 2005

Release of *Born To Run: 30th Anniversary* CD and DVD package by Columbia Records.

NO CAMERAS/RECORDERS

BRUCE SPRINGSTEEN
SOLO ACOUSTIC TOUR
CONTINENTAL ARENA
* * *
THU NOV 17, 2005 7:30PM

J 3 V-RELO
FLOOR SECTION FC 0.00
ADM$
SUBJECT TO REVERSE SIDE

Nov. 19, 2005 — Seminole Hard Rock Live Arena, Hollywood, FL

Clarence and Steven join Bruce at this show for "Drive All Night" and "Thundercrack." Steven also sings "Two Hearts" with Bruce.

Nov. 21, 2005 — Sovereign Bank Arena, Trenton, NJ

To commemorate the life of Link Wray, who has just died, Bruce opens the show with the instrumental "Rumble." He also plays "Song to Orphans" for the first time since 1973.

Nov. 22, 2005 — Sovereign Bank Arena, Trenton, NJ

Final night of the *Devils & Dust* tour. "Zero and Blind Terry" is performed for the first time since 1973.

Continental Airlines Arena, East Rutherford, New Jersey, May 19, 2005

of the most obscure songs from *The Ghost of Tom Joad*, "The New Timer," which is the story of a tramp whose best friend is senselessly murdered in a hobo camp. He sleeps with a machete by his side, and as the song ends, he prays to know who to kill. Not just this night but the night after that and the night after that and the night after that and the night after that.

Bruce sang "The New Timer" eleven times in the last six weeks of the *Devils* tour, which is one more time than he sang it on the entire *Joad* tour. Every time he sang it, it was just one song after "Jesus Was an Only Son." Usually the song in the middle was "Two Hearts," the song from *The River*, where he declares he's abandoned playing "tough guy scenes" and "living in a world of childish dreams." That he has come to the conclusion that such childish dreams must end, "to become a man and grow up to dream again."

HE ENDED THE SHOW with "Matamoros Banks," the sequel to "Across the Border," the anthem of quiet hope in the face of desperation that closed out the *Joad* concerts. This time, the illegal Mexican immigrant is dead from the first line.

He did several other songs in the encores. The last night, in a chilly arena in Trenton, two nights before Thanksgiving, the first three were beyond upbeat: "Growin' Up," on the ukulele; "Thundercrack," as a glorious return to that youth; "Santa Claus Is Coming to Town," with his children singing behind him, his son Sam sitting beside him on the piano bench.

But that's not how the story ends.

He sent the kids offstage and picked up his guitar and began to beat it as the drum it sometimes is and created a haunted rendition of "The Promised Land," which brought the whole thing back to those devils, that dust, without surrendering an inch of his belief in the reality of that promise, that land.

He took some bows and then he sat down at the pump organ and started in on a seesaw riff. After a few bars, he sang.

"Dream baby dream. Dream baby dream." The organ droned on. "Dream baby dream. Dream baby dream. Come on and dream baby dream."

That's all he sang, just those lines, over and over and over. After a couple of minutes, he added a little more of what Alan Vega wrote when he originally did the song with his post-punk group Suicide: "Keep

the fire burning, you gotta keep the light burning, come on, you gotta keep the fire burning, come on, dream baby dream."

He invited us to dry our eyes—we were, after all, the baby he sang to, each one of us, all children, even or especially if we also were parents. "Come on and open up your heart, come on and open up your heart, come on and open up your heart. Come on and dream on, baby. Yeah, I just want to see you smile. Yeah, I just want to see you smile. Yeah, I just want to see you smile. Come on and dream on baby."

The lights were on in the house, and Bruce stood up and began to stalk the stage, his head uplifted as if to look even the cheap seats straight in the eyes. It was a chant, it was an exhortation, it was a lecture, it was a criticism of the way we live our lives day by day, it was an offering of possibility. The organ kept on, reaching a crest and surpassing it, over and over again—played now from backstage, but the way it looked, the music just keeping on by itself, locked into Bruce Springsteen's vision along with the rest of us.

"Come on and open up your heart! Come on and open up your heart! Come on and open up your heart!" He sang it a dozen times, and he wouldn't stop, and you could look out at the people around you and see in their eyes what you felt in your own as tears rolled down cheeks and the smiles he commanded appeared, bewildered, in this light that leapt from that dark show.

Ten minutes into it, he kept on, insisting he just wanted to see us smile, but not really smiling himself, insisting we ought to dry our eyes, that we must stoke our fires. He told us to dream. He asked us what we were doing with our lives, how we spent our time. He didn't shout. He didn't rant or preach. He just sang.

"Come on and dream baby dream," he crooned one last time, and took his bows. The organ raved on regardless, the music, not the words, the last thing that he gave.

You could call it benediction. I'd call it definition.

BRUCE SPRINGSTEEN IS A VERB. Its primary meanings are these: To dream. To live. To live the dream.

Photography Credits

Mary Alfieri: 93 (timeline), 164 (timeline)

Mike Banos: 201 (timeline), 217 (timeline right)

Joel Bernstein: 122 (timeline), 124, 134, 141, 145, 153 (left)

Lois Bernstein: 108-109, 112 (timeline left), 114-15 (all)

Lewis Bloom: 132 (timeline)

Watt Casey: 5 (top center; bottom center), 125, 148 (top right, bottom right), 150-51, 159 (right), 165 (timeline right)

John Cavanaugh: 263 (timeline), 268 (timeline)

Phil Ceccola: 47, 48, 52 (bottom), 53, 54 (timeline), 55 (timeline), 57 (timeline right), 58, 59 (bottom), 59 (timeline), 60-61 (all), 62-63, 66 (timeline), 74, 233 (timeline)

Danny Clinch: 14, 15, 228, 231, 232-33, 234, 235, 236-37, 238, 239 (all), 240, 241, 244, 245 (inset), 246-47, 252, 257, 260-61 (all), 267 (timeline), 271 (all), 274, 275, 276, 282-83 (all), 286, 289, 290, 292, 295, 296, 298-99 (all), 300, 301, 302-303, 306-307, 308, 309, 310

Anton Corbijn, 297

Peter Cunningham: 57 (timeline left), 71, 72 (timeline left), 75, 79, 83, 196

James Davis: 11, 5 (top left)

David Englehardt: 78 (timeline), 88, 90-91 (all), 92 (timeline), 96-97, 98

Sharon Farmer: 278, 284 (timeline), 285, 291

Jayne Fazio: 121 (timeline), 122-23

Jim Fuller: 56-57, 64, 65, 66 (timeline), 68, 76

David Gahr: 2, 80-81, 156-57

Barry Goldenberg: 112, 118

Stan Grossfeld: 270 (all), 272, 273

Mike Jones: 257 (timeline)

David Kennedy: 137 (timeline)

Annie Leibovitz: 146, 147 (timeline), 150 (timeline right), 158 (timeline), 174

Index